Mothers United

Mothers United

AN IMMIGRANT STRUGGLE FOR SOCIALLY JUST EDUCATION

Andrea Dyrness

University of Minnesota Press

Minneapolis

London

The poem "Extranjera" is reprinted with permission of the poet.

Published by the University of Minnesota Press
111 Third Avenue South, Suite 290
Minneapolis, MN 55401-2520
http://www.upress.umn.edu

Library of Congress Cataloging-in-Publication Data

Dyrness, Andrea.
    Mothers united : an immigrant struggle for socially just education / Andrea Dyrness.
        p.   cm.
    Includes bibliographical references and index.
    ISBN 978-0-8166-7466-4 (hardback) — ISBN 978-0-8166-7467-1 (pb)
    1. Children of immigrants—Education—California—Oakland—Case studies.   2. Children of minorities—Education—California—Oakland—Case studies.   3. Education—Parent participation—California—Oakland—Case studies.   4. Community and school—California—Oakland—Case studies.   5. School improvement programs—California—Oakland—Case studies.   I. Title.
    LC3746.5.C2D97 2011
    371.826'9120979466—dc22

                                                                    2010050106

Printed in the United States of America on acid-free paper

The University of Minnesota is an equal-opportunity educator and employer.

24 23 22 21 20 19 18 17 16   10 9 8 7 6 5 4 3

To all mothers everywhere
who fight for a better life for their children.

Para todas las madres en todas partes
quienes luchan por sacar adelante a sus hijos.

Contents

Abbreviations

API	Academic Performance Index
BACEE	Bay Area Center for Educational Equity
BART	Bay Area Rapid Transit
CPEPR	Center for Popular Education and Participatory Research
ELAC	English Language Advisory Committee
GED	General Equivalency Diploma
JSN	Just Schools Network
OCCA	Oakland Coalition for Community Action
PICO	Pacific Institute for Community Organizations
RFP	Request for Proposals
SSC	School Site Council
UCS	United Community School

Acknowledgments

This book is the product of a long and remarkable journey. First and foremost I would like to thank the five members of Madres Unidas—Amelia, Baudelia, Carmen, Carolina, and Ofelia—for their *confianza* and *convivencia*. Their courageous honesty and collaborative spirit inspired and enabled this research, and their friendship enriched my life in ways beyond measure. The journey that we undertook together has forever transformed me.

Unconventional research must be nurtured by unconventional spaces: collectivities of people who together make it possible to challenge received norms. At the University of California, Berkeley, Graduate School of Education, I was fortunate to be part of a tight cohort of students who were committed to participatory action research and to making space for different ways of being in the academy. As first-year graduate students, we founded the Center for Popular Education and Participatory Research (CPEPR), which supported all of us in engaging in community-based research for social change. Just as the space created by Madres Unidas supported the mothers' transformative work at their children's school, so my own work with the mothers was nurtured by the space of CPEPR and my graduate school colleagues, Kysa Nygreen, Patricia Sánchez, Soo Ah Kwon, Emma Fuentes, and Shabnam Koirala, and our dedicated faculty sponsor, John Hurst. Ten years after its founding I do not know if CPEPR still exists or exists in the same way as it did for us in our PhD years, but I acknowledge it here to encourage all students who feel they cannot find a home in the academy: there are others like you; seek them out and build your own home. With a group of people behind you who will say "we've got your back," you will find that anything is possible.

There are very few people whose interest in one's project endures unwaning over many years. Among my CPEPR colleagues, I owe special thanks to Kysa Nygreen, my research partner during the first year of research and writing partner thereafter, whose insights, encouragement, and friendship helped bring this book to where it is today. I am deeply grateful to my PhD adviser and mentor, Carol Stack, whose belief in the work, in the Madres, and in me encouraged me at many difficult points from the inception of the research through the completion of this book, and whose writing is an inspiration. Years out of graduate school and thousands of miles away, I would send Carol and Kysa every new chapter draft, and I relied on their thoughtful feedback as the work moved from dissertation to book. Of course, responsibility for any errors in judgment or interpretation is mine alone.

Monetary support for my research came from the James Irvine Foundation, the Spencer Research Training Fellowship, and the University of California Regents/Dean's Normative Time Fellowship. I am especially grateful to Craig McGarvey, then a program officer at the James Irvine Foundation, for encouraging me to submit the grant that first funded the work of Madres Unidas and for affirming the principles of participatory research in the grant-making process. An early result of the research supported by this grant was a video documentary, the production of which contributed greatly to my own analysis of the data. I owe much to my associate producer and video editor, Jennifer Ho, who encouraged me to record the teachers' testimonies that later found their way into this book and whose insightful questions and suggestions sharpened my own thinking about this story. I am grateful to Alfred Hernández, our video instructor, whose patience, good humor, and skill as a teacher gave the mothers and me the confidence to undertake this new technology. I especially appreciate the individual staff members at the new small school and partnering community organizations who supported our research and helped make it possible: I cannot name them here, but they know who they are.

In the field of anthropology of education, I am indebted to several godmothers and godfathers who, through the example of their own work and their support of mine, helped make this book possible. Sofia Villenas and Janise Hurtig, collaborating with me on a panel at the meetings of the American Anthropological Association in 2003, first made me aware that I had something important to say for the field, and they have encouraged me ever since. The humility, respect, and feminist praxis with which they approach their own work with Latina mothers have inspired me, and their comments on several versions of this manuscript have been helpful beyond measure. I am grateful to Doug Foley and Bradley Levinson for their leadership in support of activist research and for their encouragement in publishing my work.

This is a book about mothers, and so it is fitting that maternity leave finally allowed me the time to complete it. I wrote the bulk of this manuscript while on maternity leave and living in El Salvador with my husband and baby daughter. Experiencing motherhood for the first time and living in El Salvador (not for the first time) gave me new lenses through which to understand the mothers' experience. I am grateful to my daughter, Sofia Elena, for showing me what is worth fighting for at all costs and for the new reserves of joy and hope her life has given me. My time in El Salvador also brought me face-to-face with the conditions and struggles that cause so many to migrate, and so I offer this story with renewed respect and admiration for immigrants. In El Salvador I relied on the help of a nanny and housecleaner, Angela, whose careful attention to Sofia allowed me to write this book in peace and who taught me much about El Salvador.

I would be remiss if I did not acknowledge my family, the people most responsible for my own wholeness as a person, a scholar, and an activist. I am indebted to my parents, William and Grace, for the example of a life rooted in faith, love, and joy, and for the natural expression of solidarity and activism that shaped me from my earliest days. And to my husband, friend, and colleague, Enrique Sepúlveda, who has been my sounding board, inspiration, sage, who together with our daughter has reminded me why this book is worth doing.

Introduction
A FRAGILE PARTNERSHIP

How do Latina immigrant mothers without college education, U.S. citizenship, English literacy skills, or economic resources organize to create change on behalf of their children and their community? What experiences and cultural resources support and sustain their efforts for change, and what stands in their way? This book tells the story of a group of Latina mothers who became activists, researchers, and vocal advocates for their children in a citywide community organizing movement in Oakland, California. The small schools movement aimed to reverse inequities in the Oakland Public Schools in part by giving new roles to parents and community members in the design and creation of new small autonomous schools. At the heart of the movement was a celebrated but fragile partnership between progressive educators and low-income parents of color whose children attended the most overcrowded and underperforming schools in the city. How could a partnership of such unequal parties flourish? How would professional educators come to see low-income Latina housewives and low-wage workers as equal partners in reform, and how would Latina mothers come to see themselves that way? This book explores these questions, charting the movement of five Latina mothers from isolation and marginality to founding parents in a new small school and coresearchers along with the author in a participatory research team called Madres Unidas (Mothers United).

The mothers in Madres Unidas began their personal journeys in home-towns far from Oakland: in rural El Salvador, Guatemala, coastal Mexico, and one of Mexico's urban centers. With one exception, they immigrated to the United States as young, single women under the age of twenty, and had their first children within two years of arriving in the country. As young girls in their hometowns, they would scarcely have believed they would one day be raising American children, much less that they would become leaders in a movement for new small schools in a U.S. city. They could not

1

have imagined how they would become caught up in, and make their mark on, the enduring U.S. struggle for racial equality and justice. Theirs was in many ways an unlikely story, and yet, as this book argues, the mothers drew from their life experience as immigrant women and the cultural resources that sustained them to become agents for change in Oakland. In doing so, they were forced to confront images of "Latina mothers" that sought to limit or neutralize their roles as leaders in reform. These images came from reformers, teachers, politicians, the media, their husbands, and sometimes from deep within themselves—memories of a brother's words in El Salvador, of dreams deferred, of sacrifices deemed inevitable for daughters, mothers, and housewives. So much conspired to dissuade them from their quest for change that confronting the controlling images became a daily ritual, and as they shared battle stories in Madres Unidas, a collective awareness of struggle strengthened their determination to persevere. The controlling images, to borrow Patricia Hill Collins's words (2000), became sources of mobilization, something to organize against, an invitation for the mothers to reinvent themselves.

Teachers, on the other side of the unlikely partnership, had barriers of their own. For educators in the small schools movement struggling with how to include parents in their plans for reform, Latino parents' lack of education, poverty, and linguistic and cultural difference were seen as formidable barriers to their "involvement." The question teachers wrestled with was how to involve parents who most likely lacked the time, motivation, experience, or know-how to engage in reform. Underlying this dilemma were certain assumptions about what motivates and enables people to work for social change. Education and specialized training, skills, resources, and professional experience were seen as natural precursors to participation in school reform. Parents who lacked these things would be difficult to involve. Seeing parents through the lens of deficit, the prospect of involving them as "partners" in reform was inordinately stressful, overwhelming, and perplexing. But what if it were the case that the barriers to parents' involvement in reform were none of the usual suspects: not their lack of English literacy, not their low socioeconomic status, not their unfamiliarity with the U.S. educational system or their patchy educational backgrounds? What if these same parents were already dynamic change agents with a sharp social critique and cultural ways of responding to structural injustice that had uniquely prepared them to engage in educational advocacy for their children? What if the barriers to their involvement came not, in fact, from their own deficits, but from progressive educators' inability to see them as change agents—from controlling images that closed off the possibilities for change before they had even been explored? In the journey that this book describes, the mothers in Madres Unidas raised these questions, first among themselves and later publicly, among teachers at their children's new small school. Some teachers listened. Some change happened.

Many stories were told about the reform as the movement unfolded and began to attract headlines across the county and country. There were stories of a troubled urban school district undergoing a renaissance; of city officials responding to the demands of an organized community; of district leaders, NGO professionals, and teachers collaborating to effect change for Oakland's most disadvantaged children; of philanthropists recognizing the unique momentum of this partnership and infusing it with unprecedented donations. In the midst of this excitement were other stories that did not get told. Backstage stories, stories that countered the euphoric forward momentum of the reform or punctured the reform's ideals of racial equity and inclusion, or stories that simply lacked storytellers powerful enough to be heard, were lost from the chorus of voices that heralded a new era for Oakland's schools. This book, based on more than three years of ethnographic fieldwork, represents some of these backstage stories. Latina mothers, as I will argue, were both the most celebrated and the most vulnerable and excluded actors in the reform. They were praised as the initiators of the reform, the voice of urgency that demanded change, the face of an oppressed community whose fate stood to be reversed by the new small schools. They were positioned in the spotlight as they testified in school board meetings and public actions about the trials their children faced in large, overcrowded schools. But they were also silenced, and nowhere more so than when they sought to define their roles in ways that diverged from the dominant images of Latina mothers, or challenged progressive educators' self-image as inclusive and democratic reformers. The friction of everyday interactions behind the public drama of the reform was not the stuff of newspaper headlines or glossy fund-raising reports, and it was not likely to win more policy victories for Oakland's schools. But it was the site where important changes were being enacted, beyond the reach of public policy, changes in how ordinary people came to see themselves and others as partners in the struggle for social justice.

In telling the story of reform as experienced by the mothers in Madres

Unidas, this book offers both a *testimonio* (testimony) and a counterstory, from the traditions of Latina feminist and critical race theories. As *testimonio*, it represents not an objective account of "what happened" during the reform (if such an account were possible), but rather the reflections and responses of a group of mothers bearing witness to the effects of the events on their lives.[1] Critical race theorists Solorzano and Yosso describe counter-storytelling as "a method of telling the story of those experiences that are not often told . . . and a tool for analyzing and challenging the stories of those in power and whose story is a natural part of the dominant discourse" (Solorzano and Yosso 2001, 475). In contrast to "majoritarian stories," which recount events from the perspective of those with racial and social privilege, a counterstory recounts the experience of domination and resistance from the perspective of those on society's margins (Yosso 2006).

Within education, writes Tara Yosso, majoritarian stories often feature Latino/a parents "who supposedly do not care about educating their children" (ibid., 9). Lacking an awareness of structural inequality, majoritarian stories fault Latino communities and students for unequal schooling outcomes.[2] The small schools movement, as I will show, intended to be a counterstory against such narratives: highlighting inequities that disadvantaged children and families in Oakland's flatlands faced, and publicly shaming city officials for allowing such inequities to go undisturbed for so long. But even within the small schools movement, as within all social movements, power relations and hierarchies privileged some perspectives and voices and marginalized others. Within the constellation of district actors, professional reformers, community organizers, teachers, and parents that formed the unwieldy partnership of the small schools movement, Latina immigrant mothers were among the least powerful actors. This book features the stories of five of them, who came together along with the author to form a participatory research team as a way of countering the marginality they experienced in the process of planning their children's new small "community school." Through their stories, other parents' stories are featured too, as the mothers in Madres Unidas systematically sought out the stories that had been silenced and brought them to the fore of public debate.

Although a counterstory necessarily disrupts the dominant story, the purpose of this story is not simply to challenge the narrative of reform in the small schools movement or its primary narrators, who considered themselves allies of Latino parents in the struggle for social justice. Rather, by illuminating the perspective of Madres Unidas, this book aims to highlight the alternative possibilities for change found in Latina mothers' organizing on their own terms in "private" spaces, and in their own efforts to confront the barriers standing against them. *Mothers United* draws on a central insight of U.S. third-world feminist theory: that the position of women of color at the margins of society provides them with both a privileged understanding of domination and unique tools or tactics for resisting and outlasting it (Sandoval 2000; Collins 2000; hooks 1990). U.S. feminists of color have pointed out that marginality, the "outsider/within" or "in-between" status experienced by women of color in their daily lives, nurtures political skills and strategies for change that are often not recognized by the white power structure, white feminists, or leftist activists (Sandoval 2000; Collins 2000; Anzaldúa 1987; Hurtado 1989, 2003). Living at the interstices of racism, sexism, and classism, Latina mothers learn to read and respond to shifting currents of power as a mode of survival, and draw on an "eclectic paradigm for political mobilization" (Hurtado 2003, 265). As Chicana feminist Cherríe Moraga wrote in 1981, "Our strategy is how we cope" (Moraga 1981, l).

The book thus has two parallel aims: first, to describe in ethnographic detail how Madres Unidas mobilized for change and the barriers they encountered even within a progressive reform movement, and second, to illuminate how participatory research methods, as practiced by Madres Unidas, created a "counterspace" that supported the mothers' agency and transformative resistance at their children's school. Corresponding to these aims I develop two central arguments. First, in engaging in reform, the Madres drew on cultural resources, experiences, and strategies for change that differed from those of professionals in the movement and were not often recognized or granted legitimacy by professionals. The Madres found themselves up against "controlling images" (Collins 2000) of what Latino parents could and should do, stereotypical images that prescribed certain paths of involvement while invalidating others. Second, through their work in Madres Unidas, the mothers deconstructed these images and supported each other in recasting their roles at the school. I argue, then, that participatory research from a critical Latina feminist lens offers a way to build upon and expand Latina women's own capacities for social critique and transformative resistance, and to extend their strategies for change from Latina-controlled domestic spaces into the public sphere. In doing so, it disrupts essentializing views of social change movements and activist research methods that leave change in the hands of specially trained "experts."

In pulling together the Madres' testimonies of their experience (written reflections, public presentations, and a video documentary we coproduced) with my own ethnographic observations of the reform over three and a half years, the book is part *testimonio*, part counterstory, and part cultural critique of the small schools movement in the tradition of critical ethnography. Critical ethnography, according to Foley, Levinson, and Hurtig (2001), "aims to illuminate the workings of power in a way that may help transform oppressive power relations" (42). Although it has often been posed as separate and distinct from activist or collaborative research (Hale 2006; Foley and Valenzuela 2005), I will argue that my collaboration with Madres Unidas best enabled the cultural critique that is elaborated in these pages. Finally, this book is my testimony: the story of a graduate student researcher who hoped to contribute to a social-change movement, and stumbled upon fault lines I was ill prepared to navigate. As much as the story highlights the fraught partnership between immigrant mothers and progressive teachers, it also spotlights another partnership, equally unlikely, between a doctoral student and a group of Latina moms who had never done research before, who wagered together that research could be a process of both knowledge building and action for change. In the remainder of this introduction, I describe the context of the reform and introduce the major actors who coalesced, and sometimes collided, on the journey to bring new small schools to Oakland. All personal and institutional names in the book have been changed, with the exception of elected officials, whose complete names are given, and three members of Madres Unidas, Baudelia, Ofelia, and Carmen, who are identified by their first names, by their choice.

History of the Movement

Two momentous events set the stage for the small schools movement and the distinct roles that parents and teachers would play in the months to follow. The first was a large community rally, or "action" in the language of organizers, which drew more than two thousand parents, pastors, and teachers to an elementary school auditorium to demand new small schools for the Oakland flatlands. Organized by the Oakland Coalition for

Community Action (OCCA), a grassroots, faith-based group with a long history of organizing the neediest communities in Oakland, the Action for New Small Schools assembled parents of students in severely overcrowded, underperforming Oakland schools and teachers and community members who cared about them to testify before public officials about the trials of large, overcrowded schools. Primarily people of color, largely low-income, and many of them immigrants, this was a group that does not usually feel its power in citywide matters, least of all in educational policy. And yet on this November evening they had captured the attention of the most powerful players in Oakland education: Mayor Jerry Brown, state senator Don Perata, Superintendent Allen Arnold, and members of the city council, the school board, and the Oakland teachers' unions.

In the public spotlight, these officials listened to the testimonies of parents and were asked to publicly commit to supporting the creation of new small schools: by providing funds, policy, and facilities. One by one, the officials answered yes to all of the parents' demands. It was a euphoric moment. In the most surprising turn of all, Mayor Brown led the crowd in chanting, "¡Sí, se puede!" (Yes, we can!). The November action was an unquestionable victory for OCCA and the parents and students of the Oakland flatlands. Not only would it set in motion a chain of events that would lead to new small schools in Oakland, but, equally important, for the first time, many Oakland parents and community members who had previously been ignored by the city felt their own power. It was an experience everyone remembers.

Eleven months later, in October 2000, one hundred people gathered in the library of a local school for another momentous event. The Oakland school board had passed the "New Small Autonomous Schools" policy five months earlier, and on this Tuesday afternoon, the district was releasing the "Request for Proposals" (RFP) for new small schools. Leaders from OCCA and BACEE (Bay Area Center for Educational Equity), a partner school-reform organization, introduced the meeting as a "celebration" of the accomplishments of their organizing. Through the RFP, local groups of teachers and parents—design teams in the language of the RFP—would have the chance to make their dreams of new small schools a reality. The new Superintendent Costas, the new assistant superintendent of school reform, and several reform leaders were on hand to answer questions about the RFP process. The room was abuzz with positive energy, and there was lots of laughter and jokes. But the most striking feature about this

[handwritten note at top of page: — 2000 parents / people gathered to demand small schools @ next rally, only 100 — what happened?]

meeting was the absence of Oakland parents—or, more precisely, the absence of parents of Oakland flatland students who would be served by these new schools. In stark contrast to the crowd at the November action, this group was primarily white, and primarily teachers. Although at least two Spanish-speaking parents had found their way to the meeting, no translation was provided, and the Request for Proposals distributed that day was only in English.

And so it happened that the parents who were there to demand that the city provide their children with new small schools were not there to find out how these new schools would be created. Moreover, this seemed to everyone present a perfectly normal and acceptable state of affairs. To everyone, perhaps, except for one Spanish-speaking mother who could not understand the meeting. Why were there no other parents there to celebrate the victory of the RFP? Was this in fact a victory won *by* the parents *for* the teachers?

As both a grassroots-driven community organizing movement and a professionally driven educational reform, the small schools reform highlights the tensions surrounding the meaning of "community" and "participation." There was no question that it was the crowds of parents and community members in dramatic public actions that was attracting public attention and signaling the community's prominent role in this movement. But as the district's RFP meeting reveals, teachers were also promised ownership of the new small schools, in ways that implicitly contradicted the reform's community-based roots. The small schools movement embodied two potentially conflicting goals: it aimed to answer an urgent community need for new schools and greater participation in those schools, while also offering educators greater professional autonomy and an invitation to "dream" again. It would accomplish these twin goals through a "partnership" of both teachers and parents, supported by professional reformers and organizers, working together for supposedly shared interests. The movement thus brought together two distinct constituencies to collaborate in the creation of new schools: professional educators who helped design and later taught in the new small schools, and urban parents who lived in the community and sent their children to the new small schools. The tensions between professional autonomy and community participation were everywhere apparent, but seldom publicly addressed. Instead, as I will show, a parallel discourse of celebrating the community roots of the reform coexisted with a discourse of doubt, concern, and misgiving about the ability of parents (at least these parents) to be equal partners in school design and reform.

From its inception, the movement for new small schools in Oakland was framed by its supporters as being fundamentally about a new relationship between schools and their communities. Unlike most reforms, they argued, this reform arises from and is driven by the community. OCCA organizers and BACEE staff like to trace the history of the movement to a group of Latina mothers from a large elementary school in Oakland, who began meeting at a Catholic church on Saturdays while their children were in catechism. The "Washington moms," as they came to be known after the name of the school, met to discuss what they could do about the problems at their children's school. Gradually, they realized that most of the school's problems stemmed from its large size, and particularly from the overcrowded building. They began to see the need for small schools.

The problems of Washington School, it turned out, were not unique, but part of a troubling citywide pattern that disproportionately affected Oakland's flatland neighborhoods. The movement for small schools was quickly framed as a movement for equity. Organizers of the movement drew a map that graphically illustrated the disparities in size and academic achievement between schools in the flatlands and schools in the hills. The hills schools, which ranged in size from 246 to 374 students, boasted dramatically higher academic indexes than the flatlands schools, which ranged in size from 490 to 1,400 students. Unspoken in the map, but known to almost everyone in Oakland, was that the flatland neighborhoods are overwhelmingly made up of people of color, while the hills residents are predominantly white. Mirroring national patterns, the schools with the most overcrowding and the poorest achievement records were the schools with the highest concentrations of Latinos and other students of color.[3] The map asked, "Is this fair?"

As the Washington moms discussed the problems at their children's school, an OCCA organizer working with the mothers read *The Power of Their Ideas* by Deborah Meier. This book, which quickly became the progressive teachers' bible, tells the story of the creation of new small alternative schools in New York City's East Harlem. Serving an inner-city population of mostly low-income kids of color, the small schools became hugely successful, and national icons of reform in urban education. The OCCA organizer shared the book with the Washington moms, and the seeds for a small schools movement in Oakland were planted.

When asked about the roots of the movement, key leaders mention both the Washington moms and Debbie Meier's book. The significance of both of these elements symbolizes what they believe is unique about the Oakland movement: the pairing of an urgent need in the community with a demonstrated educational reform solution, the coming together of community organizing and research-based school reform. On the one hand was a body of research showing that small schools could boost achievement for minority and low-income students, and lead to more equitable outcomes (Fine and Somerville 1998; Meier 1995). On the other was a critical mass of parents and teachers determined to change Oakland education. To bring these two together, OCCA organizers invited school officials and parent leaders on a trip to New York to visit some of the small schools there. The trip is regarded as a watershed event in the lives of the organizers and in the life of the movement. OCCA's director says the movement "got legs when we went to New York. That's when it became real, people saw it. People came back you know, just full of energy . . . and that energy never got lost."

New York thus became a model for Oakland organizers, along with the reform example of Debbie Meier. It was also the impetus behind OCCA's partnering with a local school-reform organization, in what was to become another unique aspect of the Oakland movement. The Bay Area Center for Educational Equity (BACEE), part of a national, university-affiliated network of restructuring schools, was sponsoring its own reform work in local schools along similar lines of the small schools in Harlem. The partnership with OCCA seemed a natural next step for both organizations.

The Partnership

The partnership between a grassroots community-organizing group and a research-based school-reform organization, unique among urban reform movements, represented in the minds of participants the coming together of "what the community wants" with "what research says is best," or the merging of "political will" with "educational expertise." As a BACEE staff member wrote early in the partnership, "The collaboration between

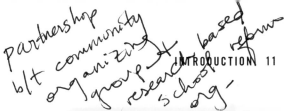

OCCA and BACEE has created an *educationally informed political will* serving to reform an entire system" (emphasis added). In this view, each organization brought something the other lacked and needed in order to achieve reform that would be sustainable and citywide. But the juxtaposition of "political will" and "educational expertise" deserves close examination, because it has important ramifications for how the reform played out and, in particular, how "parents" and "community" were constructed in the reform. Because OCCA represented parents and the community, and BACEE represented professional educators, an analysis of each organization's goals and perceived roles lends insight into the respective roles ascribed to professional expertise and "the community" in the partnership for new small schools.

OCCA

OCCA is a federation of forty congregations and neighborhood-based organizations representing forty thousand families in low-income and moderate-income communities in Oakland. Founded in 1977 by Jesuits inspired by the teachings of Saul Alinsky, the organization has become the largest civic organization in Oakland. OCCA is part of a growing national movement of faith-based organizing.[4] It is an affiliate of the Pacific Institute for Community Organizations (PICO), a nationwide network of congregation-based community organizations representing one million families. As a PICO affiliate, OCCA draws on an established method of faith-based organizing that has been well documented by Richard Wood (2002). I will elaborate on OCCA's organizing method in later chapters, but here I will highlight those aspects of its method that allow OCCA to represent the "political will" of the city, and that brought OCCA to spearhead the campaign for new small schools.

The Latina mothers who met every Saturday at St. Isabel's Church while their children were in catechism illustrate a core feature of OCCA's organizing model: the church as a community gathering place, a place to assess the concerns of the community, and a natural organizing base. The roots of the small schools movement at St. Isabel's also illustrate how OCCA begins with local concerns to build citywide campaigns. The primary method of culling the concerns of the community is through "one-to-ones": individual, face-to-face meetings between OCCA organizers or parent leaders and community members, usually parishioners or congregants in OCCA member congregations. These meetings, described as "a deliberate process of relationship building," are to learn the needs of the community, identify potential leaders, and enlist their participation in OCCA organizing activities. Martha, an OCCA organizer since 1998, sums up the organizing process this way: "It means going to people's houses and sitting down and listening to their stories. And then getting them to a meeting."

When enough of the same concerns start turning up in different parts of the city, OCCA mounts a citywide campaign. Only after months or years of organizing can OCCA confidently present city officials with a specific agenda for change. In citywide actions, such as the action for new small schools described earlier, OCCA members confront public officials in a planned, strategic way and make concrete requests that the officials have the power to grant. The legitimacy of OCCA's demands is always backed up by numbers: the number of community members who participated in one-to-ones, the number of people who came to the action, the number of families OCCA represents. This last number is always cited at the beginning of each action or meeting during the "credential," as a reminder to those in attendance (especially public officials) of the political power of OCCA. It was this organizing model that allowed OCCA to confidently say of the small schools agenda, "This is what the community wants."

In framing Oakland's small schools reform, OCCA looked to the New York small schools for hope, as an example of what was possible. But OCCA leaders also recognized that Oakland's context was different from that of New York and required a special role for community organizing. OCCA leaders wanted Oakland's small schools reform to be different from New York's in some fundamental ways, and these ways hinged on new roles for parents and the community in the design and functioning of the new small schools.

Martha was one of the OCCA organizers who had gone to New York, and she explains OCCA's role this way: "OCCA has insisted that parents be involved at every step and at every level of the school, and that is different from what they did in New York. In New York it was all directed by teachers, because teachers initiated the schools according to their visions of pedagogy. And they created a lot of choices for the parents. In New York, the parent is like the consumer of educational services and they've got a great menu. And they told us when we were there, 'Here the parents are

-diff. b/t NY & Oakland models: NY did not have much parent involvement

working-class, a lot of parents have two jobs, they don't have time to be on committees. That's not what the parents want, the parents want to be able to trust in the school, so they can leave their kids there and know that the teachers will teach them well. That's what the parents want.' That's what they told us very brazenly and I remember when he said that, Lucy [an OCCA parent leader] and I were like: 'Well, in Oakland it's not going to be that way.' So it's like a contradiction, because here we are using District 4 as a model, but in District 4 it was all teacher-led, and what we want here is a much greater role for parents."

In entering into the partnership with BACEE, OCCA assumed the responsibility of "making sure that parents are at the center of the new schools." OCCA's director explains it this way: "small schools [are] a vehicle [for creating] a place where parents can have real power and can own their schools and have a sense of . . . that connectedness that they are truly invested in the education of their kids." One of the goals of the movement, for him, was to create "an understanding and a culture where parents and community feel like these are really *our* schools."

At the same time, OCCA recognized that opening small schools was a new kind of organizing and demanded a level of educational expertise that OCCA leaders did not have. Joining up with BACEE was a way to take a community-initiated reform to a broader, more systemic level. "BACEE are the educational experts," OCCA organizers frequently said. As Martha explained to some parents, "They [BACEE] have studied all the reform efforts across the country." "We need them. We're not educators," said Laura, another organizer. "BACEE is indispensable. We totally need BACEE," said Martha. "It really is the kind of partnership where it really couldn't happen without either party.

"What are our roles? It's sort of like, the work we do, we go out, it's like plowing the ground, tilling the soil, you know, creating that readiness, that hunger, reawakening people's imaginations and the ability to dream, you know, and getting people to trust again . . . So it's like we're out there working the soil, and planting seeds, and then, as they start to grow, they really need to be cared for, and that's sort of where BACEE comes in. You know, because if you don't have what BACEE has you're gonna end up with a bunch of crappy schools." In this analysis, the community provides the hunger for change, while reform experts provide the solutions. OCCA and BACEE staff alike described BACEE's role as providing technical assistance and professional development. BACEE was seen as a repository of knowledge about school reform; as one staff member said, BACEE brought "a wealth of ideas" about what it takes to create a different kind of school.

The BACEE–OCCA partnership was also frequently described as a marriage of theory and practice. Erica, a former teacher at Washington who became the Small Schools Coordinator for BACEE, explained: "BACEE had always kind of had a theory around small schools and had not really found a way to do the work [before partnering with OCCA]." Erica was working with the group of moms at Washington who were attempting to start a new small school at the time BACEE joined up with OCCA. "At that point [BACEE] came in and sort of became the voice of research and theory and, you know, experience with small schools, and was a nice marriage for the community voice, which brought the urgency and the heartfelt, you know, 'this is what we want for our kids.'"

As a regional affiliate of the Just Schools Network (JSN), BACEE was part of a school-reform movement that began in the early 1980s. Founded in 1984 by a university professor, the Just Schools Network connected new and restructured schools around a set of common principles emphasizing personalized teaching and learning to stimulate intellectual engagement. However, the principles did not directly address issues of equity and community involvement, which were paramount in Oakland. In the late 1990s, under pressure from Bay Area affiliates, JSN added a tenth common principle, dubbed the "democracy and equity" principle. This principle stated that "the school should model democratic practices," and "the school should honor diversity and build on the strengths of its communities, deliberately and explicitly challenging all forms of inequity."

Addressing inequity had been a focus of BACEE for some time, and community organizing was gradually seen as a necessary tool for this. For BACEE, partnering with OCCA was part of an emerging recognition that "the community must be engaged for reform to be sustainable." As one BACEE staff member put it, "This was the community piece we were missing." BACEE's director explained, "Our theory of action includes connecting school reform to the issues that the community cares about. Can there ever be equitable school reform without organizing the voices that are least heard? I think not."

In this way, two community-based organizations decided together that they were going to change the face of Oakland public education. BACEE brought the wisdom of past reform efforts and a set of principles about how to create schools that work, while the organizing of OCCA ensured that the reform would answer the needs of the community. Enter a new superintendent, who arrived in Oakland promising "reform, renewal, and renaissance." George Costas was charismatic, enthusiastic, and experienced, and he raised the hopes of BACEE and OCCA leaders that they might have a third partner in the Oakland Unified School District. The new assistant superintendent of school reform, hired specifically for the small schools reform, put it this way: "OCCA is the engine, the District is the legs, and BACEE is the brains." What would drive the success of the movement, he said, is the parents, the community. But BACEE had the knowledge about school reform, and the District would provide the infrastructure to carry it out.

The Oakland Renaissance

When Superintendent George Costas took over the Oakland schools in March 2000, he inherited one of the most troubled urban districts in the country. School board member Dan Siegel later wrote in a public memo that before Costas arrived, "the District was mired in failure, corruption, incompetence, and neglect. An attitude of institutionalized racism prevailed. People within and outside the District acted upon the explicit or implicit understanding that since the majority of our students are low-income African American and Hispanic children, failure was both predictable and acceptable." Reflecting this sentiment, a headline in the *San Francisco Examiner* on July 15, 2000, read, "Lousy Test Scores No Surprise in Oakland." The article reported that in the latest round of standardized testing, Oakland students were among the lowest performing in the nation. Data from the California Department of Education show that roughly three-quarters of Oakland's fifty-six elementary schools received an Academic Performance Index (API) ranking of 5 or less, classifying them as "low-performing" by the state's performance measure.[5]

George Costas arrived in the superintendent's office like a knight in shining armor. He was uniquely positioned to harness the grassroots organizing and reform work that had begun and lead the Oakland schools in a renaissance. As an Oakland native himself who graduated from Oakland public schools, Costas had the respect of the community. He often said that as a student he had hated school and that both his parents were dropouts. This struck a chord with parents who were frustrated and disillusioned with the city's schools and tired of being told that their kids were "bad kids." Costas showed himself quick to collaborate with community partners who were pushing for change. As one OCCA organizer said, "Costas truly supports us. I mean, he really gets it."

But Costas's special affinity was with teachers. Perhaps because he credited teachers with having turned his own life around, Costas understood the critical importance of good teachers in changing the life chances for struggling students. As Oakland's new superintendent, attracting new and talented teachers to the district was one of his top priorities. Oakland faced a particularly severe shortage of qualified teachers when he arrived in March 2000. Hundreds of posts were filled by temporaries on emergency credentials. Demonstrating his commitment to changing this, one of Costas's first moves in office was to authorize a three-year, 24 percent salary increase for teachers. That decision, coming on the tail of the school board's unanimous vote to approve the New Small Autonomous Schools policy, seemed to signify the dawn of a new era for Oakland teachers. Oakland, so long a neglected backwater in public education, was finally becoming a place to be. As one reform leader commented, "There was nowhere to go but up."

Costas embraced the small schools reform for many reasons, but to him the most exciting part about it was the opportunity to reawaken the creative energy of teachers—as he put it, to get teachers who were burned out by the system to "start dreaming again." A district flyer announcing the release of the Request for Proposals for new small schools asked, "Have you ever dreamed of creating your own school?" The flyer was put in all teachers' mailboxes in advance of the special meeting to introduce them to the RFP. It is no surprise, then, that the teachers who packed into the school library that fall afternoon were bubbling over with enthusiasm and anticipation. Costas knew many of them, and greeted them with hugs. It was a friendly, collegial atmosphere. Teachers were right to believe that Costas respected them, and that they were at the forefront of a major district change effort. They were right to believe that they were the wooed party in this reform.

Teachers

Who were the teachers who were drawn by the call to start their own new schools? In some ways, they were like teachers everywhere; in other ways, they were a very distinct group. Demographically, the teachers who responded to the district's Request for Proposals for new small schools mirrored teachers across the state: they were overwhelmingly female, and overwhelmingly white. California's teachers that year were 70 percent female and 75 percent white; within Oakland Unified, the figures were 70 percent female and 50 percent white, with African Americans and Latinos comprising a much larger share of the teaching staff than statewide (30 percent and 10 percent, respectively). Among teachers who completed surveys at the RFP release for new small schools in Oakland (fifty-nine total), 81 percent were female, and 68 percent were white.[6] The thirteen teachers who formed the design team and teaching staff for United Community School (UCS), where Madres Unidas took shape, exemplified these demographic patterns to an extreme: all were women, and all but two were white. Another factor made them similar to urban teachers across the country: few of them lived in the neighborhood where they taught, and even fewer had children in the local public schools. The same survey at the district's release of the Request for Proposals revealed that of fifty-nine teachers hoping to start new schools, only eight, or 13.6 percent, had children enrolled in Oakland public schools. Teachers, then, were not motivated by self-interest or concern for their own children or communities.

Instead, a passionate commitment to social justice and equity characterized the teachers who assembled to design new small schools for Oakland's flatlands. A pervasive idealism infused small schools meetings, teachers' writing in proposals, and their interviews. For both veteran teachers who had endured years of frustration in underfunded public schools and newer teachers who often faced the worst teaching conditions, new small schools represented the chance to finally enact their dreams about what education could be. The language of "dreaming," actively promoted by Superintendent Costas and other reform leaders, was pervasive in teachers' talk about new small schools. Dreaming allowed teachers to temporarily ignore—and transcend—the realities of inequality that had plagued their schools thus far.[7] As one teacher on the UCS design team explained to me, confessing that their team had proposed a design feature that would be logistically difficult, if not impossible, to achieve, "We were told, 'Dream. What would your ideal be?'" Many of the teachers had seen their ideals deferred for too long to pass up this invitation. As we will see in chapter 1, laboring within the overcrowded multitrack year-round school had been a frustrating exercise in futility, and teachers longed for a clean slate to try out their reform ideas.

But beyond transcending the constraining conditions of existing schools, teachers saw in the new small schools the opportunity to live out their ideals for a more just, equitable, and democratic society. "I've never really given up on my sixties ideals," said one retired teacher, explaining his motivation to join a design team for a new small school. "I still feel it's possible to create a society that's much more equitable, and I've been trying to do that. So, something about a vision of an equitable society. And being a part of, being a part of a movement." Linda, a teacher on the UCS design team, said, "The greatest thing is that this thing came out of the need for a more just and equitable education for kids here in Oakland, who were in overcrowded schools, so it's kind of like continuing that legacy." She explained that the teachers on her design team identified with each other because they shared "[the] same ideals . . . I mean, that's why we're doing this. Same interests in, our theme is social justice, and we had one meeting where we all went around and shared about our histories, our personal histories, and the level of activism that there is and has been in this group is really, really, incredible." These are teachers, she said, "with the same kind of vision about a just society."

Given the sincerity with which these teachers wanted better opportunities for the families of Oakland's flatlands, many were surprised at how difficult it was to achieve the kind of collaboration and community involvement they envisioned on their design teams; how, in spite of their best intentions, parents were still often angry and disillusioned about the school design process. As Erica, the small schools coordinator for BACEE, said, "the [teachers] that are coming forward are some of the most well-intentioned people in the district, you know, people that have wonderful relationships with parents." The contrast between the ideals and intentions of educators in the small schools movement and the realities of parent participation on design teams was one of the greatest paradoxes of the reform. It would take the persistent involvement of determined parents to push the translation from good intentions to more equitable relationships.

Enter the Ethnographer

I entered the small schools movement as a doctoral student in the spring of 2000, at the peak of excitement surrounding the passing of the New Small Autonomous Schools policy. As a graduate student with personal roots in the Bay Area, I was motivated by an idealism of my own: a conviction that research could contribute to social change, and that academic researchers could work in partnership with local activists to benefit the community. I hoped to conduct an ethnography of the movement that would be both useful to movement organizers and acceptable to my dissertation committee. I strongly believed in the importance of the small schools reform as a movement for equity and social justice, as it was framed by movement organizers, and I wanted to lend my research to their goals. To that end, I approached the leadership of OCCA and BACEE to gain permission for my research and seek their input into its direction. OCCA staff directed me to meet and build rapport with parent leaders first before attempting any formal research. So, at their suggestion, I began attending local organizing committee meetings in the neighborhood that became the focus of my research. I joined the design team of parents and teachers who were planning a new small school, and I offered my services as a translator. Nearly all of the parents at these meetings were Spanish-speaking Latino immigrants, and although some of the teachers and OCCA organizers spoke Spanish, translation was spotty and haphazard. I began translating and interpreting informally for a group of parents, and soon was asked to translate formal documents for both teachers and parents.

It was through my role as a translator that I gained "access" and eventually earned the trust of parents and teachers on the design team for United Community School. My own racial and cultural identity placed me in a unique position with respect to the teachers, who were 90 percent white (all but two), and the parents, who were predominantly Spanish-speaking immigrants from Central America and Mexico. As a bilingual, bicultural Central American Latina who is racially white and class privileged, I had multiple poles of commonality and difference with both teachers and parents. My role as a graduate student from a prestigious school of education gave me an "in" with teachers and access to meetings and information about the reform that parents did not always have. It was in this capacity of "translation," not just from English to Spanish and vice versa, but from the world of education research and reform to the world of Latino immigrant parents, that I first felt the need for a participatory research project that would involve Latino parents as partners in research. But it would be a year of painstaking ethnographic research and relationship building before a participatory research project would be possible.

During my first year of research, I gathered data through the methods of participant-observation, interviews, and examining key documents and newspaper articles on the small schools movement. I attended as many city-wide meetings on small schools as I could, including school board meetings, district workshops, citywide and neighborhood actions, and local organizing committee meetings. I interviewed key players from both partner organizations and the district to learn their goals for the movement and their views of the roles parents were and should be playing in the reform. In the fall of 2000, I began attending the weekly design team meetings for United Community School (whose name was still undecided), then meeting at Whitman Elementary School. One of the most overcrowded schools in the district, Whitman Elementary was designated "high priority" for the creation of new small schools, and was recommended for my research by OCCA and BACEE because of its strong parent leadership that had been active in OCCA's organizing. At the time of my research, the school enrolled roughly 1,400 students in grades K-5, of whom 77 percent were Latino, 10 percent Asian American, 9 percent African American, and 3 percent Caucasian. Seventy-seven percent of its students were designated limited-English-proficient, and 86 percent were eligible for free or reduced-price lunch. The school had some of the lowest achievement scores in the district.

It was on the Whitman design team that I met and got to know Baudelia, Ofelia, and Carolina, three of the mothers who later helped form Madres Unidas. Baudelia, a mother of three in her late thirties, had been active in citywide organizing and was somewhat of a public figure in the small schools movement. Recognized as an articulate, fearless, and tireless parent who could both speak up to powerful officials and listen to the concerns of less confident parents, Baudelia had leadership skills that were lost on few. In a testament to her outgoing nature, she welcomed my presence at design team meetings from the start, and soon allowed me into her confidence, sharing the latest developments from the school and the trials, frustrations, and breakthroughs she experienced as she fought to keep parents at the center of school planning. It was in no small part owing to Baudelia that I came to see a participatory research team with parents as an increasingly possible and necessary response to the politics of exclusion.

Madres Unidas

On a late Friday afternoon, a group of women are seated around a small kitchen table in animated discussion. Half-empty cups of coffee and the remnants of Ofelia's famous enchiladas are surrounded by notebooks, papers, and pens on the table before us. The sounds of children playing in a nearby room intermingle with the mothers' excited voices as they discuss last night's meeting at the school and the latest affronts to parents. Finally, after much venting, the question is raised, "What do we *do* about this?"

Here Baudelia takes out a sheet of paper she has typed up (in her spare time, she says) called "Preliminary research plan." She proceeds to read the following out loud to the group (in Spanish; I offer the translation):

> Justification. Based on our own experiences and previous needs in a large school, and our participation as parents in the organization of a new small school, we are motivated to carry out an in-depth research study, with the goal of arriving at a positive conclusion after learning the causes and effects of each of the problems.
>
> General objectives. (1) To get to know and analyze the most pressing problems of parents, teachers, students, and community within the school. (2) To get to know and compare the academic progress of each student in all major subjects in the bilingual program.
>
> Specific objectives. (1) To learn the history of the new small school and its origins. (2) To identify the main problems in the school and their causes. (3) To learn what role parents are playing within the school. (4) To discover the differences between United Community School and Whitman. (5) To determine the level of interest and enthusiasm of parents in participating in the school. (6) To find out what is the relationship between parents and teachers.

Baudelia then reads a list of a proposed research activities, resources, and possible outcomes. When she finishes, the group around the table breaks into spontaneous applause. Amelia, the first to speak, asks in admiration, "How did all of that occur to you?" The mothers agree that Baudelia's ideas are all wonderful. Carmen, laughing, says, "I would have proposed exactly the same thing!" Then, reflectively, she says that this is where she could tell that Baudelia "has studied" (translated roughly as having gone to school). She says, "I realize how important school is, and I have missed out."

"No, no!" Baudelia immediately counters. "It's not about that. We're all equals here. I have ideas, but you have ideas, too." The women debate the importance of being educated, but agree that they all have important experience to contribute.

This scene characterizes many of our meetings, which took place in Ofelia's kitchen every Friday for nearly a year. Baudelia, who had been a social worker in Guadalajara, Mexico, before immigrating to the United States, was the most educated member of the group, and often took the lead in proposing research activities. The other mothers greatly admired her ability with words, her experience in social work and activism, and her confidence in dealing with school staff. But Baudelia also played a leadership role in encouraging the other mothers and affirming their right and ability to contribute, regardless of their level of experience or education. It was this quality that made her a natural leader and helped create the atmosphere of mutual respect, *confianza* (trust), and *convivencia* (living together) that made Madres Unidas possible.

Madres Unidas began meeting a week before the new small school opened.[8] The group consisted of five immigrant mothers: two from Mexico, two from El Salvador, and one from Guatemala. All but one of them had been active on the design team for United Community School and had children in the new small school. We had shared impressions, observations, and frustrations after many meetings at Whitman Elementary School. This collective experience formed a natural basis for a participatory research project. When I approached Baudelia and Ofelia with the idea of forming a parent research team, both were immediately enthusiastic. Ofelia, an energetic and outspoken young mother from El Salvador, offered her home as a meeting place. The mother of two children in first and second grades, Ofelia worked full-time as a housecleaner and nanny for a wealthy San Francisco family, and still found time to be a parent leader on the UCS design team. Like Baudelia, Ofelia was frustrated with the process on the design team and eager to see parents included more meaningfully in school planning. She saw the research as a natural extension of her work in organizing the new small school: "Las dos cosas, o sea están juntas, porque es lo mismo, Madres Unidas es como algo que queremos hacer para mejorar la nueva escuela . . . Y todas estamos aquí porque nos interesa el futuro de nuestros hijos, y queremos algo mejor para ellos, y para nuestra comunidad" (The two things, I mean, they're together, because it's the same thing, Madres Unidas is like something we want to do to improve the new school . . . And we're all here because we care about the future of our children, and we want something better for them and for our community).

Other mothers in the group had less experience with organizing and were motivated by the desire to learn, to develop themselves in new ways, and to be in community. Amelia, a mother from Guatemala with a son in first grade and an older daughter in high school, worked as a housecleaner for several families in nearby suburban Orinda. Amelia explained, "Lo que a mí me llamó la atención [fue] la investigación, porque yo no sabía que era investigación. Quería saber cómo se formaba, qué significado tenía, y eso fue lo que más me motivó" (What caught my attention was research, because I didn't know what research was. I wanted to know, how do you do it, what does it mean? And that was what most motivated me). At Ofelia's urging, Amelia had participated in the meetings at Whitman to plan the new small school, and was slowly becoming more involved. In spite of being what she considered to be a shy person, she saw the importance of being involved at the school for her son: "[Los padres] representan a la escuela de sus hijos, y debemos de dar una participación . . . Nuestros hijos se sienten orgullosos que nosotros estamos en esta investigación, no sólo por nosotros sino por ellos" ([Parents] represent their children's school, and we should give our participation . . . Our children feel proud that we're doing this research, not just for us but for them).

Carmen, Ofelia's sister, was also charting new territory in joining the research team. "Para mí la investigación fue algo que me pareció muy importante cuando me dijeron, pero al mismo tiempo pensaba que una madre normal como yo que siempre estaba con mi niño, pensé que no iba a poder" (For me, research was something that seemed very important when they told me, but at the same time I thought that a normal mother like myself who was always with her son, I thought I wasn't going to be able to). A self-described housewife (ama de casa), Carmen was not working when Madres Unidas began, but had volunteered in school classrooms for more than ten years, first for her niece and later for her son. When her older son reached junior high school, Carmen and her husband were so dismayed with the conditions in his public school that they decided to pull him out and sent him to El Salvador to finish school there. Carmen's youngest son, Alex, was now in preschool, and she hoped to send him to the new small school. At the encouragement of her sister and the rest of us, Carmen joined the research team.

The final member of the group, Carolina, was a young single mother from Nayarit, Mexico, who worked as a waitress in a local restaurant. Her son Paco was starting second grade at UCS. Carolina was an animated participant in the Whitman design team meetings, and I always appreciated her cheerful commentary afterwards and whenever I saw her at the school. She joined the research team at Ofelia's invitation, eager for the chance to keep company with other parents and to learn things that would help her son's school. She later said, "Yo tampoco no sabía nada de investigación. Para mí era como algo, como un trabajo, que tenía que cumplir, y de allí también sacar muchas ideas buenas que nos ayuda para nosotros mismos y para los demás padres" (I didn't know anything about research either. For me it was like something, like a job that I had to carry out, and from there also get a lot of good ideas that could help us and the other parents).

Participatory research, in the words of Patricia Maguire, is "a process of collective, community-based investigation, education, and action for structural and personal transformation" (1993, 157). Although the process is often instigated by an outside researcher, ideally the research question or problem is defined by the community.[9] In Madres Unidas, the research problem we collectively chose to explore grew out of the year we had spent together on the design team before the participatory research began. Most broadly, the problem addressed the role(s) that parents were playing in the new small school and the ways these roles were being defined (and limited) by school staff. We wanted to start by examining the history of school and recording the experiences of parents and others who had participated in its development. Another goal was simply to understand how the reform was working at UCS. If UCS was a story of reform, what exactly was this reform and how was it being put into practice? This was the question most compelling to the mothers, who, as parents who had participated in planning the school, were desperate to understand their experience and figure out how closely the school was adhering to its vision.

In gaining support for the participatory research project from the leadership at BACEE, OCCA, and UCS, I invoked the goals of the small schools movement. If the reform was coming from the community, why shouldn't the research and evaluation also come from the community? Involving parents as researchers was another way for parents and community members to take ownership over the new small schools. Initially, the idea sold. In collaboration with BACEE, I wrote and obtained a grant to fund the parent research as part of a larger evaluation of the reform. Although conflicts would arise later as to the nature, purpose, and prod-

ucts of the research, in the beginning we felt we had a rare window of opportunity to follow the parents' own desires.

Madres Unidas met weekly in Ofelia's home for the first year of United
Community School. We planned and carried out focus groups with parents, teachers, and students, and individual interviews with the principal,
parents, and OCCA organizers. With the grant I obtained, we were able
to buy a video camera and hire a video instructor who taught the mothers how to use the video camera. We recorded most of our research activities and watched videotape together as a means of evaluating our performance and analyzing what we learned. We also recorded several of our own
meetings. One product of this research was a video documentary, *Madres
Unidas: Parents Researching for Change*, produced in 2003 and intended to
speak to a broader audience of parents, teachers, and activists than my dissertation would reach.

But our formal research activities and products were only the skeleton
of our work together. The heart and lifeblood of Madres Unidas, what sustained our engagement in research and action at the school, was the *being
together*—in Spanish, *convivencia*—the relationships built through the sharing of daily struggles and victories, which extended, for many of us, beyond
the scope and time frame of our formal research. During the years of my
research, the mothers' lives and families were stung by tense marriages,
alcoholism, drug abuse, illness, divorce, accidents, and death. We attended
funerals and vigils together, weathered personal and national tragedies, and
mourned the death of a child's classmate in a hit-and-run accident outside
the school. But there were also birthday parties, first communions, and
baby showers, full of laughter and pride. These contrasts, I came to realize,
the collective responses to the "sadnesses as well as joys" of life (González
2001), were the source of the mothers' resilience and *sobrevivencia* (survival
and beyond). I came to recognize the mothers' ways of building community
as an integral part of our research process, dissolving the artificial distinction between research and everyday life, and offering a sharp critique of
school practices that aimed to exclude personal experience and relationships from processes of school planning and reform. As I learned from the
mothers, I was led to Latina feminist theoretical perspectives as a way to
understand their efforts for change.

A Latina feminist framework, like other race-based feminisms (hooks
1989, 1990; Collins 2000), draws attention to the everyday lives of Latina
women as the place where oppression and inequality are experienced and

— Latine feminist perspective

resisted daily (Delgado-Bernal 2006; Villenas 2001).[10] Chicana/Latina feminist scholars have highlighted the "everyday resistance strategies of Chicanas/Mexicanas that are often less visible, less organized, and less recognizable" (Delgado-Bernal 2006, 116). Countering deficit views of Latino parents, these scholars have shown that Latina mothers are already involved in making change in everyday life, by nurturing resistance to oppression at home with their children—using the home and familial cultural practices to resist oppressive structures outside the home (Delgado-Bernal 2006; Villenas 2006b, 2001). In the informal and marginalized spaces of the domestic, Latina women interrogate their experiences with hostile institutions and find ways of being in the world that preserve their dignity and wholeness. Latina/Chicana feminist thought, according to Villenas (2006a), is about "excavating" this "resilience, *sobrevivencia* [survival and beyond], knowledge and acts of improvisation" for the struggle for social change. *Mothers United* draws on these theoretical perspectives to illuminate the mothers' critique of the small schools reform and the ways the mothers, through their research, created an alternative space that promoted personal transformation and enhanced their own capacity to make change in their lives.

In the chapters that follow, I draw liberally on the mothers' analysis of their research activities, from their written reflections and our group discussions, along with my own ethnographic observations, to illuminate their critique of reform at United Community School and their own visions for change. Chapter 1 begins by providing some ethnographic context for the scenes that follow, describing the conditions at Whitman Elementary School and the motivations of teachers, reformers, and parents for participating in the movement for new small schools. I aim to show that teachers and parents brought vastly different motives and frames of reference to the reform process, which set the stage for later conflicts in school planning and design. Chapter 2 provides a close-up look at the Whitman Elementary design team as they organized to plan their new small school. I profile Baudelia and describe in detail her efforts to claim a role for herself and other parents in the design process. Baudelia's organizing, which sought to draw upon parents' personal experiences and reflections in the school planning process, was gradually marginalized by teachers who had other views of parents' roles and subscribed to different sources of legitimacy and authority. I argue that teachers' failure to recognize parents' experience as resources led them to reproduce neocolonial relationships between white professionals and parents of color. Chapter 3 explores competing visions of "community" that surfaced in the planning of the school's admissions policy, as teachers and parents negotiated the difficult question of who should get into the new "community school." Profoundly different values and understandings of "community" caused friction between teachers and parents, but they were never openly addressed. Whereas teachers constructed "community" in the service of their educational goals, the mothers in Madres Unidas articulated a view of community derived from the Latino cultural concept of *educación*, which prioritized reciprocal relationships as the basis for all learning and school reform.

Chapter 4 turns to a central theme of the book, controlling images of Latino parents, and examines how these became both sources of control and sources of mobilization in the negotiation of parents' roles in the school's first year. While teachers attempted to use controlling images to limit the subject positions of parents and punish parents who transgressed accepted roles, Madres Unidas recognized and resisted these dynamics through their research and work at the school. In a dramatic example of this resistance, Baudelia resigned from her position as cochair of the school's leadership council. Chapter 5 takes us inside Ofelia's kitchen to examine the space that nurtured our work together. I profile Ofelia and illustrate her hosting of the group as part of her commitment to the home as a site of healing and resistance, and a base for community change. Highlighting key concepts from Latina feminist thought that were core aspects of our group, including *confianza* (trust), *testimonio* (testimony), and *convivencia* (living together), I examine how Ofelia's kitchen became a counterspace that supported personal and collective transformation and enabled public acts of resistance at the school.

While the safe space of the home nurtured our work together, it was the mothers' planned actions at the school that best expressed their visions for change. Chapter 6 explores the mothers' efforts to take the lessons from their research into the public realm, educating teachers and parents through two major research products: the public presentations on their research to teachers and the parent center they founded at the school the following year. I highlight Carmen and Amelia, two mothers most visibly transformed in their roles at the school, as examples of new leadership that Madres Unidas made possible. In telling the story of the mothers' hard-won changes, I describe how professionals both obstructed and supported the process. This chapter reveals the difficulties Latino parents face in

earning legitimacy as change agents, and ends with some lessons for educators who wish to work collaboratively with immigrant parents.

The final chapter steps back to reflect on the value of participatory research as a form of activist ethnography and some theoretical and practical
challenges it presents for researchers who wish to support social-change
movements. While collaborating with Madres Unidas as coresearchers allowed insights into and impacts on school change that would have been
unattainable for me as a lone ethnographer, it also brought conflict from
movement organizers who saw it as an intrusion on their own change efforts. This conflict, I argue, reveals much about the barriers facing the
least powerful actors in social-change movements. In strengthening Latina
women's capacity for critique and resistance, a *mujerista* vision of participatory research unsettles dominant assumptions about social change, and
makes space for new voices and visions on the path to reform. If the small
schools movement privileged the perspectives and discourses of professional educators, participatory research provided a way for Latina mothers
to "talk back" (hooks 1989), and, in their words, new visions of community,
justice, and rights are sketched.

1. Separate Journeys
THE ROAD TO NEW SMALL SCHOOLS

Whitman Elementary School in 2000 exemplified the conditions in Oakland's worst schools that mobilized parents and OCCA leaders to push for new small schools. It provided suitably dramatic images of chaos, contamination, and crisis to conjure up shame among Oakland's liberal power holders, especially when compared to the orderly and relatively high-performing smaller schools of the predominantly white and affluent hills neighborhoods. One of the most overcrowded schools in the district, Whitman Elementary School served 1,400 students in a building designed for 700. At least 700 was the number most frequently cited by advocates for new small schools, but I also heard 500; and official reports (such as the figures released by the district for the newspapers) said that the building was designed for 1,200 students. In any case, what was clear was that there were 1,400 students, and there was not enough room for them. The school managed to serve this many (if "serve" is an appropriate word) through a year-round, multitrack schedule in which four tracks of students had staggered vacation breaks, and a system of "roving," in which teachers and students packed up their classrooms every month and moved to another classroom, to make room for an incoming class that was coming back from vacation. I never quite understood how the roving system saved space, the official reason for its existence, but my confusion was apparently shared by many students, teachers, and parents who experienced this system daily. Both advocates and opponents of new small schools agree that roving is a terrible, detrimental practice, extremely disorienting to children, and ultimately harmful to learning.

How was it possible that 1,400 mostly Latino children (at Whitman Elementary School alone) could be allowed to go to school in such conditions for so long? The demand for new small schools was quickly sutured to a discourse of equity and social justice for Oakland's communities of color, creating a seemingly unstoppable force that had the potential to unite dispossessed parents and community members, progressive teachers and administrators, and city officials behind a clear agenda for change. But while the deplorable conditions of multitrack year-round schools and their racial implications were irrefutable, different parties had distinct relationships to these conditions, and distinct vantage points from which to envision new small schools. In the first year of United Community School, when Madres Unidas interviewed parents and teachers about their reasons for joining the small schools effort, a pattern of distinct motivations and experiences between parents and school staff emerged. Teachers and parents brought different memories of Whitman Elementary School, of what it had taken to open the new school, and different ideas of what the small school was about. These distinct imaginaries, shaped by varying personal relationships to the "injustice" represented in schools like Whitman, set the stage for ensuing conflicts over the vision, values, and planning process of the new small school.

To set the scene for the chapters that follow, this chapter explores the perspectives of reformers, organizers, teachers, and parents on the history of small schools in Oakland and their reasons for getting involved in the reform, beginning with the conditions at Whitman Elementary School that served as the impetus for the small schools movement. I draw on my own ethnographic observations and interviews with reformers and organizers, as well as focus groups and interviews conducted by the Madres to highlight key differences between professionals (teachers and administrators) and parents around a central question of this book: what motivates and enables people to work for change? The patterns in the responses hint at a tension that would later become significant, around the relative importance of experience in the community versus professional expertise. Teachers' motivations to start a new small school were rooted in their professional experience, including the desire for increased professional development and autonomy to better implement their educational philosophy, revealing a value system that eclipsed the role of community participation in the school-reform process. For educators who did not live in the community and did not send their children to the overcrowded schools, the effort to reform these schools was experienced less as an effort to work *with* the community than to do *for* the community—to put one's professional training to work to improve the outcomes for disadvantaged children. The unquestioned commitment to professional training and expertise, coupled with sincerely held social-justice values and ideals, had the unintended effect of blinding educators to the importance of personal experience of injustice as a resource in the struggle for school reform and social change.

The need for new small schools might have been apparent to anyone visiting Whitman Elementary School in 2000. My own introduction to the disorder governing the school came when I began my fieldwork with the small schools working group, the team of teachers and parents forming to design a new small school. As I followed this group over an eight-month period, I was given firsthand experience in the chaos and confusion that teachers and students at Whitman faced daily. Whitman had two adjoining campuses, spanning two city blocks. The small schools working group's first meeting, which was my first visit to Whitman, was held in the main building. When I entered the school from what I thought was the main entrance, overstuffed boxes were stacked precariously on either side of the hallway, as if the school was moving, or in a permanent state of transience, overflowing. Several repeated visits confirmed that this was in fact the school's permanent state. The meeting was in the library, a cramped room much smaller than most classrooms, and I had to ask someone if this was the school's only library. I was told that it was, and that the school was lucky to have this.

The second meeting, two weeks later, was held in the cafeteria of the adjoining campus, called Dalton School. Not knowing, I parked my car in front of the main building where the first meeting had been, and had to follow a janitor's directions through several long corridors and two playgrounds to the adjoining campus. On my third visit to Whitman, I arrived several minutes late for a parent meeting to find the parents standing in the hallway by the front entrance, waiting expectantly. Baudelia joined us shortly. She explained that there was some confusion about the room assignment: the principal claimed not to know about our meeting, although Baudelia insisted that she had told her. Finally, the principal came out, saw us, suddenly "remembered" about our meeting, and apologized laughingly to Baudelia. We were shuffled off to an empty classroom.

The third meeting for the small schools design team was held in a Dalton School classroom. We had so far never met in the same room twice, although the last two meetings had both been on the same campus. For the fourth meeting, on its now regular Thursday evening, expecting the meeting to be at Dalton School, I parked my car in front of Dalton School, but ended up following a mother with a stroller and two kids across the enormous campus to the Whitman cafeteria. By this time I wondered if the

constant change in meeting place was a reflection of the principal's unwillingness to give the small schools working group a regular space. Baudelia
had mentioned a similar problem with the "parent support group" sponsored by a community clinic—that group was also moved to a different
room each week, for which Baudelia directly blamed "la directora."

Each week, several parents trickled in late, perhaps partly because they
had arrived at the wrong campus. Indeed, it was difficult to recruit and motivate parents to participate without a consistent meeting place. I found
it hard to believe that there was no classroom that was available every
Thursday evening for this meeting: it was held, after all, at 5 p.m., long
after school let out. What, then, was responsible for the constant shuffling
of meeting places? Was it, as Baudelia suspected, a sign of the principal's
opposition? Or was it simply negligence, the failure to plan properly and
reserve a regular meeting place? More likely, both were true. Negligence
on the part of the principal was likely a sign that she did not care to accommodate the small schools working group, and the parents left to shuffle
around felt distinctly their lack of value in the school. So too must students
and teachers feel who are subject to the indignities of the roving system.

Multitrack, year-round schedules, and the practice of roving that ac-
companies them, were a major factor motivating activists for new small
schools in Oakland. At the OCCA action for new small schools described
in the Introduction, OCCA leaders also pushed district and city officials
to put an end to multitrack year-round schedules in all Oakland public
schools by 2003. This reflected the desire of small schools activists to create
system-wide change, not just a few new options for some students. Anyone
who was involved with Oakland public schools—whether as a teacher, parent, student, or organizer—knew about the suffering that roving caused,
and knew this was no way to educate children. When OCCA organized the
action for new small schools, which drew more than two thousand people,
it was not because a New York reformer had written a book that said that
small schools work for urban kids. It was because around the city, over and
over again in house meetings and one-to-ones, mothers, fathers, and grand-
mothers were complaining about their children's overcrowded schools.
Overcrowding was a condition that required a citywide solution. OCCA's
Martha recalled, "We'd done like hundreds of one-to-ones with teachers
that worked in multitrack year-round [schools], thousands of one-to-ones
with parents whose kids were in multitrack year-round, so we *knew* when
we went for the action that ending multitrack was like this total no-brainer

that everybody, absolutely everybody, could say yes to . . . And the idea of the small schools also resonated deeply with those folks, of course, because those were the most horrendously overcrowded schools in the city."

Erica, a former teacher at Washington, explained the practice of roving from a teachers' perspective: "Once a month, pretty much anywhere from three weeks to six weeks, you pack up your room and your kids and you move into someone else's room who's out on vacation . . . So the people that are roving never really have a classroom that's theirs. So you can imagine like with first-graders, if you're in one classroom for a month, and then you're across campus, so they often don't even know where they're supposed to go. And a really important part of education is having routines, and things in the same place, so that those kinds of things don't take up your educational time. You don't have to look for the pencils, you just get your pencils and you start working. So every sort of hour that's eaten up by reacclimating children, and often children who are struggling the most academically, are finding school the most emotional, and suddenly they're in this room that's not familiar, a space that's not familiar, with, you know, an environment that's not familiar, and you don't know where your books are, and you often have, if you're lucky you get a couple hours on a Friday to rove, so you can start school on Monday in your new classroom. So the teacher that's moving out has to move her stuff out, the teacher that's moving in has to move her stuff in, and if you're lucky you'll have a couple of extra hours, they'll let you have, like, a minimum day to do that. And then on Monday morning your kids show up, hopefully to the right room, and you are expected to teach."

Linda, a bilingual teacher at Whitman, explained how the practice was a fact of life for Whitman teachers: "I roved my third year when I taught first grade, and that was every two to four weeks . . . I had taught two years of K where you share a room, and then my first year on my own with my own classroom, I didn't have a classroom! So that was really horrific, that was really, really, horrific, and the attitude was like, 'Oh, you know, everyone has to do it. It's part of the game, part of the job.'"

Baudelia, a parent of three, described the sadness of seeing "the teacher rotating every month, from room to room, running all over the school, going around carrying her books and all her classroom materials, and the children, too, carting their classroom around." The year-round schedule, she said, was especially hard on small children who take a while to adjust to school. As soon as they adjust, she said, it's time for vacation, and then when they come back, they have to adjust all over again. During one small schools meeting, another mother angrily complained, "The children are moved from room to room as if they were monkeys!"

Trying to juggle the multitrack schedule presented a particular burden for parents of more than one child in the school. Leticia, a parent of three, explained: "They put one of my daughters in one track, another in another, and another in a third track. And when it was time for one of them to go on vacation, the others couldn't go. And when I would go to ask permission [to take the others out], they would tell me, 'I don't know anything! Go away! Go away!' And then, when you go ahead without permission, they come and tell you that they're going to take your kid out of that class because she didn't come! And that's wrong, [if something happens with a relative], you can't go because they don't give you permission."[1]

Stories about life at Whitman often sound more like a three-ring circus than a school. My first impression of a state of permanent transience turned out to be a more accurate descriptor of the school than I could have imagined. In the fall of 2000, 150 students were evacuated from Whitman because of a contaminated classroom building. The mold was not detected until students and teachers started getting sick. Up to the last minute, parents were not informed about what was going on. Linda explains: "We had to be evacuated for three months because of the mold. And we were given like forty-five minutes to gather what we wanted, and they wanted to throw our stuff away . . . So they said, 'Collect the things that you're going to use for the next month' (well, they said they were going to take a month, but things always take longer than they say), and so we had to move. We were used to team-teaching in the same classroom, and then we had to be in two separate classrooms and do all this transition, and our stuff was put into these big bins, and a lot of it was thrown away . . . So we had to go through that last year."

It was conditions like these that created the urgency behind the small schools movement. As Martha from OCCA explained, "There was so much suffering at Whitman School that it was imperative to take out the greatest number of students that we could take. Because it was a physical suffering. The children were getting sick, the teachers were getting sick. I mean, they were horrible conditions." At a community meeting to discuss the construction of new schools in the neighborhood, Superintendent Costas bellowed at the crowd, "We should be ashamed that we've let kids go to school in this *warehouse* for so long!"

But although everyone could agree on the need to eliminate multitrack year-round schools, the urgency was felt differently by parents and teachers. When Madres Unidas began conducting interviews with teachers in the first year of United Community School, they were surprised to discover that many teachers had been happy at Whitman and had not originally intended to start a new small school. The mothers would later recall this as one of their most striking findings, and one of the first to alert them to the dramatically different perspectives of teachers and parents on the road to new small schools.

The Principal

Perhaps most revealing of the distinct values and motivations of teachers and parents on the road to new small schools was the Madres' interview with the principal of United Community School, Marie, who had been a teacher at Whitman Elementary School and a member of the design team. Mexican-American and Spanish-speaking, Marie had been chosen by teachers and parents on the design team to be the new school's principal. Parents appreciated the fact that she spoke Spanish and could relate to the local community. However, by the time the new school opened, Marie had already had a number of conflicts with parents, and was often nervous and short with parents in school meetings. The Madres decided to interview her individually early in the year, to better understand her perspective on the school's founding and in hopes of developing a more personal rapport with her. They wanted to know, how had she become involved in the process of planning a new small school? What motivated her to participate in the reform? What motivated her to take the post of director? What did she think about the relationship between the school and the community? How did she view the role of parents in the school? Baudelia and Ofelia conducted the interview as a pair, with myself as observer and note taker. They reported on the interview to the other mothers at our next Friday meeting.

If Marie believed that the needs of the community were central to the school's founding and existence, she did not reveal as much in the interview. When asked what motivated her to get involved in the small schools reform, her response was, "theory": ideas, she explained, from professional journals and conferences. She explained that the situation at Whitman had limited her ability to carry out these ideas, and even the limitations of Whitman were explained in terms of theory: "research shows that it's hard to create schools within schools," she said. Foreshadowing what the mothers would learn from the teachers, Marie saw the new small school as an opportunity to develop and implement her professional expertise. Most surprisingly to Baudelia and Ofelia, Marie said that she had never had the goal of starting a new small school or becoming a principal. She was approached by teachers and parents at Whitman, who enlisted her participation on the design team and later convinced her to consider the directorship. Far from the mothers' image of the school as a symbol of a long-fought struggle for safety, respect, and a better education for their children, Marie had practically stumbled onto the new small school. The nonchalance with which she described her decision to become principal was shocking to Baudelia and Ofelia. Ofelia wrote in her reflection:

> Lo que más me impresionó fue que ella no tenía la visión de ser directora, no tenía esa meta, mencionó que fueron las maestras las que la involucraron, y también padres. Su sueño siempre fue ser maestra, y creo que hay mucha diferencia en ser maestra y desempeñar un trabajo como directora. Siento que ella no estaba lista ni preparada para esta posición.

> What most struck me was that she did not have the vision of being principal, she didn't have that goal, she mentioned that it was the teachers who got her involved, and also parents. Her dream was always to be a teacher, and I think there's a big difference between being a teacher and carrying out a job like the principal's. I feel that she was not ready or prepared for this position.

Lacking from Marie's interview was any evidence of her vision for being principal or her awareness of the community's struggle in the history of the school. In the mothers' view, Marie was an unlikely candidate for a leader. Although she was certainly aware of the community organizing behind the new school, it is significant that she did not choose to mention this in her interview with two parent leaders from the community. When Baudelia and Ofelia asked her what she thought about the school's relationship to the community, Marie responded, "We haven't had a lot of interaction," and added that the school was just beginning this journey.

For Madres Unidas, to consider the school's opening just the beginning of its relationship to the community was to ignore the long history of community struggle that had led to its creation and to omit the critical role of parents in its founding. The discovery of a distinct teacher consciousness, in which parents' roles and realities figured little or not at all, was dismaying to the mothers. But, as we shall see, their insights into this consciousness would empower them in future interactions with school staff. Examining the history of the new small school from the perspective of teachers and parents allowed the mothers to uncover the roots of parent silencing, and to see how this history shaped parents' roles once the new school opened.

Teachers: "It's Time to Leave This Comfortable Place"

Madres Unidas conducted two focus groups with teachers: one for bilingual teachers and a second for Sheltered English teachers. "Sheltered English" teachers were trained to provide academic instruction in English in a way that would be accessible to students who spoke English as their second language. Because it was a small school, with one bilingual and one English classroom in each grade, these two focus groups included all of the school's classroom teachers (only physical education and prep teachers were excluded). All of the teachers had taught at Whitman and had been part of the design team that created the UCS proposal. The principal, who was interviewed separately, did not participate in the focus groups. The bilingual teacher focus group was conducted in Spanish, with Baudelia and Carmen as facilitators; the Sheltered English teachers were interviewed in English. Ofelia, as the parent in the group with the best English skills, was nominated to facilitate the English focus group. Both teacher focus groups, as all the focus groups, were videotaped and transcribed. These focus groups were eye-opening for the Madres in many ways, yielding sometimes painful insights into teachers' perspectives on parents and on the purpose of new small schools.

The most surprising discovery to the Madres was around the question of why teachers became involved in the new small school. From both teacher focus groups, the Madres learned that many teachers had not planned to open a new small school, but became involved in the effort primarily to improve their collaboration with each other at Whitman. Teachers viewed the small school reform effort as a professional development opportunity for themselves. When they decided to join the team to design a new small school, it was often to stay with colleagues they had worked with at Whitman. As Susan, a first-grade Sheltered English teacher explained:

> I realized that the teachers who were staying and coming back to the meetings were teachers that I wanted to work with or already worked with, and I realized that if I wanted to push myself as a teacher, these were the kind of people I wanted to work with. I didn't know if that meant in a new school, if that were truly a possibility, or if it just meant a different way of working at Whitman. And it was a long time before I really decided that I [did] want to leave Whitman . . . So it was getting involved with a group of people who stimulated me and help[ed] me, 'cause I'm not very visionary, become more visionary, and say, it's time to leave this comfortable or relatively comfortable place and do something different.

For Susan, it was her fellow teachers who convinced her that it was "time to leave this comfortable or relatively comfortable place." Similarly, Helen recalled, "Just looking around the room and seeing the faces of the people that were there, they were all people that I would have been honored to work with . . . I think it was the teachers that really drew me."

Many of the teachers had been part of a teaching collaborative at Whitman that had tried to implement some instructional innovations—particularly team-teaching and teacher collaboration—within the unsupportive context of a large, multitrack, year-round school. For Janice, a fifth-grade Sheltered English teacher, the experience of collaboration was powerful, and when her colleague from the collaborative system, Dora, joined the small school design team, Janice followed her. She explained:

> Working with another teacher challenged me in new ways that were very exciting for me . . . So Dora was the one who got involved with the collaborative first, with the people who were looking at forming a small school, and I wasn't really that interested, but Dora said she was going . . . So, basically, I got involved because Dora was involved, but the more I started looking at the things that really were making me unhappy and started thinking about the possibility that things could be different for the children, and that I could be a teacher in a different way, the more excited I got. So I got dragged into it.

As these quotes reveal, the teachers were motivated by profound respect for their colleagues and a desire to continue collaborating with each other in a more supportive context. Teachers were often ambivalent about leaving Whitman Elementary School. Janice told us, "I had been at Whitman for ten years and loved it there; there were many, many things that I loved about Whitman . . . And there were a lot of things that I wasn't happy with, but that I just kind of accepted as being inevitable in such a big setting." Similarly, Susan said, "There were a lot of things that I really liked about Whitman. And the things that frustrated me, I just tried hard to ignore." Linda recalled that she and a colleague began attending small schools meetings to show their support for the movement, but not to start a new school themselves, because, they said at the time, "we're happy and we probably wouldn't want to leave Whitman."

But teachers also realized that many of the instructional reforms they hoped to implement were doomed to failure in the context of Whitman. Laurie, a bilingual kindergarten teacher, put it this way: "After thirty years of teaching children in Oakland, I know that it is impossible to make the changes that need to be made when every month there are teachers coming and going, one day they're there, and the next day they're gone." Yvonne, another bilingual teacher, explained:

> One of the hard things that we found when we started the collaboration was passing our kids from one grade to the next at the end of the year was very difficult, because there were all these pressures to move kids around, or teachers were moving, or we never even knew really what teacher was going to stay from year to year, and just working with 1,400 students when it came time to figure out which kids were going to which classrooms, we got less support than we needed in order to make sure . . . that there was a smooth way of passing students.

Teachers hoped that a small school would facilitate the reform work they had attempted at Whitman. As Helen said, "I think that by having the consistency here, by having really excellent teachers in a smaller environment, a lot of the things that we attempted to do at Whitman will really finally come to fruition here."

Teachers were also motivated by their commitment to equity and their belief that children in Oakland, particularly in flatland schools, were being underserved. Although inequities between hills schools and flatland schools were mentioned as a driving factor by several teachers, they arrived at this understanding in different ways. Susan said she first learned about inequities in graduate school:

> I went to a suburban school district that had pretty good funding and very good schools; it worked out great for me and I got a really good education. But once I got to graduate school, I realized that the education I got wasn't equitable. That there were a whole bunch of kids even in the community where I lived who did not get the same education that I got. And once I started getting my credential and getting my master's degree and teaching, it became even more apparent that the vast majority of children in public schools were not getting the education that other children got . . . So I started doing research in graduate school on inequities in education, and when this project [the small school] came up, I just saw, this is the chance, at least for 240 kids, to make a difference.

Susan's understanding of inequity, and her desire to change it, was framed in the world of educational research and theory. Others were motivated by firsthand experience teaching children in underfunded schools. As Janice put it:

> For me, wanting to be involved with reform has to do with ten years in Oakland, loving these children, and thinking that they deserve so much more than they got. And feeling frustrated that no matter how hard I worked, the way it was set up, I couldn't give them what they needed, and it broke my heart.

Certainly, teachers and parents shared the desire to create something better for the children, and hoped that the new small school would provide better opportunities for the children of Oakland. But, as the quotes above suggest, teachers differed from parents in the nature of their experience with inequities, and in their understanding of how a small school would translate into better opportunities. For the teachers, the most hopeful part of the small schools reform seemed to be the new opportunities for professional development and collaboration. As Lorraine put it, "The thought of having a whole school of incredible teachers and dedicated teachers is—was—like a foreign concept!"

For Ofelia, the parent facilitator of the English teacher focus group, what was missing from the teachers' responses was the role of the community in the reform. Ofelia wrote in her reflection:

> Me pareció muy interesante escuchar a la mayoría decir que nunca pensaban en tener una escuela pequeña, que sólo pensaban trabajar juntas en Whitman. Me he puesto a pensar desde que escuché esas respuestas y siento que esta escuela está fundada más por el esfuerzo de padres y de la comunidad porque las maestras no tenían esa meta o no pensaban ni luchaban tanto para que fuese así. Siento que todas querían trabajar en una escuela pequeña pero no pusieron fe y lucha para que juntos comunidad, padres y maestros lo pudiéramos lograr.
>
> También reconozco que sí han trabajado bien duro y muchas horas, he sido testigo de eso. Pero siento que ellas trabajaron para lograr que aseptaran su propuesta, para saber cómo y quiénes asistieran a la escuela, se frustraban pensando que no tenían suficientes niños en las clases de inglés, pero siento que no se enfocaron en lograr el terreno para la escuela.
>
> *En ningún momento mencionaron que trabajaron con padres o representantes de la comunidad . . . Esto me hace sentir poco triste.*

It was very interesting to hear the teachers say that they never planned to have a new small school; they only wanted to work together at Whitman. I have been thinking about this ever since I heard those responses and I feel that this school was founded more by the effort of parents and the community because the teachers didn't have that goal, or didn't struggle for that. I feel that they all wanted to work in a small school, but they didn't commit themselves to the struggle so that the community, parents, and teachers could achieve it together.

I also recognize that they have worked very hard and many hours, I have been witness to that. But I feel that they worked to get their proposal accepted, to know who would attend the new school; they got frustrated thinking that there weren't enough children in the English classes, but I feel that they didn't focus on getting the land for the school.

At no point [in the interview] did they mention that they worked with parents or representatives from the community . . . This makes me feel a little sad.
(Emphasis added)

It was significant to Ofelia that the teachers did not mention the struggle for the land on which the school opened, which many parents remembered as a dramatic chapter of the school's history. Community members organized by OCCA had fought for several years and overcome strident opposition to secure access to abandoned city property for the construction of new small schools. Although some teachers had participated in this organizing, attending at least some community meetings that I observed, they did not recall this as central to the school's origins.

Given their own experiences as parents organizing for new small schools, the mothers in Madres Unidas were surprised to discover how little these experiences figured in teachers' accounts of the history of the school or the movement. Whereas the Madres' own memories and their interviews with other parents emphasized "the need" and "the struggle" behind the new small school, teachers confessed to being motivated more by ideas and professional collaboration to leave the "relatively comfortable" place of Whitman Elementary School. When asked about the origin of the new small schools, few teachers talked about the role of the local community or OCCA's organizing. For most teachers, the reform was seen as emanating from the ideas of Deborah Meier in New York's Harlem. The following response of Tracy, from the English teacher focus group, is illustrative:

> I read *The Power of Their Ideas* when I was in Texas [other teachers nod in agreement], and I read it and I had been teaching for a year and a half, and I thought, man! I gotta start a school! Yeah, so, it mostly started on the East Coast, right? In New York and Chicago. I don't know much about here.

Tracy's response is interesting because she did not seem to remember that she was speaking to a parent (Ofelia) who had been involved in small schools organizing in Oakland, and who might not know what *The Power of Their Ideas* was. I often wondered whether teachers would adjust their responses for parent interviewers. In this case, it seemed that Ofelia's identity as a parent was irrelevant—or insignificant—to the teachers. Tracy assumed shared background knowledge about an educational reform book, and claimed ignorance about the local context, in spite of the fact that she was speaking to a parent who had been active in the local organizing: "I don't know much about here." I interjected, "in case Ofelia didn't know," that *The Power of Their Ideas* was a book written by Debbie Meier, a teacher who started a small school in New York.[2] It turned out that most of the teachers had read the book. The following exchange reveals their esteem for the New York educator:

Helen: One time there was a conference in Emeryville at the Holiday Inn . . .
  and we snuck in to hear Debbie Meier! [everyone laughs]
Susan: You crashed?!
Helen: We crashed. She was the keynote speaker and we were just like, Oh!
  If we could just start our own school! But I have to confess, I used to
  think, oh, you know, piece of cake!

Lorraine, a kindergarten teacher, revealed a vague knowledge that the community had been involved in the Oakland reform:

And then a group of parents, I don't if this was before or after Washington,[3]
but a group of parents, school board members, and, of course, no teachers,
some people from OCCA went back and looked at the New York City small
schools . . . And no teachers were involved at that point.

Lorraine's reference to the fact that teachers had not been included on the
trip OCCA organized to visit small schools in New York reveals the separateness with which teachers and parents experienced and participated in
the movement.[4] Lorraine had heard about this trip but didn't know much
about it. Her comment that "of course, no teachers" went suggests some
resentment that parents should have had this opportunity, and not teachers. Again, the source of expertise and inspiration for the reform was seen
as New York, and parents' participation in the reform, in her mind, hinged
on their exposure to the schools in New York. There was no recognition
of the urgency of the situation in Oakland, or the organizing of parents
locally, which had given rise to the movement in Oakland.

Some teachers did discuss the role of parents and the community in the
origins of the reform. Yvonne, a bilingual teacher, explained: "The idea is
from the East Coast, New York, but also from OCCA and what they tried
to do at Washington [Elementary]. Washington parents . . . organized for
a new small school, but the district didn't grant it." In Yvonne's mind, it
was the coming together of these two forces that created the new small
schools in Oakland:

It sounded like there were two things coming together; there was the
OCCA and the movement, and I'm not sure where that started, I'm not sure
if that started after hearing about what was happening back east, or if they
just happened to come together at the same time . . . But it definitely was
coming from the community, from Washington, and I think from BACEE.

In general, bilingual teachers were more familiar with OCCA and better informed about the community's organizing than were Sheltered English teachers. Those who had participated in OCCA meetings had received some training on working with parents. As Linda recalled, "Erica [BACEE coach] and Evelyn [OCCA organizer] were always talking about parents and teachers working together." Still, references to the roles parents had played were vague and fragmented—in this case, tied to something the BACEE coach or OCCA organizer had said—and not the result of first-hand experience with parents. More to the point, the role of parents in the reform, or the experiences of parents at Whitman, were not central in the teachers' minds about how the reform had come about or what had motivated them as teachers to get involved.

Parents, by contrast, spoke exclusively of bad experiences at Whitman and the role of community organizing when discussing their reasons for becoming involved in the new small school. Parents had countless stories of being mistreated by school staff at Whitman in what they perceived as a hostile environment to Spanish-speaking parents. Stories of their children's suffering in an overcrowded school were often intertwined with stories of their own experiences in an unresponsive bureaucracy. Recall Leticia's story earlier, who, when asking for permission to take her three children out at the same time, was shooed away by the administration, only later to be told that her children were dropped from the roster for having missed classes. The confusions of roving and the multitrack schedule were exacerbated by poor communication between school staff and parents. Parents often complained that the principal and office staff at Whitman did not speak Spanish—in spite of the fact that 77 percent of the student body was Latino—and did not respond kindly to Spanish-speaking parents. In the small school, they liked the fact that the principal and secretaries spoke Spanish and attended to them respectfully when they came to the office. The need for better relationships ("relaciones más familiares") between staff and parents was often cited as a reason for joining the small schools effort.

Baudelia explained her motivation for organizing for new small schools by describing the myriad problems she and her children faced at Whitman Elementary School: "en base de la necesidad que estaba viviendo yo en Whitman" (based on the need I was living at Whitman). Like most parents (and teachers), she did not like the year-round, multitrack schedule of the school. But beyond the obvious organizational problems of an overcrowded school like Whitman, Baudelia was concerned by what she saw as a lack of respect for parents' rights. This was a theme echoed by several parents in discussions at design team meetings. Like the mother who said that children were moved around "as if they were monkeys," Baudelia was angered by the administration's tendency to pull children out of classes and put them into other classes without communicating to the parents. In some cases, she said, children were moved from the bilingual program to all-English classes simply because of space constraints. When parents confronted the principal, they were told that there was no room for their kids. "Son cosas que no tienen que estar pasando, ¿si me entiende?" (These are things that shouldn't be happening, do you understand?).

Baudelia recounted several incidents in which there were problems at the school that the principal failed to communicate to parents. When asked about the administration's communication with parents, Baudelia responded, "Pues, ¿cuál comunicación? ¡Es nula! . . . En primer lugar, el 75 por ciento de la población es Hispana. Ella no habla nada de español" (What communication? It's null! In the first place, 75 percent of the population is Hispanic. She [the principal] doesn't speak any Spanish).

In the end, Baudelia's firsthand experience with the deep problems at Whitman provided the motivation for her to continue to work for new small schools:

> Yo veo que necesitamos un cambio, necesitamos una escuela pequeña, necesitamos que haya comunicación . . . Eso me involucró, dije yo quiero ver un cambio en la escuela y a la vez que la nueva escuela haga la diferencia de, en todos los aspectos, en la educación, en la comunicación, en la organización, en todo.

> I see that we need a change, we need a small school, we need there to be communication . . . That got me involved, I said I want to see a change in the school and at the same time for the new school to make the difference in all aspects, in education, in communication, in organization, in everything.

Ofelia, when reflecting on her own reasons for joining the small school design team, shared the following: "Me daba mucha tristeza ver todos los problemas que existían en la escuela donde iban mis niños. Seguido mis niños estaban con sangre en la camisa, porque tenían problemas con los niños afuera . . . Entonces yo me sentía frustrada, yo no sabía qué hacer, o

sea, ¿qué hago? Decía yo, yo no me puedo mover, no tengo esa posibili-
dad. ¿Qué puedo hacer yo para mejorar la escuela de mis hijos?" (It made
me so sad to see all the problems that existed in my children's school. My
children would regularly come home with blood on their shirts, because
they had problems with children outside . . . So I felt frustrated, I didn't
know what to do, like, what do I do? I said, I can't move, I don't have that
option. What can I do to improve my children's school?). Other parents,
too, shared stories of fights in the bathrooms and on the schoolyard at
Whitman—violence that might be more expected at a junior high or high
school than an elementary school—stemming from overcrowding and a
lack of oversight. In these circumstances, as Ofelia put it, the small schools
reform was "like an exit, an open door," to be able to change the problems
at Whitman.

If the conditions provided the motivation, for parents, OCCA offered
the means to organize for change and make new small schools a reality.
Baudelia, responding to the answers of other parents in a focus group, reflected, "A lot of people already explained [the reasons for new schools], to
eliminate overcrowding, so that the children wouldn't have to rove anymore, but why? I think it's because somebody felt this need and these problems that we are facing. Because there is a lot, a lot of need, but if nobody
feels that need and nobody understands us, nobody is going to take initia-
tive. I think [this school] was founded because there was somebody who
took an interest in our problems and thought of giving us a solution. And
that somebody for me was OCCA." Baudelia's assertion that "if nobody
feels that need" suggested her awareness that parents' experiences alone,
as members of a marginalized class, were not sufficient to mobilize for
change; they needed allies with power to take "an interest in our problems."
The significance of OCCA, as an organization that represented parents and
the community and took their concerns to the public sphere, figured prominently in Baudelia's narrative about the origins of the new small schools.

Although not all parents recognized OCCA or the role it had played in
organizing for new small schools (a fact that Baudelia would later lament),
for all parents, the new small schools were seen as an answer to intensely
personal need based on their own experiences at Whitman Elementary
School. Many had participated in the large actions to demand new small
schools and appropriate facilities, and recognized United Community
School as the product of community struggle. The experience of injustice

was a powerful shared narrative that explained both the need for new smɑ..
schools and their participation as parents in the reform.

In this chapter, I have tried to highlight the different perspectives teachers and parents brought to the new small school based on their differing social locations. Teachers had a choice in joining the design team, and they described their motivation very much in the language of choice: the small school was an option they hoped would enrich their professional lives as well as their students' learning. For parents, it was a necessity. Their children's educational survival in no small way depended on it. In the following chapters, I explore how these distinct frames of reference shaped interactions between parents and teachers as they struggled to collaborate in the design of a new school. For it was not just that parents and teachers came from different places. Parents, as the Madres would discover, would have to fight for the recognition that the place they came from was a legitimate one from which to engage in school reform, and that their experience, no less than the teachers' training, had uniquely positioned them to work for change.

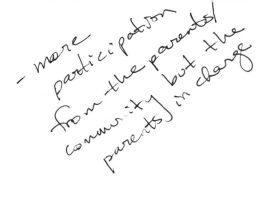

— more participation from the parents [from the community but the parents] in change

2. Baudelia's Leadership
CLAIMING SPACE FOR PARENTS IN SCHOOL DESIGN

On a Wednesday evening in October, one week after the Request for Proposals (RFP) release,[1] a group of parents and teachers met in the small library of Whitman Elementary to discuss plans for a new small school. The teachers had already met on several occasions, but this was their first meeting with Whitman parents, at the school site. The small school design team did not have the blessing of Whitman's principal and, according to teachers, had met "in secret" until then. Now, thanks to the organizing work of a parent leader, Baudelia, the group had been granted meeting space at the school, and parents were brought into the conversation.

Present at the meeting were seven Whitman teachers, all women, sitting along one side of a long table, and ten parents, including Baudelia. There was also an OCCA organizer, Evelyn, a representative from BACEE, and myself. The meeting, which was called and led by Baudelia, was conducted almost entirely in Spanish, with periodic translations into English by Evelyn for two teachers who could not speak Spanish. The purpose of the meeting was to introduce parents to the teachers' plans to date, and to devise ways for parents to collaborate in the design of the new small school.

The meeting began with one of the teachers, Linda, explaining that teachers had begun the process of creating a new small school. Although they did not yet know many details, they had definitely decided to submit a proposal. Another teacher added, "We do know that what we want to do as teachers, we can't do in this school."[2] A parent asked, what did they want as teachers? The teacher replied, "We want a sense of community and more participation from parents and the community in the school."

From the outset, teachers publicly framed the design of the new small school in terms of a desire for greater participation from parents and the community. And yet the parents were made to understand that the teachers had already been meeting and planning for the school, without the participation of parents. Baudelia's work to bring the two groups together

49

was the first of many steps toward the elusive partnership between teachers and parents. This chapter describes the efforts of Baudelia to claim a space for parents in the design process, and highlights differences between her organizing strategies and those of the teachers. While the meetings called and led by Baudelia were interactive and participatory, privileging discussion of parents' experiences and concerns, meetings directed by teachers consisted mainly of giving parents information or soliciting parent input in predetermined areas. I analyze these differences as a struggle over legitimacy in the social-change process, in which Baudelia fought for parents' right to participate in school design based on their experience with, and not necessarily training in, their children's education. Teachers' failure to recognize parents' experience as a legitimate source of expertise resulted in silencing parent voice and reproduced neocolonial relations between white professionals and parents of color.

Once teachers had made known to parents their intention to open a new school, Baudelia addressed them: "Do you have specific plans for the instructional program or philosophy of the school?"

A teacher responded with what sounded like a well-thought-out vision statement, including a list of beliefs about children, ending with "children have the power to create social justice in their communities." This was the first parents were to hear about the "social justice" focus that teachers had chosen for the new small school.

Immediately responding to this vision statement, Baudelia asked, "What role will parents have in creating this education?"

Another teacher replied that they hoped that teachers and parents would design the school "together."

From here on, a volley of questions was directed at the teachers from the parents, as teachers explained their ideas and the constraints under which they had to work. One father, wearing an Alameda County Transit cap, asked what would happen to Whitman Elementary School if a new small school opened up at another site. Would this school grow back to its original size? Would it have the same problems? How would children be selected to attend the new small school?

Baudelia, as a fellow parent, responded to his question by saying that this was a major concern, and that they would have to work to improve the education at Whitman, too, because they are all "part of the same family."

She said, "We don't know which of our children will attend the new small school, and we have to be concerned about all of our children. We can't abandon this school."

Throughout the meeting, Baudelia encouraged other parents to express their concerns and assured them that they would plan another meeting. As the meeting drew to a close, Baudelia announced that at the next meeting, teachers would hear from the parents about their concerns about new small schools. "During today's meeting, we parents have listened to you teachers," she said, "and now at the next meeting, the teachers will listen to the parents!" She suggested a list of questions, which she had evidently prepared ahead of time, that teachers should pose to parents at the next meeting:

What do you understand by "small schools"?
Would you like for your children to attend a small school in the future?
How would you like your child's school to be?
How can we organize as parents and participate in this?
What do you propose to make this dream a reality for the education of our children?

She said that they would write the questions on butcher paper, and parents in groups could write their answers. Of all the meetings on small schools I had attended, this was the first time J had seen a dialogue initiated about what the small schools should look like. It was significant that this dialogue had been initiated by a parent. Teachers then added to Baudelia's list of questions:

How do you understand the "self-governance" *(autogobernanza)* of the school?

Here Baudelia asked whether everyone in the room would understand the word *self-governance*. The teacher who had proposed the question said that the point was to see what parents understood by it, and they would discuss it at the next meeting. Teachers then added the following questions:

If you could name the school, what would you name it?
What is the responsibility of the child, of the parent, and of the teacher?
How can we include parents of other ethnicities who don't speak Spanish?

Baudelia took down all of their suggestions and assured them that they would be discussed at the next meeting.

In this first meeting, Baudelia worked to affirm and validate parents' concerns, and to signal to teachers and parents the existence of a community in which relationships were paramount. As she had said to the father, all children at Whitman were "part of the same family," not just those who would attend the new school. At the end of the meeting, she publicly observed that the teachers had controlled the meeting ("we parents have listened to you teachers"), and announced that this would not be the format of future meetings. To guide teachers in initiating a conversation with parents, she prepared a list of open-ended questions that teachers should ask in order to encourage parent reflection and discussion. The questions teachers added, by contrast, focused on specific areas that reflected their view of parents' roles: in naming the school, for example, and reaching out to other parents. This was the first parents would see of teachers' attempt to manage parent participation, a topic that will be explored further in later chapters.

Two weeks later, Baudelia called me to remind me about the next parent meeting. She told me she was not sure how many parents would come, because the school had scheduled another parent meeting for the same time. "Why?" I asked, surprised. Baudelia told me that City Councilman Ignacio de la Fuente had asked for a parent meeting at Whitman, and the principal had scheduled it for the same time as the small schools parent meeting. "The principal is always creating obstacles for me," Baudelia said.

In spite of this complication, forty-eight parents showed up for the small schools meeting the next evening. Although Baudelia asked them if they were all in the right place, and gave them the opportunity to go to Ignacio de la Fuente's meeting if they wished, no parent left. It appeared they had all come to talk about new small schools. In addition to the parents, there were nine teachers, two OCCA organizers, and myself. Baudelia had secured child care from the school so that parents would be free to concentrate on the meeting.

Baudelia was in charge of the meeting. She had an agenda, in English and Spanish, and a list of questions for the parent and teacher working groups, also in English and Spanish. "Today we didn't come to listen," she announced, "but to work together, parents and teachers." Baudelia explained that parents would discuss in small groups the questions being passed out, questions that had been generated at the last meeting. She encouraged parents to express all their ideas in the small groups, to not feel embarrassed because no idea was silly, all ideas would be taken into account. They then broke into five groups, each with five to ten people, parents and teachers. Baudelia asked each group to appoint a note taker so that all their ideas would be recorded. Then, at a later meeting, they would put all their ideas together.

The room buzzed with activity. Parents were being asked about questions that mattered to them, and they had a lot to say. In addition to the questions generated from the last meeting—including "What do you understand by 'small schools'?" and "How would you like your child's school to be?"—were some new ones: "Do you have any concerns about the education of your children?" "If you could choose the principal of your school, what qualities would you want that person to have?"

The following excerpt from my field notes reveals some of the rich discussion that occurred:

> Baudelia asked me . . . to join a group that was all parents, to help lead them along. (All of the other groups had at least one teacher.) This group was in the midst of an animated discussion about the importance of small classes, citing all the things that go wrong when a teacher has too many students to deal with. The one father in the group, Don José, who sat in a wheelchair, was taking notes on his questionnaire. The other three parents were Ana, Maria, and Veronica. All three women were very articulate and impassioned about the problems their children face at Whitman. One complaint they had about Whitman was that students are not treated with respect. Children are moved from classroom to classroom abruptly, with no explanation. "They move them from room to room as if they were monkeys!" Ana said, and the others laughed, and wrote down that phrase. Ana said, "My daughter is not a puppet."

We were not even halfway through the list of questions when Baudelia called time. It was already 6:30, and she had promised the group that the meeting would not take longer than an hour. Several groups wanted to continue working, but some teachers started to get up and one of them flashed the lights on and off to indicate that the meeting was over. The child-care lady let out the kids, who came streaming into the room. "Not yet!" Baudelia tried to say. "The meeting isn't over yet!" But it was too late.

She told the group to turn in their sheets, and that we would continue this at the next meeting, the same time next week.

Baudelia

Baudelia had three children at Whitman in PreK, first, and third grades. I first met her at a local organizing committee meeting for OCCA, where she immediately began talking to me about the conditions at Whitman. As an OCCA parent leader, Baudelia had been invited to accompany a delegation to Chicago to tour the small schools there, but she didn't know whether her husband would let her go. She had never been separated from her children. She told me she was trying to convince him that it would be a great opportunity. "¡Yo voy a preparar la maleta aunque sea!" (I'm going to pack my bags anyway!). This first interaction illustrated a great deal about Baudelia that I would later come to appreciate: her public status as a recognized parent leader, set against the conflict she faced at home with a husband who was not always supportive of her public role. Yet, far from being a constraining force on her activism, her ability to negotiate and navigate between multiple identities was a resource for her mobilization, providing a strength and a political savvy that would be useful in confronting a range of obstacles at the school. Analyzing Baudelia's organizing as an example of what feminist Cherríe Moraga (1981) termed "guerrilla warfare," a "way of life" for women of color, illuminates her engagement with teachers as part of an "eclectic paradigm for political mobilization" (Hurtado 2003, 265).

Baudelia immediately strikes one as articulate, confident, and self-assured. Before immigrating to the United States, she was a social worker in Guadalajara, Mexico, and had begun a law degree. She dropped out of law school to accompany her husband to Oakland, in what was intended to be a short trip to "fix his papers." They ended up staying ten years and counting. Still, Baudelia had not become a U.S. citizen, and did not consider her stay in this country permanent. Although her husband was also highly educated in Mexico, he now worked as a janitor at the Coliseum, the city's baseball stadium. Baudelia and her husband still talked about returning to Mexico, but she was committed to staying at least until her children learn English well:

> Me gustaría que mis hijos . . . aprendieran bien el inglés, que agarraran una carrera, porque yo no quiero que ellos pasen por lo que yo estoy pasando.

Para mí ha sido bien difícil, del idioma . . . Y no me gustaría que mis hijos pasaran por lo que yo estoy pasando ahorita en este país . . . O sea, yo estoy pensando en mis hijos, ya no en mí.

I would like for my children . . . to learn English well, to get a good career, because I don't want them to go through what I am going through. For me it's been very difficult, because of the language . . . And I don't want my children to go through what I am going through now in this country . . . I mean, I'm thinking about my children, not about myself anymore.

Baudelia was committed not only to her own children. In the five years that she had been living in her neighborhood, across the street from Whitman Elementary School, she had been active in neighborhood affairs, from getting more streetlights installed, to getting a liquor store closed, to getting a roving patrolman for the neighborhood, where crime and drug dealing were major concerns. She was a volunteer for the Neighborhood Action Team, the Unity Council, and the People's Clinic. She was also a member of St. Isabel's Catholic Church, where she was first introduced to OCCA. It was through her involvement in OCCA, and because of the need that she saw at Whitman, that Baudelia first became involved in the small schools reform.

Baudelia was one of the parents who gave a testimony at the November 8 action for new small schools, and she remembers this as a pivotal experience:

Yo me acuerdo que me dijo Eric [de OCCA], "¿puedes dar un testimonio?" Y yo, ¡no! Pero ay, ¡no! Con 2,500 personas y todos enfrente, y yo llegué y Dios mío, veía a todo lleno allí en el gimnasio, y yo me sentía nerviosa . . . Estaba nerviosa, pero dije, "Bueno, yo voy a hablar lo que yo pienso, a mí nadie me está diciendo que yo tengo que decir algo, yo voy a decir lo que piensa." Como que yo sola me di el valor, y aprendí, desde ese momento yo siento que aprendí a dejar el miedo a un lado.

I remember that Eric [an OCCA organizer] asked me, "Can you give a testimony?" And I was like, no! No way! With 2,500 people and everyone in front, and I arrived and my God! I saw the gym all full, and I felt nervous . . . I was nervous, but I said, "Well, I'm going to say what I think, nobody is telling me that I have to say anything, I'm going to say what I think." Like

I found the courage within myself, and I learned, from that moment I feel that I learned to put fear aside.

Her courage and passion compelled other Latino parents at Whitman to seek her out when their children were having problems. Baudelia had many stories of parents coming to her with problems: from frozen cafeteria lunches that made children sick, to classrooms without air conditioning or drinking water on hot summer days, to teachers who were physically and psychologically abusive to children. In each case, Baudelia advised the parents to confront the administration, accompanied them to meet with the principal, or confronted the principal herself. She also encouraged parents to come to the school's parent meetings, where they could air their concerns or hear critical information about the school. As Baudelia explained it, helping parents was what she most loved doing.

En primer lugar, lo que se trata de la comunidad o de la gente, allí estoy yo. Si me ponen detrás de un escritorio, no funciono, pero . . . algo que sea por el bien de la comunidad, allí estoy yo. Los niños, la gente . . . eso es mi mayor satisfacción, la gente, la gente, la gente.

First of all, whatever has to do with the community or with people, I am there. If you put me behind a desk, I'm useless, but . . . anything that is for the good of the community, I'm there. The children, the people . . . that is my greatest satisfaction, people, people, people.

But Baudelia struggled with English and felt limited in what she was able to do in Oakland, compared to her previous experience in Mexico. In Mexico, she told me,

Me sentía más satisfecha en el trabajo, lo que yo hacía . . . no tenía ninguna barrera como aquí que es el idioma. Aquí aunque yo quisiera irle a acompañar, "O mire, vamos a tal hospital, vamos al MediCal," ¿a qué voy? No hablo el idioma. Entonces me limita, es una limitación bien grande que tengo. Yo pienso que es lo único que a mí me limita mucho, porque yo con el idioma yo, no me importara que no tuviera el conocimiento, pero adquiría la experiencia como sea, ¿si me entiende? Pero el idioma, el idioma, la forma de entender con los demás, eso es lo que a mí me limita mucho.

I felt more satisfied in my work, what I did . . . I didn't have any barriers like I do here, with the language. Here, even if I wanted to accompany someone, "Oh, let's go to the hospital, let's go to the MediCal office," what am I going for? I don't speak the language! So it limits me, it's a very big limitation that I have. I think it's the only limitation I have, because if I knew the language, I wouldn't care if I didn't have the right knowledge, I would find the experience one way or the other, you know? But the language, the language, the way to understand other people, that's what really limits me.

Interestingly, Baudelia felt that any other knowledge she might need to help people get by in the United States she could easily acquire through experience: it was the English language that was most difficult for her. Baudelia had taken a series of English classes at local public colleges, none of which had given her the confidence to speak English well.

Then there were the challenges at home. Although Baudelia explained her organizing work in terms of her children and the community, it conflicted with traditional family expectations that her husband held. Before leaving for meetings, she would have to leave the house clean and dinner cooked for her husband. As she said to me, "No me gustara que mi esposo me llama la atención, 'Oye, por andar en la calle mira cómo tiene la casa o la comida o la ropa,' entonces es difícil para mí" (I wouldn't want for my husband to say to me, "Hey, for gallivanting around, look what a state the house is in." So, it's difficult for me). Her husband did finally let her go on the Chicago trip, after much persuading:

Pues, traté de decirle, "Mira, es una oportunidad, piensa en nuestros hijos, yo lo estoy haciendo por mis hijos, no lo estoy haciendo por un paseo." "¡No, no! ¡Ya te dije que no!" Y al día siguiente yo seguía . . . "Pero, mira José, dame la oportunidad." "¡Qué no!" Entonces venía nuestro aniversario. Me dice, "¿Qué quieres que te regale para nuestro aniversario?" Dije, "¿Me vas a dar lo que yo te pida?" "¡Sí!" "¿De veras? Mi deseo es que me dejes ir a Chicago." . . . Y me dejó ir.

Well, I tried to tell him, "Look, it's an opportunity, think about our children, I'm doing this for my children, I'm not doing it just for a trip!" [And he'd say,] "No, no! I already told you no!" And the next day I would keep it up . . . "But, look, José, give me the opportunity." "I said no!" Then our anniversary came. He asked me, "What do you want me to give you for our anniversary?" I said, "Are you going to give me what I ask for?" "Yes!" "Really? My wish is that you would let me go to Chicago." . . . And he let me go.

On the Chicago trip, Baudelia visited small schools where students and teachers weren't roving, where the buildings were clean, where parents, teachers, and students worked as a team, and parents told her they had excellent communication with the teachers. "You could see the difference," she explained. She returned from the trip even more determined to make a difference at Whitman.

Baudelia encountered obstacles not only from her husband. Her work on the small schools design team brought her into frequent contact with the principal, and she had many stories of confusing communication episodes. Not all of those were caused by a language barrier—Baudelia's English was better than she gave herself credit for. In Baudelia's view, the principal was not supportive of any kind of parent organizing at the school and felt threatened by the prospect of change. Baudelia constantly encountered opposition from the principal. The first time she tried to post flyers about the small schools parent/teaching meeting, the principal told her that she could not distribute any flyers in the school that did not have the district's stamp. Baudelia got around this by standing right outside the front door, and handing flyers to parents as they walked into the school. As she explained to me, "Yo sabía que estaba haciendo algo por el bien . . . Me bajaba la moral, pero yo también lo hacía afuera de la escuela" (I knew that I was doing something for the good [of the school] . . . It hurt my morale, but I just did it outside the school). On another occasion, the principal was not going to grant child care for a small schools meeting, because she said that Baudelia represented an outside group (OCCA). Baudelia had insisted that she was a Whitman parent and that the meeting was for other Whitman parents, and the principal finally gave in.

Baudelia did not hesitate to tell the principal exactly what she thought. As she frequently says, "Me gusta decir las cosas directas, lo que estoy sintiendo" (I like to say things directly, what I am feeling). One time, she told me, she had tried to tell the principal in her broken English that the principal needed to listen more.

Yo le dije, "¿Sabe qué? Usted le hace falta mucho escuchar." Le dije, "Yo siento que usted me oye—you listen me! But no me escucha," le digo, "¡no me escucha! No me escucha, porque no hace nada." . . . Y no soy la única que lo siento, pero no todos los padres tenemos a veces el valor de decírselo a ella directamente.

I said to her, "You know what? You need to learn how to listen." I told her, "I feel that you hear me, but you don't *listen* to me. You don't listen to me, because you don't do anything." . . . I'm not the only one who feels this way, but not all of us parents have the courage to tell it to her face.

Baudelia's direct style was difficult for some teachers and administrators to take. However, she felt it was a way for them to know what other parents were simply saying behind their backs. Sincerity was a quality she highly valued and found to be in short supply at Whitman.

In the end, Baudelia's refusal to tolerate the injustices at Whitman motivated her to work for a new small school. "Yo veo que necesitamos un cambio, necesitamos una escuela pequeña" (I see that we need a change, we need a small school).

Worrying about Parents in the Incubator

About a month after the Request for Proposals for New Small Schools was released, BACEE held its first "Incubator" session for design teams. The Incubator, in the words of the RFP, is "a unique organization designed to help new school Design Teams birth and nurture New Small Autonomous Schools." A collaboration between the district, BACEE, and OCCA, the Incubator was intended to provide coaching and technical assistance to design teams as they responded to the RFP and planned their new small schools.

This meeting was to be a proposal-writing workshop, and design team members were discussing challenges and giving and getting feedback from each other and from BACEE "school coaches." Thirteen teachers from the Whitman design team were present. No Whitman parents were present, and it appeared that no parents had been invited.

In my small group, Nancy, a teacher from Whitman whom I had not met before, shared that one of the main challenges their design team faced was how to involve the parents. I told her that surprised me, since I had been at the parent meetings and had seen a lot of parent interest. She then clarified that the challenge was to involve more non-Spanish-speaking parents. It is true that there had been no non-Latino parents at the meetings until now; and this was primarily because Baudelia was doing the organizing and she knew mainly Latino parents.

Nancy said that teachers at Whitman wanted parents to help in the writing of the proposal, and that this was a big challenge. The other member of our small group, a retired elementary school teacher, responded that parents probably wouldn't *want* to help with the writing of the proposal, and that at most they could critique it once it was written. Nancy liked that idea.

Baudelia might have had something to say about this had she been there, but as it turned out, she had never been told about the Incubator meeting. The next morning when I saw her at the school, I told her about it. She said that parents had not been invited, and she wanted to know more about it. "I could have gone," she said. It also turned out that she had not seen a copy of the RFP. Although she had been one of the two Spanish-speaking parents to make it to the RFP release, she had not been given a copy, and since the meeting was not translated, she didn't understand what it was for. So she did not know what specific criteria teachers were working with. Without the RFP, parents were effectively excluded from participating meaningfully in the planning process for a new small school. Why had it not occurred to teachers to share this with parents? The RFP, a document from the district invested with supreme importance by all teachers who held it in their hands, had become a gatekeeper.

At this point Baudelia expressed her frustration to me about trying to collaborate with the teachers at Whitman. She said that she felt teachers were not taking her work into account. For example, she told me, the teachers had held an all-day planning meeting on Veterans Day, but did not tell parents about it until the day before. Baudelia did not know how to get to the college where it was being held, so she didn't go. In her opinion, teachers should have posted flyers and gotten the word out to parents well in advance.

Listening to educators talking about parents at Incubator meetings brings to mind images of colonial officials discussing in hushed tones what to do about the "natives." Although the comparison may seem far-fetched, a growing number of scholars have pointed out that education in the United States unfolds in the context of colonial relations (Moll and Ruiz 2002; Tejeda, Espinoza, and Gutierrez 2003; Valenzuela 1999). The relations between education professionals and parents in the small schools movement reflect racial and cultural politics that have been inescapably shaped by the history of colonialism. As I observed teachers struggling with how to include parents in their plans for reform, I thought of the question W. E. B. DuBois once asked of African Americans: "How does it feel to be a 'problem'?"

Latino parents were a problem for education reformers in the small schools movement. They were a problem for reformers' work, needing to somehow be "involved," and they were victims of educational inequality and injustice that the reformers hoped to change. But they were often not present at the table when decisions about reform were being made. Why were parents so often talked *about* and not *with*? Why were the very real organizing efforts of Latino parents not seen or counted by the same teachers who aimed to involve them?

African American feminist scholar bell hooks (1989) writes of being excluded from the feminist movement by white women who claimed to be antiracist. White liberal women requested and longed for the presence of black women, yet "wished to exercise control over our bodies and thoughts as their racist ancestors had" (hooks 1989, 112). Liberal whites, like the progressive educators in the small schools movement, have become so used to speaking for the "Other" that they are not aware of how their speech silences those who most need to be heard. Hooks writes, "When liberal whites fail to understand how they can and/or do embody white-supremacist values and beliefs even though they may not embrace racism as prejudice or domination ... they cannot recognize the ways their actions support and affirm the very structure of racist domination and oppression that they profess to wish to see eradicated" (113). Hooks calls our attention to the deep paternalism underlying many progressive change efforts initiated by whites, where people of color are spoken about, rather than invited to speak as experts of their own experience. "Often this speech about the 'Other' annihilates, erases: 'No need to hear your voice when I can talk about you better than you can speak about yourself'" (hooks 1990, 152). Recall Baudelia telling the principal, "I feel that you hear me, but you don't *listen* to me."

The construction of Latino parents as "Other" has important implications for the way educational policy is implemented, Enrique Murillo (2002) points out. Within this discourse, Latinos become objects of white benevolence or discipline. Describing the reception of Latino immigrants in a Southern town, Murillo writes, "Many who claimed to welcome the newcomers nonetheless tried to change them (using awkward presumptions of benevolence) and enjoyed the self-righteousness of not seeming overtly racist" (225). This aptly captures the contradiction Baudelia encountered between teachers' professed goals for meaningful parent involvement and their attempts to manage that involvement to suit their own needs. Teachers requested the participation of parents in planning for new schools, but, as we will see, continued to act as if they preferred parents weren't there. Bell hooks writes, "Our very presence is a disruption" (1990, 148).

Silencing Parent Voice at Whitman Elementary

I told Baudelia that I would translate the questions from the RFP into Spanish and bring them to the next meeting, which I did. But by the next parent–teacher meeting, Baudelia was no longer in charge. The forty-some parents who had come expecting a continuation of the previous week's discussion found something rather different. The following description from my field notes illustrates how the agenda was taken over by teachers:

> The parents' responses to the questionnaire (from last week's meeting) were written on poster board, posted all over the room. When it came to that item on the agenda, Cristina, a teacher who is bilingual, told parents she would give a summary of what had been said for each question. She did this in both English and Spanish. For some questions she didn't read any answers at all, for example, the question, ¿Cómo le gustaría que fuera la escuela de su hijo? (How would you like your child's school to be?). She said she wouldn't get into the specifics, because there were many different ideas, and she invited parents to go read the posters after the meeting. But in my opinion that was the most important question, and it would have been well worth reading aloud all of the answers. For that matter, why weren't the parents reading their own answers? Why was a teacher reading it for them? By summarizing and paraphrasing, and never reading parents' answers in their own words, Cristina was taking the authority to decide what was most important; taking the parents' words away from them.
>
> During the reading (or summarizing) of the answers, the parents sat quiet. It occurred to me as slightly tragic that this exercise, which had

started out being about parents' generating their own ideas, ended up being such a boring drill! With all the energy seemingly stolen away from them.

After the review was complete, Baudelia spoke up to encourage parents who had not been present at the last meeting to add their ideas. "Por eso estamos," she said. ("That's why we're here.") One father made a comment about class size. But after that, Cristina moved to the next point on the agenda. No other parent had a chance to add anything. Cristina explained that part of the teachers' vision for the new small school was to have control over their budget, so that no class would have more than 25 students. While this was relevant to the father's concern about class size, it was unfortunate that this closed off the opportunity for other parents to add their ideas. Cristina had moved the meeting on to the "teachers' vision."

Following this was a question-and-answer period with the parents asking various questions about the school's program. Finally, Baudelia held up the RFP I had given her and explained that it was from the district. She said that many of the questions they discussed in the last meeting are in the RFP and that that's why they were discussing them. She also said that parents have the right to know what the teachers are proposing, and that she would make copies of the questions available for the parents.

At this point several teachers chimed in to say that they needed parents' help in preparing the proposal. Cristina said, "We can't submit this to the district without your help." Marie said, "You have to sign off on the proposal!" Linda said that teachers had been working on their days off, and had started writing the proposal, taking into account the parents' concerns, "but we feel that we can't go on writing without your help."

Linda told the parents that the teachers wanted to share with them what they had written so far, an answer to the question in the RFP about the school's educational philosophy. She read aloud the description in Spanish. Another teacher read the same thing in English. Clearly, their choice of words mattered enough to them to want to read it out loud word for word. Why was the parents' choice of words not equally respected?

It was because she understood the power of written words that Baudelia had asked each parent group to appoint a note taker at the last meeting, and each parent's thought had been painstakingly recorded. Yet the parents saw their words summarized or brushed over, while the teachers' words were read exactly as written. Furthermore, parents might have wondered what had been the point of recording their views if the teachers' vision remained separate, unchanged by the parents' ideas? While the parents wrote in public, at a meeting designated for them to record their thoughts, the teachers wrote in private, at a place and time unknown to the parents, and ultimately it was the teachers' written product that would become the proposal for a new small school.

After the teachers' vision had been read, Baudelia asked the teachers for copies of what they had written to distribute to the parents, and she also said she would make copies of the translated questions from the RFP for parents. As the meeting drew to a close, Baudelia urged all parents to write down their ideas and bring them to the next meeting.

Because Baudelia understood that teachers were preparing written responses to the RFP questions, she went home and wrote out her own answers to the questions. When I called her on the phone one morning the next week, she read one of her answers to me. Although she said she didn't know the proper terminology to use and that the teachers could edit her words, I thought what she read demonstrated no lack of eloquence. The following is her answer to the RFP's question, "What serves as the impetus for you and your team to seek to create a school at this time?"[3]

El objetivo de crear una nueva escuela, es en base a la necesidad de un cambio en los aspectos de: organización, académico, de participación, de comunicación, de seguridad, de limpieza y estructura, en la que podamos tener una visión diferente del proceso de enseñanza, en lugar de que se considere al maestro como único responsable de manejar la educación de los estudiantes que esta responsabilidad sea compartida entre padres, maestros, directores, incluso del entorno comunitario.

Nuestra misión es despertar la comunidad para que se de cuenta cada uno de nosotros está aquí para servir, así como para que se sirva, para respetar y ser respetado. Todos trabajaremos juntos con un máximo compromiso de responsabilidad de vocación, para lograr escuelas autónomas y el mejoramiento de su calidad. Éste es un deber y un derecho de todos y cada uno. Tomando como base principal la comunicación, ésta será la clave del éxito, y esto sea reflejado a través del rendimiento escolar de los alumnos.

The purpose of creating a new school is based on the need for change in the aspects of: organization, academics, participation, communication, security, cleanliness, and structure, so that we can have a different vision of the teaching process, where instead of considering the teacher the only one responsible for the education of students, this responsibility is shared between parents, teachers, school directors, and the larger community.

Our mission is to waken the community so that each one of us realizes that we are here to serve, just as to be served, to respect and be respected. We will all work together with the maximum commitment and responsibility of our vocation, to achieve autonomous schools and the improvement of their quality. This is a right and responsibility of each and every one of us. Beginning with the foundation of communication, this will be the key to success, and this will be reflected in the academic performance of the students.

In this excerpt, Baudelia emphasizes the mutuality of roles and egalitarian relationships in her vision of a school community, offering a direct critique of the current hierarchical structure. Her use of the words "each one of us" and "each and every one of us" signals the equality between parents and teachers, posing school design and school change as a "right and responsibility" of both. It is important to recognize this vision statement as the product of an oppositional consciousness, in the terms of U.S. third-world feminist theory, reflecting Baudelia's keen awareness of power differentials and her commitment to equalizing them. In this framework, Baudelia's experience of marginalization was a privileged standpoint from which to envision an alternative school: put differently, her vision could only be articulated from the lived experience of injustice. Given this, Baudelia's answers to the questions in the RFP should have been taken seriously by teachers who aspired to a school for social justice.

Baudelia told me that she had given her answers to the teachers at a meeting the Friday before (the day after the last parent meeting). The teachers had never officially invited parents to write responses to the RFP. And yet, Baudelia was meeting them on their own ground. In reading their statement of educational philosophy aloud to the parents, teachers had signaled that their privately written responses would be privileged over parents' oral responses. Baudelia responded by also writing in private. Her words had now entered the mix. Bell hooks describes the bold and courageous act of writing for women who have been silenced. "For us," she says, "true speaking is not solely an expression of creative power; it is an act of resistance" (1989, 8). In submitting her written statements unsolicited, Baudelia was challenging the teachers' domination of a process that was meant to include parents. "It is that act of speech, of 'talking back,'" writes bell hooks, "that is the expression of our movement from object to subject—the liberated voice" (9).

Negotiating the Right to Speak at Whitman

For the fourth Whitman parent–teacher design team meeting, on its now regular Thursday evening, parent attendance dropped from about fifty to twenty-five. Teacher attendance was also low: although normally at least nine or ten teachers would be present, only five arrived for this meeting. The group had seemingly lost some of the momentum it had in the early meetings that Baudelia had organized. Whereas the meetings Baudelia led had been interactive and participatory, the last meeting had been teacher-driven, with parents playing largely listening roles. The following excerpt from my field notes shows teachers continuing to dominate the meeting:

> Since I arrived a few minutes late, the meeting had already begun. Cristina, a bilingual teacher, was standing in front reading from a piece of paper, what sounded like a response to one of the RFP questions. She read in Spanish. I asked Baudelia whose response she was reading, and she said it was the teacher's own response. I asked her if they had read her (Baudelia's) response out loud. "No!" she said, as if surprised that I should ask such a thing. Had they said anything about what she had written? I asked. "No," she said, "I guess they didn't like it." I told her she should ask to read what she had written. "Did you read it?" she asked me. "Of course! I typed it up for you!" I said. "Really?" She looked happily surprised, but darted off to the front of the room before I could ask her again to read it.

All of the parents had copies of the questions from the RFP that I had translated into Spanish. These questions got to the heart of starting a new small school, asking design teams to describe the needs of their community, the vision and philosophy of the school, the proposed instructional program, and the role parents and community partners would play. On the basis of their answers to these questions, the district would decide whether or not to grant the new small school. But throughout the whole meeting, these questions were never addressed. Instead, posted around the room were four questions written by the teachers, which the parents were to discuss in small groups. This was explained after Cristina had finished reading her piece. The questions were

(1) What are your thoughts about discipline? What will your contribution be to support our agreements?
(2) What do you need to feel comfortable and capable to participate actively in the development of the new school?
(3) Should we organize a group of parents to observe a multiage classroom?
(4) School schedule. What is most convenient for the parents? What is most convenient for the students? (My translation from the Spanish)

Each group of parents, with one or two teachers, was to focus on a different question and report back to the large group what they had discussed. This activity was on the agenda as "Break into small groups and discuss parents' component of proposal," or "Trabajo en equipo: el componente de padres de la propuesta." So these four questions were "the parents' component of the proposal"? Who had decided that? The parents' role had swiftly been circumscribed to one of discipline, scheduling, and observing classrooms.

And yet, animated discussion was happening at each of the four tables. In each group, parents were discussing things that mattered to them, in ways that did and did not comply with the teachers' questions. Teachers often had to steer the discussion back to the question at hand. In some cases, parents' responses to the question seemed to deliberately resist the teachers' intent. For example, when it came time for the groups to report back to the large group, the parents who had discussed discipline shared the following comments:

- all kids should wear a uniform
- teachers should require *(exigir)* their students to turn in homework
- homework should not only be sent to school signed by parents, but should be sent home signed (corrected) by teachers
- kids who don't turn in their homework should be punished—made to stay in during lunch, for example
- parents should know the rules of their child's classroom(s)
- kids should not be moved from one classroom to another

Although the question had asked parents what would be *their* contribution to support *our* (teachers') agreements, all of the parents' points referred to the responsibility of the school or teachers, who to these parents weren't holding up their end of the discipline bargain. The parents had effectively subverted the teachers' question. Where the question implied that discipline problems are at least partly parents' responsibility, parents turned their critique to the school. In effect, parents were saying the school is not strict enough with their children. Baudelia added a comment about the homework, saying that while parents sign their children's completed homework, they never see it again, so they never know what their child did right or wrong. How can they help their children in this case? Again, the consensus of the parents appeared to criticize lax teacher policies, which shortchanged their kids.

Baudelia facilitated discussion after each group presented, inviting other comments and passing around the microphone. There was some ruckus as the microphone was passed around, as parents laughed and joked at the prospect of speaking into a microphone. One mother came forward and joked into the mike, "Well, I'm not going to talk to you folks tonight, I'm going to sing!" (field notes, November 30, 2000; my translation from the Spanish). Everyone laughed. Often after a parent spoke into the microphone, other parents would clap. I wrote down in my notebook, "Does the microphone empower?" Parents were clearly reveling in the opportunity to speak their mind, and in the possibilities for voice and play that the microphone allowed.

There was a heated discussion about multiage classrooms, a topic of one of the groups. The parents appeared to be unanimously against these classrooms, which were a part of the teachers' plan for the new small school. Parents expressed the concern that, if mixed in a classroom with two grades, some kids would lose out. As Baudelia explained to me, children were usually thrown into mixed-age classrooms because there was no room for them anywhere else. In other words, she objected to multiage classrooms as a makeshift practice, not as an educational strategy. But other parents were opposed to it even as an educational strategy. Teachers would only teach to one grade level (the lowest), so some kids would be repeating content. One father said emphatically, "It doesn't work to have two grades with one teacher." When Baudelia asked the group at large whether they were in agreement with multiage classrooms, there was a loud, resounding "NO!"

The parents had communicated their opinion to the teachers. The teachers, represented by Marie, responded by saying that parents needed to visit successful multiage classrooms at Whitman and in San Francisco. But later, when Baudelia asked the parents who would be interested in making such a trip, Marie said, "That doesn't need to happen now. That can happen in January or later, after we find out whether our school was accepted." There was no attempt to win the parents' agreement before the proposal was due, or to defend or explain the teachers' educational vision for multiage classrooms in light of the parents' concerns. I got the feeling this had already been decided.

And yet, I have tried to convey that this meeting was not a one-sided narrative. Although teachers clearly had an agenda, parents appropriated and subverted it in various ways and took advantage of having "the floor" to make their voice heard. Baudelia's asking the parents whether they were in agreement with multiage classrooms was in a sense a rhetorical question, because she knew that they were not. But it gave the parents the opportunity to shout a unified "no!" in front of the teachers, communicating their opinion loud and clear.

And the loudest expression of resistance was still to come. The next day, Baudelia called an emergency meeting to express her frustration to the teachers. She told me what happened the following week. After the meeting, Baudelia had stayed behind to talk to Laura, an OCCA organizer who had been present, and two of the teachers. "I have to tell you how I feel," she explained to the teachers. "I can't continue working this way." She said she felt that the teachers were working with the parents only as a requirement—"como un requisito"—and that they were working very separately. Baudelia said she expressed everything she felt and that Laura was amazed. The teachers offered to call an emergency meeting with the other teachers and parents the following day to discuss the issue. So, on Friday, seventeen teachers (far more than had been at Thursday's meeting) and several parents showed up. Baudelia explained everything she felt to the whole group, and argued that parents have the right to know the information the teachers are using, and the way they are working on the proposal. She told them, "You think that we as parents can't understand the process [of writing a proposal], but we do understand!" Furthermore, she said she was not going to keep organizing parent meetings if nothing important would be discussed. "I don't want what happened last Thursday to ever happen again." If teachers didn't have the proposal to share with the parents, Baudelia would simply not schedule the meeting.

British social critic Paul Gilroy (1987), writing on race, says, "The idea that blacks comprise a problem, or more accurately a series of problems, is today expressed at the core of racist reasoning. It is closely related to a second idea which is equally pernicious . . . [that] defines blacks as forever victims, objects rather than subjects, beings that feel yet lack the ability to think, and remain incapable of considered behavior in an active mode" (11). The Whitman teachers would have certainly considered themselves anti-racist, but their practices reproduced racial politics that denied intellectual agency to Latino parents. Baudelia called this out when she said, "You think that we as parents can't understand the process, but we do understand!"

In the meeting, Baudelia had wanted parents to discuss the questions from the RFP, which they had in front of them. But while she was doing the agenda with Laura, teachers had put up the other questions that had nothing to do with the proposal. "Where did those questions come from?" she had asked. She was angry, but didn't feel that she could say anything until after the meeting.

At issue here was the parents' trust for Baudelia as a parent leader, something she valued greatly. Baudelia told teachers that parents would start to think of her as a liar, "like the principal," if she kept promising them that their input was valuable when it really wasn't. Her comparison to the principal is telling, because the principal was almost universally mis-trusted among Latino parents as a poor leader who did not respect par-ents' rights. In trying to involve parents in the school, Baudelia had fought against this model of leadership and had struggled to create a place where parents' voices could be truly heard. Baudelia knew that parents' trust was a delicate thing, and she risked losing it if the teachers were not behind her.

But also at issue here, for Baudelia, was parents' right to be informed about and to have a part in a process that would greatly affect their chil-dren. As Baudelia said to the teachers, "Quizás nosotros como padres no tenemos la capacidad, pero sí tenemos el derecho" (Maybe we as parents don't have the capacity [to be involved in the proposal-writing process], but we do have the *right*). Interestingly, here she allows that not all par-ents might have the capacity to participate in substantive ways, a possibil-ity she had previously denied. But rather than an acknowledgment of par-ents' lesser capacities, this choice of words was meant to inform teachers that a parent's right to participate in the process was not dependent on his or her qualifications. Parents had a right to participate whether they felt qualified or not.

According to Baudelia, the teachers had fallen silent, stunned, but eventually acknowledged that they knew the process hadn't been right and that they needed to come up with better strategies to involve parents. Baudelia said she felt better after the meeting: "¡Me descargé!" (I unloaded!) she said.

When I asked Linda, a teacher, for her perspective on what happened, she replied:

> It was a communication breakdown. And we felt so under pressure, and I can understand where [Baudelia] was coming from, and I also know how hard we were working, and it felt really bad at the time, that "God, don't these people realize we're up until 11 o'clock at night working on [this]?" But it was a communication breakdown, and I'm glad that it happened because I thought it brought us closer after we met.

The confrontation, as difficult as it was, was a form of catharsis, bringing parents and teachers the relief of finally being honest with each other. As Linda said, "I think that's how people are brought closer together. There's always going to be conflict."

On Social Justice: "Aren't We Also Going to Talk about *Us*?"

The Whitman design team's proposed new small school centered on a theme of social justice. Part of the teachers' vision statement read:

> We see social justice curriculum as the portrayal of history and current events from multiple perspectives, participation in community activism and service, and the cultivation of respect. Our school community will act as a model of a tolerant and just society through our ongoing efforts to celebrate our diversity, to offer an equitable education, and to govern ourselves through a participatory democracy.

In early conversations with teachers about the new small school, Baudelia did not understand what they meant by "social justice." "They're talking a lot about 'social justice,'" she told me in our interview. "But I don't understand it." Finally, she had asked a teacher to explain it to her. Here she recounts the conversation:

Pues que los niños conozcan sus derechos, que esto lo apliquen afuera, y que tengan más conocimiento pues de lo que es una justicia social. Dije yo, "¿Pero no vamos a hablar también de *nosotros*, de lo que nosotros pensamos, de lo que nosotros queremos, de lo que nosotros queremos para esos niños?" Dijo, "¡Sí! Claro, también se va a hacer eso."

Well, so the children know their rights, so that they can apply this outside, and so that they have more knowledge, you know, about what is social justice. So I said, "But aren't we also going to talk about *us*, about what *we* think, about what *we* want, about what we want for those children?" She said, "Of course! We'll do that, too."

Here Baudelia challenges the teachers' abstract notion of social justice with the need to "talk about *us*." Her question to the teacher seemed to symbolize the conflict the design team was facing, as teachers experimented with ideas in the abstract, away from the immediate concerns of parents. And yet, Baudelia suggested, isn't that what social justice is about? The inclusion of parents' real-world needs, ideas, and concerns in the design of the school for their children?

Tejeda, Espinoza, and Gutierrez (2003) assert, "The ideology that pervades liberal notions of social justice is that of a hopeful Americanism. For all its talk against the social ills of 'racism and economic inequalities,' it fails to translate into a lived praxis that adequately contests the multiplicity of ways racism, capitalism, homophobia, privilege, and sexism are made manifest" (21). The authors caution against any notion of social justice that is divorced from the experience of those who most suffer from injustice. In order to enact a "decolonizing pedagogy," they argue, social justice must be defined by historically colonized people; our notions of social justice must be "derivative of and informed by the experiences and interpretations of those living an internal neo-colonial existence" (ibid.). Like bell hooks, they urge us to be conscious of our "neo-colonial condition," lest we believe that we have shed our racist past.

"Internal neocolonialism," which characterizes the U.S. context today, according to the authors, is a condition produced by mutually reinforcing systems of colonial and capitalist domination and exploitation. This concept emphasizes the continuity of colonial relations from our colonial past, reproduced in new forms (*neo*colonialism) and within the same country (internal). In our context it amounts to a condition of white privilege and control. Drawing on Barrera's (1979) definition of colonialism, they argue that "there continues to be a structured relationship of cultural, political, and economic domination and subordination between European whites on the one hand, and indigenous and non-white peoples on the other" (Tejeda, Espinoza, and Gutierrez 2003, 5). Within this context, "the forms of violence and 'microaggressions' experienced by dominated and exploited groups in the context of everyday life are both normalized and officially sanctioned by dominant ideologies and institutional arrangements in 'American' society" (3).

Tejeda, Espinoza, and Gutierrez raise the inherent contradictions in white teachers' attempts to implement a "social-justice" pedagogy without including the voices of Latino (and Asian and African American) parents who have most directly experienced educational and social injustice. In their view, the tendency of progressive teachers to think they know better than the parents themselves what parents need is neither a mystery nor an anomaly: it is the latest reinscription of colonial domination. It is made possible by cultural systems of knowledge and representation that construct inferior "Others" as the basis for domination, and by "historical amnesia" that encourages us to forget our roles as oppressors and oppressed. Importantly, "historical amnesia" can also mean the refusal to see the past in the present: a view of racism that consists in past atrocities, such as slavery and the extermination of Native Americans, and not in everyday life. Research by Lee Anne Bell (2003) showed that white professionals in the education and human-service fields went to great lengths to deny their own racist conditioning, maintaining a "color-blind" ideology that protected their innocence while seeing racism as a thing of the past. The importance of the concept of internal neocolonialism is that it highlights the new forms of colonial domination that are reproduced in our era: all of the subtle and not so subtle ways in which white privilege and control are still exercised. In the case of the Whitman small school design team, it can be seen as the violation of parents' cultural and intellectual rights in the small school design. Tejeda, Espinoza, and Gutierrez conclude, "The integrity of the indigenous mind/body is the standard by which we measure the success of any decolonizing pedagogy" (2003, 33).

Baudelia clearly had a strong understanding of social justice; it just didn't match the teachers' concept. A strong sense of justice (or, more often, injustice) lay behind all of her interactions with teachers, with the principal, with other parents, and behind all of her decisions to confront school authorities when she saw something she didn't think was right. Recall how she overcame the principal's opposition to her posting flyers because, as she said, "I knew that I was doing something for the good [of the school]." Rather than explaining social justice to Baudelia, teachers would do well to *listen* to her. They then might notice how often she uses the words *just* and *unjust*, and, most importantly, *rights*, in explaining her experience at Whitman Elementary School.

"Maybe we as parents don't have the capacity [to be involved in the design process], but we do have the *right*," she had said. According to Baudelia, parents have the right to know about their children's educational programs, to choose bilingual education and have their choice respected, and in general to be kept informed by the school:

> Yo creo que los padres tenemos derecho a saber si algo está pasando en la escuela y que pueda afectar a los niños, como eso que pasó del moho, eso que pasó a la escuela. Yo creo que tenemos el derecho de saber, por ejemplo . . . si mi niño va a ser cambiado de un salón a otro, o de una letra a otro, yo tengo el derecho de saber el *por qué*, ¿si me entiende? . . . Yo siento que es un derecho, que nosotros tenemos que mantenernos informados.

> I think that as parents we have the right to know if something is happening in the school that could affect the children, like what happened with the mold [in a contaminated classroom building], what happened to the school. I think we have the right to know, for example . . . if my child is going to be moved from one class to another, I have the right to know *why*, do you understand? . . . I feel it's a right, that we have to keep informed.

Importantly for Baudelia, these rights are accompanied by responsibilities or "obligations" that parents have: for example, to attend meetings at the school. In her response to the RFP, quoted earlier, Baudelia writes that it is a "right and responsibility" of "each and every one of us" to work together to achieve better schools. Rights are thus connected to individuals' obligations to the community.

From Baudelia's response to the RFP and her interview, a rich picture emerges of her vision of a just community, where everyone is there "to serve and be served, to respect and be respected." Respect and service to the community are important elements of this vision, and they are revealed clearly in her description of the "leadership model":

The leadership model that we would like to have in the new school is Democratic. The director should:

(1) Have the capacity to understand the community context.
(2) Have the desire to serve and make changes when they are necessary, not simply the desire to be someone.
(3) Be capable of directing, guiding, and understanding, with the potential for growth and necessary change.
(4) Be able to stimulate, encourage, and nurture supportive relationships between different people and to work on a team to support group decisions.
(5) Be secure of himself/herself, so that he or she can transmit this to others.[4]

Baudelia also believes that all children in the school should wear uniforms, and that they should receive civic education. She told me that she once approached Whitman's principal to ask why students never sang the national anthem. The principal had responded that it was because students were from all different cultures. Baudelia said:

> Yo entiendo, no les vayan a enseñar el himno de El Salvador, el himno de Canadá, sino el de *aquí*. Estamos en los Estados Unidos, es bonito que los niños se enseñan a respetar lo que significa la bandera, yo no digo que diario, ni cada ocho días, ¡pero una vez al mes! Un acto cívico, ¿cuándo les dan un acto cívico? Jamás.

> I understand, we're not about to teach them the anthem of El Salvador, the anthem of Canada, but of *here*. We are in the United States, it's nice for the children to learn to respect what the flag means, I'm not saying every day, not even every week, but once a month! A civic ceremony, when do they do a civic ceremony? Never.

Although it may seem puzzling that someone who is not even a U.S. citizen should want her children to learn the United States' national anthem, it became clear that this was part of Baudelia's vision for a community, a sense of belonging that would bestow on children both the rights and the responsibility that she feels are currently missing. And these rights and responsibilities are granted not on the basis of nationality, nor language, nor individual "capacities," as Baudelia made clear to the teachers, but by virtue of membership in the school community.

The parents' insistence on a school uniform for children shows that Baudelia is not alone in this vision of community. The parents in the design team meeting proposed a mandatory uniform as a "discipline" strategy. This reflects their belief that good behavior comes when children feel they are part of a community. As Baudelia explained it: "Si un niño se sale, usted no sabe si es de la escuela o es de la calle. Y si usted lo ve pasando un niño por ejemplo de kinder que va con el uniforme, 'Oye, ¿porque va solo?' O '¿porque te saliste?' O 'vas a la escuela, ¿no?' ¿Y cómo lo vas a identificar?" (If a child goes out, you don't know if he's from the school or from the street. [But] if you see a child passing, for example, from kindergarten who's wearing his uniform, "Hey, why are you alone?" Or, "Why did you leave?" Or, "You're going to school, aren't you?" How [else] are you going to identify him?). In this view, membership in the school community means that others will care about students and hold them accountable for good behavior. The uniform denotes membership, and with membership come rights and responsibilities.

When talking about "social justice," then, teachers need to be attentive to parents' understandings of justice, not only because it is their children whose futures are being envisioned, but because it is often the parents' experience that gives concrete expression to teachers' abstract notions of justice. As Tejeda, Espinoza, and Gutierrez assert, "The question of social justice by whom begs us to ask the question: Social justice for whom? We move away from notions of social justice that seek to create social space for the poor, dark-skinned and indigenous to be more like their oppressors" (2003, 21). From Baudelia's perspective, the first step toward a vision for social justice would be for the teachers to listen to and include parents' voices in the planning process. To talk about "social justice" and "democracy" while continually silencing parent voices was a blatant contradiction.

Fortunately, the story did not end there. Baudelia confronted the teachers, as we have seen, and forced them to engage in real dialogue with the parents. What factors enabled Baudelia to confront teachers in this way? Teachers would often see her as exceptional, explaining her behavior in terms of unique personality traits: "feisty" or "confrontational." Certainly, Baudelia had a strong personality: as she was fond of saying, "I always have to say what I feel." But it is important to understand her behavior in light of her life experience as an immigrant woman. Baudelia had been a social worker in Mexico, with a passion for helping others and the training and ability to do so, before she arrived in Oakland and found herself constrained by discrimination and a language barrier. This transition, and her "outsider/within" status in Oakland, gave her a unique vantage point from which to view the exclusion of parents by teachers. Here, Baudelia takes her place in a long line of U.S. feminists of color who share, according to Chela Sandoval, a "common border culture" . . . "comprised of the skills, values, and ethics generated by a subordinated citizenry compelled to live within similar realms of marginality" (2000, 52).

If Baudelia's experience provided the skills to engage with teachers, an essential factor in enabling her to continue struggling for parent voice at Whitman was the support of OCCA. At this point in my research, Baudelia talked again and again of how OCCA was an invaluable source of support to her. Importantly, an OCCA organizer had been there with her when she confronted the teachers. Baudelia credited OCCA with helping her learn to get past fear, and with legitimating parents' right to organize and express themselves.

OCCA provided both motivation and support when things got tough. Baudelia recounts that in times of stress, there was always Laura, an OCCA organizer, to help her out: "Siempre ha estado OCCA atrás de mí, en cualquier cosa . . . Siempre ellos han estado como apoyo" (OCCA has always been behind me, in everything . . . Always they have been a support). In the face of opposition from the principal, from teachers, from her husband, and at times from other parents, the support of OCCA encouraged Baudelia to keep on.

At the last parent–teacher meeting before the small school proposal was due, eleven parents and eleven teachers sat in a circle with copies of "A Summary of our New, Small, Autonomous School Proposal." This was a select group of parents that Baudelia had invited, because teachers had asked for a smaller group. The teachers began the meeting by reading aloud the proposal summary, in Spanish. They took turns reading, at times stumbling on the Spanish, at times correcting each other or laughing as parents giggled at their mistakes. For many of the teachers, the Spanish was a struggle. But their effort to read in Spanish, and their willingness to laugh at themselves and with the parents, created a feeling of closeness—a reminder that they were learners, too.

After the reading, the teachers asked parents to respond to three questions they had posted on the wall: What excites you? (¿Qué les emociona?) What worries you? (¿Qué les preocupa?) And, What questions do you have? (¿Cuáles preguntas tienen?) They asked parents to start by sharing what was exciting to them about the proposal.

Baudelia responded first, saying she was excited about the bilingual program and the project-based learning and community service. In the project-based learning piece, she liked the example of a community garden in which the children would harvest food that could be donated to a homeless shelter. Baudelia said that would teach children social responsibility, which she liked. A teacher responded by saying that the community-service idea is part of their vision for social justice.

"Oh, that's social justice?" Baudelia exclaimed. She looked happily surprised, as if she finally understood what the teachers meant, and she liked it.

The feeling in the room that night was overwhelmingly enthusiastic. The parents were thrilled about many aspects of the proposal, and the excitement was palpable as people imagined a school like this becoming a reality.

Of course, this was only the beginning. But through the insistence of the parents and the commitment of the teachers, a space had been opened for honest conversation. Ultimately, Baudelia had helped move the teachers closer to their goal, stated in the proposal: "We believe that we can create a school where people can come together in their urgency and pain, with passion, anger, and dreams to speak to one another in authentic voices."

3. Contested Community
NEGOTIATING ADMISSIONS IN THE NEW SMALL SCHOOL

Two years after OCCA held its first action for new small schools in Oakland, United Community School opened its doors in temporary facilities in the heart of the Fruitvale district. It was the first new school to open in the Fruitvale-San Antonio neighborhood in more than forty years. The brightly painted portables and newly laid lawn, still fenced in by bright orange netting to protect the fragile grass, stood out in colorful contrast to the surrounding urban environs: the looming concrete of the elevated Bay Area Rapid Transit (BART) tracks, a busy freeway, and still more train tracks, crisscrossing the avenues leading to the school. No one could have called this plot of land desirable property for a school. It stood at the border of a bustling commercial strip where an informal economy struggled to make up for decades of corporate and government neglect, and an industrial wasteland stretching to the Bay, traversed by commuters whizzing by on the freeway or on BART trains, on their way from jobs in the city to homes in the suburbs. And yet, community leaders with OCCA had fought for eight years to acquire this land from the city for new small schools. And on this day in late September, they were here to celebrate their victory.

Representatives from the school district, the school board, BACEE, and OCCA joined parents, teachers, and families to commemorate the unprecedented partnership that had brought them to this day. It was an overcast Sunday afternoon, with the sun trying hard to break through the clouds, and a steady wind blowing the decorative banners, balloons, and streamers that had been hung for the occasion. Colorful murals and welcome signs in English, Spanish, and Vietnamese were displayed on the wire link fences enclosing the school. Neighborhood Mexican restaurants and markets, along with several families, had donated food and drinks for the celebration, and a row of long tables was laden with platters of beans and rice, chicken, carnitas, lasagna, and potato and macaroni salads. Children's craft stations were set up around the courtyard, and in an adjoining playground a crowd of gleefully screaming youngsters attacked a succession of piñatas.

From the podium, a series of speakers addressed the crowd, sharing their pride in the new small school and thanking everyone who had helped to make it possible. "I'm very emotional, because our dream, our vision of a new school in our community, is a reality," said Lupe, a mother who had been on the design team. A second mother, Norma, told the crowd:

> I want to take this opportunity to say that I am very happy that my son is going to go to this new school where they have grass to run on, where they have nice new buildings, new classrooms, desks, and chairs. I've lived in Oakland my whole life. I was born here, I grew up here. I went to Oakland schools. And I know that Oakland schools need a lot of fixing. The schools I went to had only torn textbooks, broken lockers, and no security, and here, finally, we have the security that our children are going to go to a school that is nice, new, and safe.

After parents and teachers had spoken, an OCCA elder named Barbara spoke of the eight-year struggle to bring the school to this site—a history of, in her words, "an entire community coming together and working together towards a common goal."

The opening celebration of UCS was in many ways a celebration against all odds. In the face of urban neglect and decay, the community had chosen to open a new school, and had succeeded in overcoming innumerable bureaucratic and political obstacles to locate it there. The lot on which UCS was located, designated to house two new small schools in permanent facilities by 2004, had been the site of an abandoned department store building since the mid-1980s. In 1993, community members through the Local Organizing Committee at St. Isabel's Church mobilized to pressure the city to tear the building down and construct new schools in its place. New schools and recreational fields for children had been identified as top priorities for the community. The history of the community's struggle to obtain control of the property is in itself a remarkable story, beyond the scope of this chapter.[1] But, important for our purposes, the opening of UCS on the site represented the community's struggle to "transform the building from a symbol of despair to one of hope."[2] Many people present at the opening celebration that Sunday, including OCCA leaders, parents, and some teachers, bore the memory of the long struggle for the land, and the image of blight and abandonment that occupied that space before. When Barbara from OCCA spoke of the eight-year struggle to open the school, she was grounding the school in that community history, reminding all those present of its roots.

This history is important because it shaped community members' perceptions of the school in distinct and powerful ways. For parents who lived in the community and witnessed the transformation of the site, including many OCCA parents who had participated in the struggle to win the land for schools, UCS was indeed a symbol of hope; its purpose and existence were tied inextricably to the aspirations of the community. Teachers and reformers, however, did not necessarily share this view of the school. As discussed in chapter 1, not all teachers had been a part of the long struggle for the land or recalled it as a key part of the school's history. While teachers celebrated with the community the victory of the school on that day, they brought different memories of what it had taken to get to this moment, and different ideas of what the school was about. For this reason, the struggle of the community to gain control of the land would not end when the school opened. After participating in the struggle to bring UCS into existence, the mothers in Madres Unidas would find themselves raising the question of what it means to be a "community school," and who, after all, was "the community"?

This chapter examines competing visions of community that underlay teachers' and parents' negotiations in the process of deciding who would attend the new small school. In the months before the school opened, contentious debate to determine a fair admissions policy shaped interactions between teachers and parents, bringing tensions about the character and membership of "community" to the fore. Not only did parents and teachers bring distinct cultural values and understandings of community to the discussion, but their ability to operationalize their values in school policies was conditioned by cultural politics that privileged teachers' interpretations while silencing those of parents. By analyzing both the "ideals" for community and the discourses, spaces, and practices through which they were negotiated, I argue that teachers constructed "community" in ways that undermined the claims of Latino parents, and served to minimize Latino parents' power and participation in the shaping of the school. Madres Unidas, through their research into the admissions process after the school opened, uncovered the harmful consequences the school's mistakes had on the community, and suggested other values that should shape the school's admissions decisions.

Soon after their proposal for a new school was accepted, sixteen parents and five teachers had gathered in a classroom of Dalton School, adjoining Whitman Elementary School, to discuss a name for the school. The mood was jubilant. Parents called out ideas in Spanish, and teachers offered English translations. Both parents and teachers wanted to know how each name would sound in both languages. Early in the discussion, Baudelia said that the name should reflect the community, because, she said, "this school has been a community effort." She suggested United Community School. After much discussion and many ideas, an English-language teacher asked the group if they couldn't come up with a name that reflected their social-justice theme.

Baudelia responded in Spanish, "Social justice for whom? It starts in the community." A name that comes from the community, she argued, is a name that reflects social justice. In a struggle that would repeat itself many times in the development of the new school, the Latino parents fought to connect the school's social-justice vision to the immediate community, or the parents and families who had struggled to make the school a reality. The teacher's suggestion that the name United Community School did not reflect their social-justice vision revealed a conception of social justice that surpassed, and perhaps superseded, the local community of parents and families. This would be a point of contention that animated disagreements between parents and teachers over the next several months, but, like an undetected parasite that surreptitiously drains the body's resources, was never addressed or treated. Instead, teachers chose to run meetings in a bureaucratic format that minimized spaces for open discussion and dialogue, and prevented both parties from reflecting on and articulating their own images of "community." In the end, the group voted for the name United Community School, which they decided to translate into Spanish as Escuela del Pueblo Unido (literally, School of the United People), or, as it came to be known among Spanish-speaking parents, Pueblo Unido School. But it was not until Madres Unidas began their research, well into the school's first year, that the question was raised, what exactly is a "community school"?

United Community School is located just down the street from the old Whitman Elementary School, near the busy intersection of two main thoroughfares in Fruitvale, the heart of Oakland's largest and most established Spanish-speaking community. Across the street from the school, in front of a Goodwill store, Latino day laborers lined up each morning hoping to be picked up for jobs. Although some parents complained that they didn't want their children walking past "those men" on their way to school, other parents, including Ofelia, argued that the day laborers were "part of our community" and had the right to be there. All parents, who lived in the neighborhood and walked their children to school, knew there was much that needed to be changed about their community. In an essay she wrote for her GED called "Oakland Streets," Ofelia wrote that she worried about her children's safety. She described walking past the park with her eight-year-old son where groups of men were drinking and smoking marijuana, and having to explain to her son why they were smoking.

Fruitvale faced the challenges common to distressed urban neighborhoods everywhere, including joblessness, inadequate housing, low levels of educational attainment, and high rates of poverty. In 2000, Fruitvale was Oakland's most densely populated district, as well as one of its most diverse. A port-of-entry neighborhood in a city that was one of the top ten destinations for immigrants in the country,[3] Fruitvale experienced rapid population growth between 1990 and 2000, with the largest growth in its Latino population. Data from the 2000 census show that Fruitvale's population was 50 percent Latino, 24 percent African American, 17 percent Asian and Pacific Islander, and 8 percent white. Its total population of 54,857 represented an increase of 15 percent since 1990.

In 2000, 43 percent of Fruitvale's residents were foreign-born, and roughly half of those had arrived in the previous ten years. A third of residents were noncitizens, and nearly two-thirds of the population spoke a language other than English at home. Of these, the vast majority were Spanish-speaking. Seventy percent of the foreign-born population originated from Latin America, primarily from Mexico and Central America. Fruitvale's main thoroughfares, Fruitvale Avenue and the busy International Boulevard, are lined with Mexican restaurants, bakeries, markets, and *carnicerías* selling Mexican and Central American products, and agencies for sending remittances to Mexico and Central America. The neighborhood continues to attract many new immigrants from Mexico and Central America.

The economic obstacles and barriers to education facing the community are also evident in the census data: Only 11 percent of the population twenty-five years and older had a college degree in 2000, compared to 27 percent in the state as a whole. Nearly half of the adult population (47 percent) were not high school graduates. Twenty-one percent of families lived below the poverty level, and 25 percent of individuals did. Only a third of residents owned their homes.

In the face of these statistics, a strong network of well-established community organizations worked to support Fruitvale's immigrant population. St. Isabel's Catholic Church, a large multicultural parish more than a hundred years old, had an active Local Organizing Committee since the early 1970s. This was the committee that spearheaded the demolition of the abandoned department store and pushed for the construction of new schools. The Unity Council, founded in 1964, brought a number of important services to Fruitvale, including Head Start, the Fruitvale Senior Center, home-ownership assistance and affordable housing, employment services, and new parks. Fruitvale was also home to the People's Clinic, the Spanish-speaking Citizens Foundation, and the Latino Legal Counsel Center, which provide health and legal services, education, and advocacy for Spanish-speaking residents.

If the parents at UCS had one thing in common, it was the experience of struggle and setback that their neighborhood had witnessed over the past several years. As Baudelia had learned in her five years of organizing in Fruitvale, no service was won without a struggle. As a stark reminder of this, a tragic accident in the school's first year shook the community to its core. One morning in January, two families from the school were crossing the street on their way to school when they were hit by a speeding driver. The driver did not stop. All of the children and one of the mothers were hospitalized in critical condition; that night, five-year-old Lucy, a kindergarten student, died. The UCS community mourned the death of little Lucy with a pain all the more acute for having foreseen such a tragedy and having tried, unsuccessfully, to prevent it. Parents had organized to demand that a stoplight or a crossing light be installed at the intersection where the accident occurred, before the school opened. The city had promised them a crossing light, because it was cheaper. They got nothing. In the first few days of school, there was a crossing guard. Then even the guard was taken away, transferred to another school. With no protective measures on one of the busiest streets in Oakland, UCS parents sent their children to school with some apprehension, but without, it seemed, much choice. Now they wondered, how many children's lives would it take for the city to pay attention to this neighborhood? How many of *their* children?

At an angry meeting with city representatives five days later, parents demanded to know why the city let this happen, and why City Councilman Ignacio de la Fuente had not shown up to face them himself. They were informed by a representative of the traffic department that the intersection where the accident took place was ninth on a list of intersections in the city that needed stoplights. Ninth. At a meeting back in August, the month before the school opened, parents had been told that traffic lights cost two hundred thousand dollars apiece to install, and that the city had money for only two per year. At that rate, it would be more than four years before the school could expect a stoplight. In the meantime, parents were assured once again that flashing yellow lights would be installed. If parents had expected a public apology, and a promise for a swift installation of a new stoplight, they found instead a labyrinth of bureaucratic excuses. They had heard it all before, and they were sick of it. Many of them expressed their rejection of the city's response to the crisis by walking out of the meeting.

In fact, the city mobilized much more quickly than anyone expected. A new stoplight was installed at the intersection of the tragedy in March 2003, just over a year after the accident. Ofelia was one of the parent organizers of a ceremony to publicly thank Councilman de la Fuente for his attention to the community. But the stoplight had come at a high price— too high a price—and it confirmed what the parents at UCS already knew: progress for their children would come only with struggle and sacrifice. The memory of the tragedy remained strong in parents' minds, adding to the repository of experiences that shaped their sense of community. Collective suffering, writes sociologist Mary Pardo (1998), is a powerful force shaping community identity.

Pueblo Unido School's teachers may not have shared the local community's history of hardship and struggle, but they certainly intended for their school to be an integral part of this community, and to add to the resources that would make Fruitvale a better place. The ethic of community and collaboration, however vaguely defined, was at the core of their vision. Their proposal read: "Our school will build bridges among the diverse cultures represented within the student population, as well as within the community, through our social justice approach, collaboration, and integration . . . These bridges will be constructed in a climate of respect, safety and inclusion." This excerpt suggests how teachers believed they would achieve their goal of community. "Integration" was a key feature of the teachers' vision for a community school, reflecting their desire for an ethnically diverse, integrated school and for an equal number of bilingual (Spanish-speaking) and English-speaking students with plentiful opportunities for the two language groups to interact. Their experience of bilingual education at Whitman, a segregated school, had shown that their ideas about language learning were difficult to implement without sufficient speakers of English. They hoped to rectify this situation at UCS by having one classroom each for Sheltered English and bilingual education at each grade level.

Ironically, the teachers' goal of an integrated school, rooted in sound educational philosophy, created serious complications for carving a community school out of Whitman. In the first place, Whitman Elementary was 75 percent Latino, and nearly all the parents who had been participating in the organizing were Spanish-speaking. Where was the team going to find the English-speaking parents that their plan required? And how would they choose from among the Spanish-speaking families seeking admission to the school's bilingual program? As a small school, UCS's admission was capped at 240; and they were pulling from a school of nearly 1,400. Many dedicated parents had worked long and hard throughout the fall planning for the new school, but still were not assured of a place for their children in the school. Yet, several times these parents were asked by teachers to help recruit other, English-speaking parents. Recall that at the very first meeting with parents, called and organized by Baudelia (described in chapter 2), one of the three questions teachers posed to the group of Latino parents was, "How can we include parents of other ethnicities who don't speak Spanish?" So, from the beginning, teachers were preoccupied with the issue of diversity, and sought to involve Spanish-speaking parents in helping them bring in parents of other ethnicities. During another meeting I observed, when teachers asked for help in recruiting English-speaking parents, Ofelia had immediately objected, "How are we supposed to do that if we don't speak English?" The desire for integration thus introduced a dramatic tension into the design team, whose parents were almost without exception Spanish-speaking. The instructional ideal of an integrated, balanced student population was given priority over the needs of the parents immediately present.

Every two weeks for the several months before the school opened, more and more parents showed up at the designated classroom or cafeteria, having heard word of the new small school and eager to learn whether their children could attend. Mothers arrived with strollers and toddlers in tow, whispered among themselves, and rocked their babies while waiting for the meetings to start. There was a palpable anxiety in the air, as parents did not know who would be admitted to the new school, and parent leaders were still unclear about many aspects of the school's program. Teachers, for their part, were still waiting for answers from the district on critical issues, and found themselves explaining to parents their frustrations with the district. Facing a limited amount of time and a pressured situation, teachers opted to run these meetings in a bureaucratic format that minimized spaces for public discussion and debate. Although some teachers and OCCA organizers supporting the team made serious efforts to give parents leadership roles, these efforts were ultimately sabotaged, I believe, by a cultural value system that prioritized professional expertise over relationship building. The following examples illustrate the way spaces for authentic conversation and community building were gradually closed.

One teacher began the practice of inviting parent volunteers to help plan and facilitate the larger parent meetings. The three or four parent volunteers would meet the day before the large meeting to create the agenda. These "prep meetings" were an opportunity for parents to get to know one another and contribute their ideas to the planning process. In one such meeting I observed, the parent volunteers had a rich discussion about the challenges of increasing parent participation, and whether parent participation should be required as a criterion for admission. At this meeting, the OCCA organizer, Laura, asked me to help the parent who had volunteered to keep track of time. After the parents left, she told me and the teacher, "We have to help the parents develop that discipline." She said that it was good that "they saw what happens without discipline today," when parents were talking out of turn and talking over each other, because now they would be conscious of it tomorrow. From her perspective, the planning meeting had been undisciplined and drawn out. From my perspective, it was one of the few opportunities that parents had been able to genuinely speak on an issue important to them. This was not usually possible in the larger meetings, which were run in a question-and-answer format, with teachers dispensing information and parents asking questions.

In my observations of parent meetings for the small school design team over the course of a year, parents and teachers had remarkably few opportunities to get to know one another personally, or to discuss in any depth their goals and desires for the school. The teachers, it seemed, had had that opportunity among themselves when they first began planning the design team. As Linda explained to me, the social-justice theme had emerged from group discussions "where we all went around and shared about our histories, our personal histories. The level of activism that there has been in this group is really, really, incredible." Parents had not been present at those discussions, and had not had a similar opportunity to share their histories. The only time that I saw parents invited to share their personal experience and discuss their concerns in small groups was in the very first meetings that Baudelia had organized.

The OCCA organizer, Laura, was also concerned about the lack of opportunities for personal sharing. Sharing stories, she told me, is a "basic principle of organizing." At the next planning meeting, we suggested the idea of breaking the parents into small groups for discussion, as Baudelia had done at the first large meeting. The parent volunteers were immediately enthusiastic and incorporated it into the agenda. But what happened to this in practice the next day was illustrative.

Parents arrived to find Marie, the school's newly selected principal, running the meeting. Marie did not seem to remember the facilitating roles that were delegated to parents the day before, and ran the meeting as if no planning had taken place. Aside from Marie, there was only one other teacher present. This meeting erupted in chaos, as parent frustration reached a boiling point and Marie struggled to maintain control. As the following description reveals, controversial issues were handled in a way that served to exacerbate the conflict.

The first item on the agenda was the enrollment criteria for the new small school. This was the issue foremost on everybody's minds. At the last large meeting, many parents had spoken up to say they believed selection should be based on children's need. Several parents shared stories about injustices in the way their children had been treated at Whitman. Now parents arrived to find that the selection criteria had been decided. Marie had written the criteria on poster board in English and Spanish and taped it to the blackboard. They were as follows: (1) parent involvement in the development of UCS (United Community School), (2) parent interest and lottery, keeping siblings together, (3) special-needs kids, by teacher recommendation, and (4) waiting list.

When Marie explained the first criterion, that parents who had participated in organizing the school would have preference for their kids to go to the new small school, Baudelia immediately asked, "Participation starting from *when*? What about the parents who were very involved last fall who are not here today?" This triggered a lengthy debate about how parent participation should be measured, and how much would count to give kids preference. Marie said this was open to discussion and that the parents should help them decide this, but a little later, she said that if a parent had attended at least three meetings, that would qualify their kids for preference. It was not clear who had decided this or when.

Then Baudelia wanted to know, what was the point of inviting new parents to these meetings if there was no more room in the school? They had been told the bilingual program was full. Parents come to these meetings with the hope that their children will be able to attend the new small school, Baudelia said, and she didn't want to lead them on. As she had said to me earlier, "No me gusta que me engañen ni me gusta engañar" (I don't like to be deceived, nor do I like to deceive others). Throughout the meeting, Marie was trying to translate into English for a couple of Asian parents, but the debate was heated and parents weren't waiting to be translated.

Marie then explained that the principal of Whitman was not letting them announce the new small school from the classroom, so teachers could not recruit English-speaking parents or students from Whitman. This issue had come up during the planning meeting the day before. At that time, Marie had explained the need to recruit non-Latino parents, and had encouraged the parent volunteers (who were all Latina) to bring their non-Latino friends to the next meeting. Ofelia had asked, "How are we supposed to do that if we don't speak English?" She thought that should be the principal's responsibility. "Doesn't the principal know we're doing this for the good of the community?" she had asked. Now, Ofelia again expressed her anger that the principal was not supporting them; and the need for a group of parents to go meet with the principal was discussed as an "action item" for the end of the meeting.

Significantly, by channeling the parents' frustration toward the principal of Whitman Elementary School, the teachers shielded from public examination or critique their vision of an integrated school. The teachers' desire for an equal number of English-speaking (sheltered) and bilingual students in the new small school was potentially problematic given the demographics of Whitman and the design team. But this was never a design issue that was open for debate.

Each time Marie switched to the English translation, the room erupted in murmurs, as parents whispered and talked among themselves. At some point, Marie called order and said that they really had to stick to the agenda. She told parents that if they had a question that was not related to the topic being discussed, to write it down on a pad of paper that she placed on the floor in the middle of the circle. She said these questions would be addressed at the end of the meeting. I wondered who would write down their questions in such a chaotic environment, when there was no guarantee that they would ever be addressed. But one mother immediately came forward and took the pad.

Next, Marie explained the lottery, which unleashed many more questions, and the "special-needs" criterion. Two spots in every grade were being reserved for students with special needs, who teachers thought could most benefit from being in a smaller school. Marie explained that it was necessary to reserve these spots because some children don't have parents who advocate for them, and teachers have to advocate for them. She reminded the parents that the purpose of this school is "social justice," and implied that teachers recommending special-needs kids was the "just" thing to do. Again, the parents who had made the effort to advocate for their children were made to feel that they would take second place to families of the teachers' choosing. In the teachers' vision of a diverse, integrated school—with full inclusion of special-needs students and equal numbers of English- and Spanish-speaking students—many Latino parents who had fought to open the school might not find a place for their children.

At this point in the meeting a conflict between the parents became evident. Some of the parents tried to support Marie in quieting the group, and became angry with the parents who were whispering. Baudelia, exasperated with how the meeting was proceeding, talked to Ofelia and me the entire time. She told me that Ana, who was standing at the front of the room trying unsuccessfully to maintain order, was one of those passive parents who say to the teachers, "Sí, maestra, ¡lo que usted diga!" (Whatever you say, *maestra!*). Ana had been at the prep meeting the day before, but did not appear bothered by Marie's taking over the agenda that had been created by and for parents.

The last item on the agenda was the "parent participation contract," which Lupe, a parent, had volunteered to explain. Under the contract, parents would be required to volunteer at the new small school; their support was essential in order to get the school off the ground. Baudelia immediately objected that parents couldn't be required, because many worked long hours and could not afford to spend time at the school. She said that parent participation should be voluntary, strongly encouraged, but not obligatory. Marie said the teachers wanted parents' feedback about this, and that they would discuss this in small groups next.

The purpose of the small-group activity, which had been planned the day before, was to have the parents get to know one another in a more personal way. Marie was there when we planned this, but had apparently decided to change it. "In small groups you can discuss the parent contract and what your ideas are for parent participation in the school!" she announced. She wrote the discussion points for the small groups on the whiteboard. When I reminded her about the activity's original purpose, she added, "get to know each other" to the list. "Get to know each other" was now one of four things they were directed to accomplish in small groups, in no more than ten minutes. A chaotic period of dividing people into groups followed. In such a context, there was not even time to ask parents to introduce themselves.

At seven o'clock Marie flashed the lights on and off to indicate that the meeting was over. She asked each note taker to turn in her sheets indicating what kinds of committees parents were interested in participating on. Our group hadn't gotten to discussing the committees. Quickly, I asked for volunteers to go meet with the principal, or form a safety council, or help with registration. I wrote down a few names. By this time everybody was leaving, and parents who volunteered were asking me, "When do I have to do this? Who will tell me what to do?"

After people had left, Ana complained to me about Baudelia's and Ofelia's behavior. "They were talking through the whole meeting!" she said.

In this meeting, rising tensions between parents and teachers were exacerbated by an authoritarian leadership style that systematically shut down parent voice. First, Marie disregarded the roles parents had volunteered for in the planning meeting and attempted to facilitate the meeting herself. When parents resisted by talking over her and questioning the decisions she presented them with, she attempted to rein in the discussion by limiting their questions to writing on a pad, which would be addressed "at the end of the meeting." Then, what was intended as an open-ended small-group activity was turned into a closed, ten-minute exercise in which parents were told to discuss predetermined questions of the teachers' choosing. In an example of what Gregory (1998) has termed the "governing of deliberation" and the "regulating of dissent," the single opportunity for parents to discuss among themselves was restricted to ten minutes at the end of an already chaotic meeting.[4] It was "regulated" by the need to produce a list of volunteers for various parent committees. This function of the small-group activity served the teachers' interests, because it supplied a pool of volunteer labor that teachers could draw on for later work. However, in limiting the small-group discussions to this purpose, teachers and parents both lost the opportunity to engage in a dialogue that might have illuminated some of the underlying conflict.

Angela Valenzuela (1999), in her seminal study of a predominantly Latino high school in Texas, argues that Latino youth and non-Latino teachers held competing definitions of "caring," with harmful consequences for student achievement. Whereas teachers subscribed to an *aesthetic* or technical definition of caring, Latino students sought an *authentic* form of caring grounded in Mexican cultural views of *educación*. Under aesthetic caring, writes Valenzuela, "teachers expect students to demonstrate caring about school with an abstract commitment to ideas or practices that purportedly lead to achievement" (263). When students did not demonstrate this, teachers assumed that they "did not care" about school. Latino students, however, articulated a vision of education and caring derived from the cultural concept of *educación*, in which reciprocal, trusting relationships constitute the basis for all learning. When teachers failed to initiate these relationships, Latino students assumed they "did not care" about them. The Latino concept of *educación*, well documented by other scholars, is communal in orientation, emphasizing respect and responsibility to the community, rather than simply the individual acquisition of skills and knowledge.[5] This view of education was reflected in the work of Madres Unidas and in their expectations for their children's school, which, in their words, should "develop positive habits of social cooperation and living together *(convivencia)*." In defending this vision at the school, the mothers also found themselves battling aesthetic or technical definitions of community from their children's teachers.

Baudelia's assertion that "social justice starts in the community," like her

earlier question, "Aren't we also going to talk about *us?*" reflected a principal difference in perspective between parents and teachers. For Baudelia,
decisions ought to have been made based on responsibility to personal
relationships with people in the school community. This was especially
true in the question of selecting who would attend the new small school.
While teachers followed a rule-based, bureaucratic procedure (any parent
who had attended at least three meetings would have priority for the new
school), Baudelia felt a personal responsibility to the parents she had organized throughout the year who for various reasons stopped coming in
the spring. Teachers might not have noticed the sudden absence of these
parents; Baudelia did. She worried that some of these parents might not
make it into the small school under the new criteria. In this meeting and
in others, she repeatedly pushed teachers to seek out the parents who had
stopped coming, at one point even giving the teachers a copy of her sign-
in sheets from those early meetings.

Ironically, the teachers' decision to reserve spots for special-needs students who "don't have parents who advocate for them" was rooted in a desire to provide a fair opportunity to families who may not have participated
in planning the school. However, this decision alienated the community of
parents who had been participating, because teachers had reserved the right
to identify who had "special needs." The teachers sought to make admissions decisions according to abstract principles of fairness, even if it meant
harming or excluding parents from the community who had personal relationships with the design team. Arguably, all parents who attended the
meetings felt their child to be strongly in need of a new educational environment. Now they were being told that teachers might find other children to be more deserving of a new school than theirs. Furthermore, parents were informed of these decisions "after the fact," without being given
the opportunity to discuss or question them. When Marie announced the
special-needs criteria, she had reminded parents that this was a "social-
justice" school, thereby deflecting any criticism or debate.

I often heard it said that teachers were in a better position to enact fair
policies, because teachers had the interests of *all* the children in mind,
while parents were focused narrowly on *their* own children.[6] However,
this assumption fails to capture the cultural understandings of community that Latino parents brought to the design team. Parents more often
explained their dedication to the new small school as part of their desire
to help their community. Recall Ofelia's question, "Doesn't the principal

know we're doing this for the good of the community?" and Baudelia's linking of social justice to the community. A concern for the larger community was evident from the earliest design team meetings, when parents worried about the future of Whitman Elementary School, which they would leave behind. In the first meeting, described in chapter 2, when one father asked what would happen to Whitman after the new small school opened, Baudelia had responded by saying that they would have to work to improve the education at Whitman, too, because they are all "part of the same family." Parents raised questions about the future of Whitman in nearly every small school design team meeting. Some parents I met who were active in the organizing had either no children left in school or a child who would have only one year in the new school, but they worked tirelessly because they believed their community needed it. A web of social relationships of friends, relatives, and neighbors who had experienced the same injustices shaped the consciousness of Latino parents who struggled for the new small school. Most of the teachers did not live in the community, and would not have to face the consequences of an angered neighbor or a severed friendship that might result from misguided admissions policies. While many teachers cared about the students and parents at Whitman that would be left behind, they did not count these people among their immediate family or circle of friends. Parents, by contrast, knew that they would see them on a daily basis: at church on Sundays, around their kitchen tables, for children's birthday parties and barbeques. What happened to these other members of the community mattered, in a deeply personal way.

Thus, while teachers made decisions based on their educational philosophy and integrationist ideals, parents reacted from the very personal experience of the needs and relationships in their community. It was this difference that was at the core of conflicts between teachers and parents during the months before the school opened, and it was precisely this difference that was never openly addressed. In the absence of spaces for honest discussion of differences—between teachers and parents, and between parents—the creation of "community" remained an elusive goal. Instead, a bureaucratic and authoritarian management style fostered resentment and mistrust between parents and teachers, and divisiveness among parents. Some parents, like Ana and Lupe, thought that the demands of community required standing by the teachers, no matter what. The teachers were overworked and under pressure, and needed the support of parents to get the new school off the ground. Others, like Baudelia and Ofelia, believed that the creation of community required fighting for a real voice. As we will see, the principal and some teachers would later exploit this difference among parents, using a strategy of divide and conquer to undermine parent input.

"They Don't Think We're Capable"

In late spring, at the request of one of the teachers, Linda, and with the help of the OCCA organizer, I began meeting with some of the parents alone to discuss these issues. Linda had told me that teachers were "feeling overwhelmed and need all the help we can get." She asked Laura, the OCCA organizer, and me if we would be willing to meet with parents on our own, without the teachers, to help resolve some of the conflicts. I had spoken to her about my desire to involve the parents in participatory research, and she had been enthusiastic. "I liked your idea about empowerment and leadership training, or however you called it," she told me.

At first, the parents were not excited about coming together. By this time, Ana and Lupe and Baudelia and Ofelia were almost arch-enemies. Ana and Lupe had come to regard Baudelia and Ofelia as troublemakers, and Baudelia and Ofelia saw Ana and Lupe as puppets of the teachers. Both groups were skeptical of the other's willingness and ability to help the school. But they also recognized the need to work together and to address some of the conflicts before they snowballed.

So, on a Wednesday afternoon late in May, we gathered at the home of Ofelia. Reserving a room at Whitman had proved to be too complicated, so Ofelia had offered her house, just down the street from the school. Perhaps because of the change in scenery, the tone of this meeting was markedly different from the parent meetings at the school. The meeting began with informal conversation about the mothers' personal lives, triggered by a story from Baudelia's English class at a local college. Baudelia shared how the teacher punished her for using Spanish in the class. For every word she said in Spanish, she was made to write and say it in English five times in front of the class, and felt humiliated. The mothers immediately offered expressions of sympathy and solidarity, and launched a rich discussion on the difficulties of learning English. After the conflicts in the last meeting, they discovered that they all faced the fear that "if we say something wrong, people laugh at us." The conversation brought the mothers into a common space of fellowship and solidarity, a safe space from which to approach the conflicts at the school.

As we switched to discussion of the school, I said that I believed the teachers wanted to involve parents, but didn't know how. Baudelia responded, "They don't think we're capable." To nods of agreement, Lupe said, "We need to work together. This shouldn't be about fighting." The mothers discussed the main issues of conflict that had arisen in the past weeks: the parent participation contract, the selection criteria for students, and the issue of special-needs students. On points of disagreement between them, such as whether parent participation should be voluntary or mandatory, they addressed each other directly and openly, explaining their reasons for why they disagreed. They also shared concerns that had not been discussed in the larger parent meetings. We wrote up the major concerns on butcher paper and discussed possible ways the parents could address them. Ofelia served coffee. Now the conversation was casual and joking. And over coffee and donuts, the mothers decided to have a potluck for the teachers. They hoped to invite teachers into an honest conversation— significantly, away from the school, at a place where they could set the tone. Ofelia volunteered her house.

After the tense bureaucratic meetings at the school, the personal conversations in Ofelia's living room felt like a breath of fresh air. Conflict was no less present at this meeting than at the school's parent meetings, but it was addressed openly as between friends, rather than pushed to the margins. There was coffee and donuts and laughter and jokes. The mothers had found common ground, and perhaps a little more trust.

On a Friday evening some two weeks later, six mothers spread platters of food on Ofelia's kitchen and dining-room tables. In addition to Baudelia, Ana, and Lupe, Ofelia had invited her sister Carmen, and another mother, Carolina. The tables were overflowing. There were tostadas, enchiladas, tamales, rice, and many kinds of salad. To drink there was homemade *horchata* (a rice beverage), Kool-Aid, and soda pop. The teachers arrived together, coming directly from a business meeting at the school, and were immediately invited to eat. The atmosphere was festive and joking as everyone helped themselves to heaping plates of food. Compliments for the mothers' cooking abounded.

After a half hour of eating and socializing, Baudelia called the meeting to order. She explained that the purpose of the meeting was to have an informal conversation between parents and teachers, and to figure out a way that parents could participate in the planning and decision-making process of the school. She suggested as a way to start that parents individually share their experience with the process to date and how they were feeling about it. She began. She said she felt that parents had been working in an isolated fashion and that teachers did not take them into account in decision making. She said parents always heard about decisions after the fact—such as the decision to reserve two spots in each class for students with special needs, and multiage classrooms. The parents had been promised that the new small school would not have multiage classes, but lately they had heard word that in fact there would be combined classes. The "combined" classes Baudelia was referring to were Linda and Sandy's team-teaching arrangement. Many parents Baudelia and Ofelia had spoken to were not happy with this arrangement. When other parents shared, the issue of multiage classes kept coming up. Finally, Baudelia asked the teachers, "What is the objective of multiage classes?" And Sandy, in exasperation, responded, "Do you have another few hours? That is a whole different discussion that we don't have time for now." Baudelia seemed frustrated. Linda and Sandy were clearly upset.

During this discussion, a few people tried to translate for the two or three teachers who didn't speak Spanish, but translation was spotty and inconsistent. As the debate became heated, there was no time to translate. One teacher walked out in frustration because she didn't understand what was going on, and, she later said, "nobody was translating." The teachers who stayed explained that they were exhausted from working ten- to twelve-hour days and didn't have time for more meetings with parents. They invited parents to attend their weekly business meetings at the school, where important issues were discussed, but assured parents that these were tedious. Still, parents expressed a willingness to attend and agreed to rotate, sending two or three representatives at a time.

Ironically, the parents' first attempt to open a dialogue with teachers resulted in an even firmer, more deafening silence. The attempt went down in the teachers' lexicon as "the tostada meeting," as in, the infamous tostada meeting that left several teachers in tears. I later learned that teachers felt attacked by the parents. Marie asked to speak with me privately at the school the next week, and told me that Linda and Sandy had been deeply hurt by the parents' questioning of their team-teaching. She asked me to work with the parents to teach them how to express their concerns more sensitively, to "depersonalize" them. There was no attempt to explore the parents' concerns or the sources of their frustration. To the parents' claim that they felt excluded or did not understand the objectives of teachers'

reform ideas, teachers responded that they had no time for that. The claim
of exhaustion shielded the staff from having to examine or account to parents for their practice. Deborah Meier, reflecting on her experience founding a small school in Harlem, writes, "We were often exhausted by the
things that mattered least to us" (1995, 25). This could well capture the
sentiment of teachers on the Whitman design team, who were so frazzled
that they had neither the time nor the energy for an honest conversation
with parents. The net result of the fallout from the tostada meeting was to
silence the parents' critique, and to ban further dissent.

The Lottery

The lottery for United Community School took place one day in late June
after school had let out for the summer. The school held one lottery for the
bilingual program and a separate one for the sheltered English program,
both on the same day, and in public. But on the awaited day, the teachers
found they had a problem. Even in the "sheltered" pool, or students seeking admission to the English program, Latino students outnumbered non-
Latinos three to one. In order to get the diversity they desired, therefore,
teachers would have to handpick non-Latino students before the lottery.
There was much debate among the teachers on the design team about
how to handle this. Some thought it would be unethical to automatically
place the non-Latino families, since families had been told they would be
selected randomly by lottery. In the end, the teachers decided to bring the
problem to the parents, who were waiting in the cafeteria. In the words of
one teacher, this is what happened:

> The parents came through. The parents came through. The parent group
> that was there that day was, I believe, 100 percent Latino. And some of
> those parents had indicated that they wanted sheltered classes. But almost
> every parent in that room said, "It's more important that we have a diverse
> school than my child get in just because I put sheltered." And they said to
> factor ethnicity into the lottery process. The parents were amazing.

Teachers often retold this story as an example of how parents and teachers arrived at a shared vision of a community school. Latino parents voted
against their own self-interest, the story went, to create an ethnically diverse school. On the surface, the parents' vote confirmed the teachers'

view that this was the socially just thing to do. However, as the mothers in Madres Unidas would discover after the school opened, the story was much more complicated. The lottery vote, as perhaps all simple votes, masked a host of underlying confusions and exclusions that ultimately shaped who ended up attending United Community School.

The Chosen and the Excluded

Early in the Madres' research, Baudelia's worst fears appeared to have come true. Baudelia had mobilized many parents to attend the design team meetings, telling them that their children would receive preference for the new school if they got involved. But when the school opened, she was dismayed to discover that some of these parents were not in the new school. Through their interviews with parents, the mothers learned that these anomalies were not simply isolated cases or the inevitable margin of error: they were part of a troubling pattern suggesting that the selection process had not taken place the way they had thought at all. As they delved deeper into this question, the mothers came face-to-face with some of the harmful consequences the school's "mistakes" had on the community.

The realization first became apparent in the parent focus groups, when the Madres asked parents how they got into the new small school, and what they thought about the selection process. Many parents responded that they had been brought in by a teacher or by the principal, often after the lottery had taken place. Some parents who had participated in the planning meetings found their children excluded nonetheless, and had to struggle to get their children in. The following example, from the second parent focus group was illustrative.

> *Teresa:* A mí el sorteo que se hizo por último no me gustó. Porque yo estuve en todas las reuniones de cuando empezamos a cerca de cómo se iba a tumbar este edificio, y yo estuve allí, y muchos padres fuimos allá a pelear . . . [Pasa el BART y no se escucha] y al último no me gustó porque se hizo el sorteo y a mí no me tocó. Y habían dicho que se les iba a dar preferencia a los papás que asistían a las reuniones, y no fue así. Y a mí no me tocó porque no salió el niño en la rifa que hicieron. Entonces salieron padres que no asistieron a las juntas, y pues yo sé que fue una rifa . . .
>
> *Baudelia:* ¿Y cómo llegó aquí?

Teresa: Espéreme, ¡allí voy! [Risa de todos] No pues, lo que pasa es que, Linda, yo hablo muy bien de ella porque ella es muy buena maestra y mi hijo ha estado con ella desde el primero . . . Entonces Linda vio que yo estaba desde el comienzo, pienso que ella dijo que no estaría justo si la señora quedara a fuera, mas bien mi niño, ¿no? Entonces, pues no sé cómo fue que lo hizo pero me dijo, "Aquí está, señora, su hijo [está a dentro]." Yo la verdad me puse muy contenta porque yo estaba luchando tanto para que viniera acá.

Maria: Así me pasó.

Baudelia: ¿A usted lo pasó lo mismo?

Maria: [Indica que sí.] O sea, yo no asistí a muchas juntas, pero yo llegué aquí por la maestra. Porque ella quiso traer a mi hija para acá.

Todos: O, ¡qué suerte!

Lucia: A mí también, la maestra me empezó a decir, "Mire, esto le conviene, y esto, haga esto."

Teresa: I didn't like the lottery that they did in the end. Because I was at all the meetings since we started about how they were going to tear down this building, and I was there, and many of us went to fight . . . [The BART passes and some words are lost] and in the end I didn't like it because they did the lottery and I didn't get picked! And they had told us that they were going to give preference to parents who attended the meetings, but they didn't. I didn't get in because my son didn't get picked in the lottery. So parents were picked who didn't attend any meetings, and well, I know it was a lottery . . .

Baudelia: And how did you get here?

Teresa: Wait, I'm getting to that! [Laughter] No, what happened is, Linda, I speak very highly of her because she is a very good teacher and my son has been with her since first grade . . . So Linda saw that I had been there since the beginning, I think she said that it wouldn't be fair if I was left out, or my kid, you know? So, I don't know how she did it, but she told me, "Here, señora, your son is in." And I was very happy because I had struggled so much for him to come here.

Maria: That happened to me.

Baudelia: The same thing happened to you?

Maria: [Indicates yes.] I mean, I didn't attend many meetings, but I got here because of the teacher. Because she wanted to bring my daughter here.

Everyone: Oh, what luck!

Lucia: Me too. The teacher told me, "Look, this would be good for you, do this."

In this exchange, Baudelia and Amelia learned that a parent who had been involved since the beginning was wrongly sent to the lottery, and only afterwards rescued by a teacher who recognized the mistake. Tellingly, after Teresa shared this story, two other parents who had *not* been involved since the beginning said that they also got in because a teacher helped them. These glaring inconsistencies disturbed the mothers, who began to question the school's identity as a "community school." How could parents feel ownership of the school if they had entered so haphazardly, by chance or by "pure luck"? It was clear many of these parents did not know the history of the school and did not understand the sacrifices others had made in order to open the school. When asked how they felt about the selection process, one parent's response in the third focus group was indicative:

Veronica: Pues, ¡yo estoy contenta porque mi niña pues sí le tocó! Yo la verdad yo quería la Whitman, porque allí todas mis niñas desde chiquita . . . ¡Pero ahora hubo la oportunidad de entrar aquí me siento pues más contenta!

Ofelia: ¿Y usted le parece justo?

Veronica: ¡A mí se me hizo justo porque fue lo último pues! Que yo, me dijeron hay un cupo de pura suerte.

Veronica: Well, I'm happy because my daughter got in! The truth is, I liked Whitman, because all my girls had been there since they were small . . . But now there was the opportunity to come here and I feel even more happy!

Ofelia: And you think it's fair?

Veronica: I think it was fair because it was the last minute! I, they told me there was a spot by pure chance.

In her reflection after conducting this focus group, Ofelia wrote:

Estoy muy impresionada de escuchar de la mayoría de padres que sus hijos están en esa escuela porque les ayudó la directora o porque les ayudó una

maestra. Es muy raro escuchar que están ahí porque participaron en juntas o porque salieron en la lotería o simplemente porque el padre o madre
estaba interesada.

I am really amazed to hear so many parents say their children got into
the school because the principal helped them, or because a teacher helped
them. It's very rare to hear that they are there because they participated in
meetings or they came out in the lottery or simply because the father or
mother was interested.

Ofelia also learned of other parents who met the school's criteria but had
been excluded. One parent told Ofelia in an individual interview, "Many
parents who came to the meetings, their children are not in the school.
There was favoritism, preference." As founding parents, the mothers were
concerned about the effects of this favoritism on other parents and the
community. How did it affect the parents who had been involved since
the beginning to know that many parents were there by favoritism? What
about the parents who had been left out altogether? As Baudelia shared
during a Friday meeting:

> Son cosas que te hacen sentir bien mal, y tú tienes que reprimir ciertos sen-
> timientos. Por ejemplo, yo cuando . . . me toca estar y estoy preguntando,
> "¿Cómo se ingresó a esta escuela?" Y que dicen, "¡Yo nunca vine a esta
> reunión, yo nunca supe, yo nunca nada!" Entonces yo me pregunto, yo
> me siento mal pensando en toda la gente que participó que ni me han
> reclamado, entonces yo estoy diciendo, ¿Cómo es posible?

> These are things that make you feel really bad, and you have to repress cer-
> tain feelings. For example, . . . when it's my turn to interview and I'm ask-
> ing, "How did you get into this school?" And they answer, "I never came
> to meetings, I never knew, I never nothing!" Then I wonder, and I feel
> bad thinking about all the people who participated who haven't even com-
> plained to me, so I'm saying, How is this possible?

To answer these questions, the mothers decided to interview more parents individually, and, significantly, to interview some parents of children
who did not make it into the new school. As we approached our winter

recess, having conducted three parent focus groups and one teacher focus group, the mothers made a plan of individual research activities over the next month. They could interview anyone they wanted, as long as they could justify to the group its importance to the study. Baudelia chose to interview two parents she knew personally whose children had not made it into the new small school, and who still attended Whitman. She wanted to hear their perspective on the selection process and their experience in the school's organizing. She invited anyone who wanted to come with her. Amelia accompanied her on one of the interviews; Carolina went with her on the other.

When the mothers reported back to the group on their research, these eye-opening interviews deeply moved the group. Baudelia's first interviewee, a woman named Alicia, had participated in several meetings at Whitman, but because her name did not appear on the sign-in sheets, she was not given preference. She figured she had failed to sign in when she arrived late to two meetings. When she protested to the principal, she was told she was number 16 on the waiting list. Alicia told Baudelia she still wanted to transfer her children to the new school, and asked her to find out where she stood on the waiting list. In her reflection Baudelia wrote: "Me gustaría que los padres se involucraran en la selección de los niños dándoles prioridad a las personas que hayan participado, y me gustaría que se dieran a conocer los nombres de las personas que están en la lista de espera" (I would like for parents to be involved in the selection of students, giving priority to people who have participated, and I would like for us to find out who is on the waiting list).

The second interview, with a woman named Nora, was even more sobering. Nora had worked closely with Baudelia in the early part of the planning year, organizing parents to attend actions and meetings at the school. In the spring, she fell ill and missed the last three meetings. Her son brought home a letter saying he was being entered in the lottery. Indignant, Nora went to the school and asked a teacher, "¿Cómo es eso que él va a ser sorteado? ¡Si a mí me dijeron que les iban a dar preferencia a las personas que participaron y yo anduve ayudando y llevando gente para la acción y yendo a las reuniones!" (How is it he is going in the lottery? They told me they were going to give preference to the people who participated and I went around helping and bringing people to the action and going to the meetings!). The teacher said she did not know anything. Nora then went to the principal, who told her that only the parents who had attended the last three meetings were given preference. Nora said nobody had ever told her that they were going to count only the last three meetings.

From Baudelia's interview transcript, the following words of Nora's stand out: "A fin siempre reciben más beneficios las que no participan para nada, y yo lo digo porque a la escuela UCS entraron personas que yo conozco y familiares míos que nunca se pararon a una reunión . . . y me da mucho coraje ver a esa gente que lleva sus niños ahí y no movió ni un dedo" (In the end, those who don't participate at all benefit the most, and I say this because UCS admitted people I know and relatives of mine who never set foot in a meeting . . . And it makes me furious to see those people bringing their kids there [to the new school] when they didn't even lift a finger).

Baudelia and Carolina recounted their interview with Nora to sympathetic shaking heads and clicking tongues around Ofelia's kitchen table. The mothers were horrified that some parents who had given their time to the new school's organizing had been treated so badly by school staff. Carolina emphasized in her reflection that, after being wrongly excluded from the school, what particularly hurt Nora was her meeting with the principal:

> No encontró ninguna salida con la visita que le hizo a Mis Campos. Porque al contrario se sintió más decepcionada y triste porque Mis Campos le comentó que las últimas tres reuniones fueron las que los padres de familia tenían que haber asistido . . . Pero ni siquiera Mis Campos la comprendió lo que ella esperaba era recibir una orientación de parte de Mis Campos, pero no fue así.

> She didn't find any solution with the visit she made to Ms. Campos. On the contrary, she felt more disappointed and sad, because Ms. Campos told her it was the last three meetings that parents were supposed to attend . . . But not even Ms. Campos understood that what [Nora] hoped for was to get some guidance or encouragement from Ms. Campos, but she didn't get it.

Nora's story illustrated that the wounds of this experience were deeper and more lasting than any of them had imagined. As Carolina said, "Ella se quedó bien desconsolada y desde ese momento ella dice que ya no va a poder asistir a ningunas reuniones, y ahora . . . le aconseja a los padres que no asistan a las reuniones, porque los que asisten a las reuniones son los que no tienen el valor de quedarse" (She was left very despairing and from that moment on she says that she's not going to go to any more meetings, and now . . . she advises other parents not to attend the meetings, because those who attend the meetings aren't rewarded). As founding parents who had participated in the selection process, the Madres felt a personal responsibility to parents like Nora. Baudelia, in particular, was disturbed by these interviews. She wrote:

> Para mí fue muy difícil dirigir esta entrevista porque en cierto punto me culpa a mí diciéndome que yo no le dije que sólo iban a contar las 3 últimas reuniones, pero la verdad es que cuando yo la invité al final ella estaba enferma.
>
> Yo siento un compromiso moral de estar al pendiente de investigar en qué lista de espera se encuentra esta persona. Me gustaría que hubiera un poco más de justicia, que los maestros y la directora tomaran en cuenta dando prioridad a las personas que hayan participado antes. Porque de esto no se puede culpar a las maestras o a los padres, esta decisión de selección se tomó entre todos juntos . . . Aprendí a reconocer nuestros errores.

> It was very difficult for me to conduct this interview because to a certain extent I blame myself, telling myself that we didn't tell her they were only going to count the last three meetings. But the truth is that when I invited her at the end, she was sick.
>
> I feel a moral obligation to find out where this person is on the waiting list [for the new small school]. I would like for there to be a little more justice, for the principal and teachers to take into account and give priority to the people who participated before. Because this can't be blamed on only the teachers or the parents; this decision about the selection was made by all of us together . . . I learned to recognize our mistakes.

The mothers discussed feelings of regret, frustration, and helplessness in the face of the mistakes the school had made in the selection process. Ofelia said:

> Para mí siento que la lotería de los niños fue injusto, yo siento que yo como padre que tuve participación en eso, yo reconozco que cometí un error, y

eso ha servido para yo ver, esta investigación ha servido para yo ver mis propios errores. A mí me hubiera gustado si otra vez volviera pasar, hacer otro plan, o ser diferente.

I feel that the lottery for students was unjust, and I feel that I as a parent who played a role in that, I recognize that I made a mistake. And this research has helped me to recognize my own mistakes. I would have liked to see the admissions process happen again, to have another plan, to do it differently.

Baudelia felt there was still something to be done to make it up to these parents who had been left out, if only the teachers would involve them in admissions decisions. As she explained:

Ya cometimos un error, se puede remendar ese error. [Las maestras] tienen la lista de los padres que participaron, a ver cuáles yo conozco, compararla con la lista que yo tengo, porque yo tengo una lista, pero nunca se nos informan. Ellas, ¿cómo lo están valorando? Yo siento, eso es lo que me ha hecho sentir a mí mal, como impotente.

We already made a mistake, we can correct it. [The teachers] have a list of the parents who participated, let's see which ones I know, compare it to the list that I have, because I have a list, but they never inform us! They, how are they valuing it? This is what has made me feel bad, like impotent.

The findings about the school's admissions mistakes were painful for the Madres, because they deeply felt the hurt and resentment of the parents who had been left out. Teachers, by contrast, were unaware of any cases of parents who were unfairly excluded or admitted, and did not mention the waiting list. The Madres' interviews with teachers revealed a dramatically different perspective on the admissions process. In teachers' minds, the greatest potential for error was in not reaching enough parents with information about the new school, not in excluding some parents who should have been in the school. As Susan, in the English teachers' focus group, said, "I don't think [the selection process] was perfect, because I know there are still families who didn't get the information, and that wasn't right or fair." Teachers spoke of the challenges of conducting outreach and giving information to parents of 1,400 students at Whitman with no support from the district. But given those challenges, most believed, as Sandy said, that "it was as fair as possible." In Susan's words, "With what we could do, with the amount of outreach we were able to achieve, I mean we did, based on the knowledge we had and the advice that we tried to get from a few other people, we conducted the best selection process that we were able to." The prioritization of educational goals for a diverse, integrated school led teachers to be more preoccupied with outreach to new parents than with including all of the Spanish-speaking parents who had participated since the beginning. Outreach to a wider group of parents would increase their chances of attaining a student body that would best support their pedagogical goals. The possible exclusion of some members of the Spanish-speaking community who had participated in the organizing was not a concern. This was either inevitable, necessary, or, in the teachers' interpretation of the lottery incident, understood and supported by the parents themselves.

Madres Unidas would make the admissions process a major focus of the presentation they prepared for school staff on their research findings, in which they highlighted the consequences of the school's admissions decisions. They informed teachers that the exclusion of parents who had participated in the school's early planning meetings "brought resentment to the community, to the people who organized the meetings, and resentment to the school."

In negotiations over who should get into the new small school, and how this community should be formed, profoundly different values and understandings of "community" caused friction between teachers and parents, but were never openly addressed. For teachers, community was to be created in the service of their educational goals. Their educational philosophy called for a diverse, integrated school, with multiage classrooms and full inclusion of special-needs students, and admissions decisions had to be made to meet those goals. Like the teachers in Valenzuela's study, teachers at UCS expected parents to demonstrate commitment to these pedagogical principles, which reflected the best professional wisdom about reform, in order to support the school. The mothers in Madres Unidas, by contrast, articulated a view of community that prioritized reciprocal relationships as the basis for all learning and school reform. Even the most well-intentioned or pedagogically sound reform strategy could not compensate for the harm caused to relationships in the community, if these were not considered during the reform process. The next chapter explores how these competing views of community further shaped parents' roles and parent–teacher relations in the first year of the new school.

4. The Good Parent, the Angry Parent, and Other Controlling Images

The mothers in Madres Unidas understood that UCS was created to give parents and the community a greater voice in the schooling of their children. As founding parents, with the exception of Carmen, they knew the history they had traveled to get here: how the community, through OCCA, had demanded new small schools and had fought for this land where UCS now stood. They also had the proposal, and were aware that the school's charter document promised new roles and rights for parents. "In contrast to the disenfranchisement often felt by parents," the proposal stated, "their voices will be valued and they will play a vital role in the decision-making processes of the school." However, the Madres soon apprehended that only a certain kind of parent was considered deserving of new roles, and that parent participation could swiftly be curtailed or invalidated if it did not conform to the teachers' images of "the good parent." Their experience of the discrepancy between the school's vision and mission and the reality of parent participation shaped their emerging research agenda, and led them to focus special attention on how parents' roles were being defined and negotiated by school staff, parents, and reform partners.

This chapter examines the negotiation of parents' roles, and the mothers' analysis of this process, in the first year of United Community School. I draw on African American feminist theorist Patricia Hill Collins's (2000) concept of "controlling images" to highlight how school staff attempted to manage and control parent participation through the use of a good parent/bad parent binary, in which only certain kinds of participation were considered acceptable. I trace patterns of teacher–parent relations in the new school to the larger discourse of parent participation in the small schools movement. The mothers developed a critique of the way parents were framed based on their own experience in the movement, their experience in the new school, and their interviews with parents and teachers at UCS about parent participation. In the mothers' analysis, teachers framed the "good parent" as a puppet or a parrot, a mouthpiece for the staff, while invalidating other kinds of participation. Teachers delegitimized the Madres' participation and critique through the censorship of anger and the privileging of professional "expertise" over experience in the community.

"Controlling images," according to Patricia Hill Collins, are socially constructed stereotypical images of a subordinate group, designed to serve the interests of the dominant group. They are part of a larger process of objectification in which black women (and other subordinate groups) are constructed as "Other," as diametrically opposed to the desirable traits of the dominant group, as objects to be manipulated and controlled. Black women in the United States have been subject to, and have resisted, at least four controlling images of black womanhood: the mammy, the matriarch, the welfare mother, and the whore or "hoochie." The most relevant for the present discussion are the mammy and the matriarch. The mammy image is that of the faithful, submissive domestic servant, designed to justify the economic exploitation of house slaves. Mammies were loving caretakers of white children who were presumed contented with their subordinate status. According to Collins, "the mammy image represents the normative yardstick used to evaluate all Black women's behavior" (2000, 72). Black women were to be deferent, compliant, and sacrificial. Of course, black women in their own homes were far different than they were as mammies, and for these mothers the controlling image of the "matriarch" applied. While the mammy represents the "good" black mother—under white supervision and control—the matriarch symbolizes the "bad" black mother, the black mother in her own home. The matriarch was a "negative stigma applied to African-American women who dared reject the image of the submissive, hardworking servant" (75). Matriarchs were overly aggressive, unfeminine mothers who spent too much time away from home (working) to properly supervise their children. The controlling image of the matriarch has been used to serve the dominant ideology by explaining unequal social outcomes: the failed black mother became responsible for black children's poor school achievement.

Although black women have resisted these controlling images and have engaged in creative self-definition in numerous contexts, the prevalence of these images reveals the contours of black women's oppression and objectification throughout time. Collins writes, "Taken together, these prevailing images of Black womanhood represent elite White male interests in defining Black women's sexuality and fertility, [and] help justify the social practices that characterize the matrix of domination in the United States" (84). It is the use of controlling images to justify and rationalize domination that deserves our attention.

"Decepcionada, Defraudada, y Desesperada"

In the early weeks of United Community School, it became clear that the patterns of parent exclusion that had shaped the school's planning process were present in the new school. In spite of parent opposition to multiage classrooms and teachers promises to delay this until they could win agreement from parents, the school opened in September with multiage classrooms in the early grades: Baudelia's daughter was in a combined first- and second-grade classroom. As the days and weeks progressed, the mothers in Madres Unidas were confronted with a number of other "irregularities" that began to raise their suspicions and renew their fears that parents were being deceived. Some of these anomalies, such as the violations of the school's admissions policy described in chapter 3, were hidden, discovered only by probing investigation. Others were blatant and enraging, announced shamelessly to parents by school staff. The uniform policy voted on by parents at a meeting over the summer was disregarded by the principal and replaced by another one. When parents protested, Marie agreed to send home ballots to all parents to vote again on the policy. At the meeting designated to announce the results of the vote, Marie said she had lost the ballots, and didn't have time to count them anyway.

"In everything we have been ignored," declared Baudelia at one of our Friday meetings. The parents had opposed multiage classrooms; they got multiage classrooms. The parents wanted a lottery; then they found students had been handpicked after the lottery. The parents voted on a uniform policy; Marie disregarded it. "¡A mí me desespera las mentiras!" (I am fed up with the lies!) Baudelia exclaimed. Amelia and Baudelia said they were refusing to go to any more parent meetings, because they were a waste of time. Throughout the discussion, the mothers said they felt "decepcionada," "defraudada," and "desesperada" (disillusioned, deceived, and despondent).

Baudelia and Ofelia, as the most outspoken mothers in the group, began to perceive that they had been branded as antagonists, or troublemakers, by the principal and some of the staff, so that any concerns they raised could be dismissed. After confronting Marie privately on some of the conflicts, including the uniform policy, they concluded that she had made up her mind that they were problem parents and would not take them seriously. This was the beginning of a decisive pattern in which school personnel (and eventually, as we will see, some external reform partners) communicated the message that the parents who named the problems *were* the problems. In framing Baudelia, Ofelia, and the other Madres as angry troublemakers, or alternatively, greedy founding parents who refused to cede control of the school to new parents, the staff could dismiss their critique and delegitimate it in front of the other parents. These identity politics played out in a variety of ways.

In the second month of the school, as part of the school's plan to involve parents meaningfully in school decision making, a parent governance committee was announced, and parents voted on four representatives. Baudelia, as the parent who had received the most votes, was to be the council president. However, when Marie announced the committee composition at a general parent meeting, she also delivered a warning. As the mothers retold it to me, Marie announced over the microphone that if Baudelia wanted to serve on the committee, she would have to "change her attitude." I wished I could have been there to see the shock in the room as one of the school's most respected parent leaders was publicly chastised by the principal. But Baudelia was not upset. As she explained it to us, she could not change her attitude, and if serving on the committee required doing so, then she would not serve, because she refused to be a puppet ("¡No voy a ser marioneta!"). Further disregarding the parents' votes, Marie appointed another parent, Norma, to serve as cochair with Baudelia. An English-dominant parent who was new to the school community, Norma had a timid disposition and agreed to be cochair only at Marie's intense coaxing.

Baudelia's assertion that she refused to be a puppet revealed her doubts about the function of the council. She suspected it would be a token body without any real authority, whose purpose would be to confirm the principal's and the staff's decisions. If she would be continually chastised for speaking up, it would be a waste of her time, she told us. She preferred to work for the good of the school through the research and her parent organizing with OCCA. However, after the coaxing of the other Madres who convinced her that the council *needed* someone like her on it, and with my encouragement, she agreed to serve on the council.

In the same parent meeting when the staff had announced the parent governance council, Marie had informed parents that in the new school

they would no longer be able to switch their child from the bilingual program to the English program or vice versa. Baudelia had asked, "Isn't it
the parents' right to choose a different program, if one isn't working?"
That had been the policy at Whitman Elementary School, which Baudelia
knew well. But Marie had responded, "Not in this school." When Baudelia
then asked about the district policy, Marie replied, "This is an autonomous
school and this is what we're doing."

In our Friday meeting following this incident, the mothers were en-
raged. This was the first time the issue of "autonomous" came up as a significant and politically loaded word. While not all of the mothers understood what it meant to be an "autonomous school," they perceived that in
this instance it was being used against them. Baudelia believed she knew
what autonomous meant and that Marie was using it wrongly. As she put
it, "To be autonomous does not mean to take away parents' rights!" At this
point Amelia asked, What does it mean to be autonomous? Baudelia explained that being autonomous was supposed to mean that schools could
make decisions democratically with parents. Instead, Marie was using it to
mean that teachers could do whatever they wanted.

The meaning of "autonomy" became a platform for claiming and contesting ownership of the school, and the mothers would eventually explore
the issue in depth with other parents and teachers in their research. For
now, Marie's use of it signaled to the mothers that the representation of
the school, as well as the representation of parents constructed by the staff,
could be used to exclude and delegitimize parents' concerns.

In late October, the mothers' frustration had reached its peak. Baudelia
and Ofelia called a special meeting with the staff to discuss their concerns,
and because they were convinced that they would not be taken seriously
alone, they asked me to be there. They had decided try one more time to
have an open conversation with the staff, to try to counter the image of
them as "problem parents" that was being circulated.

We met in the staff lunchroom. As it turned out, the teachers had staggered lunch breaks, so it was impossible to meet with all of them at once.
The mothers had short conversations with pairs of them before Marie and
Diane, the instructional leader (the administrator second to the principal,
who was given this title), came in. Because Diane did not speak Spanish, I
translated as the mothers listed their concerns: about the uniform policy,
the bilingual policy. The meeting very quickly became a back-and-forth between Baudelia and Marie, with Baudelia growing increasingly frustrated,

and Marie becoming increasingly defensive. Finally, Baudelia asked Marie, why should parents come to parent meetings if their decisions would not be respected? Marie responded that if Baudelia would rather stay home and not come out to improve the school, then she had "bad intentions."

Here Marie avoided dealing with Baudelia's question by suggesting that Baudelia had a bad attitude. The question was left hanging: why would anyone want to come to a meeting to vote on something that would surely be overturned? What kind of parent participation did the school really want? But these questions were left unexplored. Instead, it was suggested that by raising these questions, Baudelia was simply looking for an excuse to "stay home." That Baudelia was one of the school's most active parents who had probably never missed a meeting and spent more hours volunteering and organizing at the school than any other parent was momentarily lost. Her long history of participation and dedication to the school should have been enough to prove that she did not have "bad intentions." However, it was the nature of her participation that was threatening to the staff. In a power struggle that would repeat itself throughout the year between parents and professionals, Baudelia was being punished for being too angry.

Attempting to defuse the situation, Diane, an elderly white woman with a sympathetic disposition, offered another analysis. "I have a feeling something else is going on here," she said. She suggested that the group of founding parents were feeling resentful that new parents were being given a voice, parents who had not been involved since the beginning. She was presumably referring to Norma and the other parents appointed to the School Site Council. Now Baudelia and Ofelia were positioned as unwilling to cooperate or share power with new parents. Diane painted this as a natural process of transition and adjustment. However, the concerns Baudelia and Ofelia had brought up were still not addressed. These concerns had to do with parents *as a collective* being ignored by the staff: their votes overturned, their rights disregarded. In Diane's analysis, as in Marie's, the mothers' long history of participation, rather than entitling them to equal partnership with the teachers, was seen as a liability. Perhaps they had been given too much power, it was suggested, and needed to be put in their place. The possibility that the founding parents never *had* any real power, as evidenced by the growing body of contradictions and deceptions they were discovering, was obscured.

The censorship of anger has often been used in public schools as a means of exclusion and control (Lareau and Horvat 1999; Crozier 2001; Fine 1991). More to the point, as Mica Pollock (2008) compellingly documents, the anger and critique expressed by parents of color is likely to trigger defensive reactions from educators who fear any insinuation of racial discrimination. Pollock's study of complaints of racial discrimination filed with the Office of Civil Rights circa 2000 reveals that accused districts went to great lengths to defend educators' intentions—and attack those of the complaining parents—while failing to explore the actual sources of the critique. The widespread refusal of educators to acknowledge even "partial, unwitting responsibility" for acts of racial exclusion meant that the only possible response to complaints of discrimination was to dismiss the parents who made them as "difficult," "kooky," "angry," or "hostile complainers" (2008, 25, 45, 62, 171). In the meeting described above, Baudelia and Ofelia's attempt to counter the staff's image of them as "problem parents" was met with similar responses from both Marie and Diane. The message from both administrators was that Baudelia and Ofelia needed to change their behavior (or their attitudes) in order to resolve the conflict: in other words, the source of the conflict was Baudelia and Ofelia. There was no recognition of error on the part of school staff nor any acknowledgment of the legitimacy of parents' frustration. As would happen repeatedly throughout the year, the mothers' concerns were held hostage to a representational battle between "good" and "bad" parents. The use of identity politics to neutralize parent activism has also been documented by Michael Apple (1996), who highlights the role of school officials, as representatives of the state, in limiting the subject positions of parents. As Apple observes, "The subject positions made available by the state were only two: 'responsible' parents who basically supported 'professional decision making,' or 'irresponsible' [parents]" (64). This was also the case at UCS.

These interactions with school staff provided rich fodder for our Friday discussions and began to suggest the shape and course of our research at the school. It was through debriefing together that the mothers were able to collectively develop an analysis that rejected the staff's image of them as problem parents, and identified the ways in which the staff attempted to manipulate the image of the "good parent" to extend their own agenda at the school. The desirable parent, the mothers recognized, was the parent who said and did exactly as the principal or teachers wanted. The mothers used the words *marioneta* (marionette puppet) and "parrot" to describe the roles assigned to parents, revealing their analysis that "good parents" were expected to be a mouthpiece for the staff, with no opinions or agency of their own.

A striking example of the "good parent" was revealed at a parent meeting in November. The principal had announced that Norma, the English-speaking parent who was cochair of the School Site Council, would be running the meeting. According to the mothers, Marie then proceeded to dictate to Norma everything she should say. Norma was reduced to repeating Marie's announcements to the parents, "como un perico" (like a parrot). Like Patricia Hill Collins's "mammy" who fulfilled her caretaker duties under white supervision and control, the "good" parent representative on the SSC fulfilled her leadership role under the supervision and control of the principal. The mothers discussed this incident with evident anger and disgust. The following exchange I recorded at a Friday meeting reveals their developing analysis of the school's view of parents:

> *Baudelia:* Siento que están violando nuestros derechos. Ahora, ¿hasta cuándo yo voy a poder cambiar a mi niño de un programa bilingüe a un programa de inglés? ¿Por qué me están quitando ese derecho? ¿Por qué están cambiando los derechos por ejemplo de un comité? Hacerlo como ellas quieren. ¿Quién les da esa autoridad de formar un comité a su conveniencia de ellas? Ser autónoma dice padres y maestros trabajarán juntos, pero ¿de qué manera estamos trabajando padres y maestros juntos? ¿Para organizar festivales? ¿O para organizar programas académicos? ¿Cuándo se nos han dicho, "Padres, vengan para hacer un programa"? ¿Cuándo? A mí no.
>
> *Ofelia:* ¡Nos llaman para organizar cosas de fiesta!
>
> *Baudelia:* Pero no están diciendo, "Padres, vengan, ¿qué programa les conviene?" ¿Qué mejoría va a tener un programa bilingüe? ¿Qué problemas vamos a ver en esto? ¿Cuándo se nos han tomado en cuenta? Sólo para lo que les conviene, han estado tomando en cuenta, para beneficios de ellas, para festivales, para reuniones de esto, para reuniones del otro, eso no está bien.
>
> *Carmen:* Y por eso ya no fui para escoger a la maestra de preschool, me invitó que fuera ayer otra vez, y yo le dije que no tenía tiempo, pero realmente yo no quise ir porque si voy, voy como monigote a decir, "Esa sí me gusta, la otra no me gusta," pero ella va a decidir por ella misma. [Risa de todas.]

Amelia: Allí lo hubieras dicho a la directora, "¿Para qué usted me está invitando a mí, si mi hijo no va a estar aceptado en la escuela?"

Carolina: ¿Entonces, a ir allí tengo esperanza de que mi hijo va a ir a preschool?

Carmen: Por eso, pero si es que hablar, yo le pudiera haber dicho más cosas, pero me canso . . . Me desespero y ya no le dije nada.

Baudelia: I feel that [the teachers] are violating our rights. Now, up to what point will I be able to transfer my son from a bilingual program to an English program? Why are they taking away that right? Why are they changing the rights, for example, of a committee? To do it as they want. Who gives them the authority to form a committee at their own convenience? To be autonomous means that parents and teachers will work together, but in what ways are parents and teachers working together? To organize festivals? Or to organize academic programs? When have they told us, "Parents, come help plan a program"? When? Not to me.

Ofelia: They call us to organize things for parties!

Baudelia: But they are not saying, "Parents, come, what program would work best for you?" What improvements will a bilingual program offer? What problems might we see? When have they taken us into account? Only when it's convenient for them, when it benefits them, for festivals, for these meetings, for those meetings, that is not right.

Carmen: And that's why I didn't go to select the preschool teacher. [The principal] invited me to go again yesterday, and I told her that I didn't have time, but really I didn't want to go, because if I go, I go as a puppet to say, "That one I like, that one I don't like," but [the principal] is going to decide for herself. [Everyone laughs.]

Amelia: There you should have said to the principal, "Why are you inviting me, if my son is not going to be accepted into the school?"

Carolina: So, if I go, do I have hope that my son is going to preschool?

Carmen: Yes, but to talk, I could have said many more things, but I get tired . . . I get fed up, and then I didn't say anything.

Carmen, in spite of hours of volunteering for the school and participating in all of the parent meetings, was still not assured of a place for her son in the preschool. Repeated inquiries to Marie always got the same answer: that they didn't know yet, and that she could not guarantee a place for Carmen's son. In the above exchange, the other mothers point out the irony of the principal inviting Carmen to help select the preschool teacher when she had no assurance that her son would be admitted into the preschool. Why, then, would she go? But Carmen believed, whether her son was accepted or not, the principal was not really seeking her opinion. She had learned from experience that expressing her opinion had no bearing on the principal's decisions or actions. She was being asked to participate "as a puppet," or a dummy. And for that reason, she refused to go.

Baudelia and Ofelia's point that parents were only called upon to organize festivals revealed their growing sense that parents were used strategically by teachers and staff to accomplish the teachers' goals. In this and other discussions, the mothers recalled how eagerly the teachers recruited them to go to school board meetings when an important decision was being made and they needed a strong parental presence to pressure the school board. As Carolina put it, teachers called parents "when they just need bodies." The pattern was for teachers to encourage parent participation "when it benefits them." In her analysis, Baudelia wrote, "Pero algo que sí puedo asegurar si llegaran a necesitar de pedir algo al Distrito entonces sí se preocupan para que los padres apoyen, se logra lo que quieren y se olvidan que los padres tienen voz y voto" (But one thing you can be sure of is if [the teachers] need to ask for something from the District, then they will make sure parents support them, they will get what they want and they will forget that parents have voice and vote). The invitation to participate in body but not in mind—to be present in the audience at an action or school board meeting, to serve on the School Site Council, to vote on a policy at a parent meeting, while their actual opinions and concerns were silenced—felt distinctly manipulative to the mothers. "Están logrando sus objetivos, no los objetivos de los padres," Baudelia observed ([The teachers] are achieving their own objectives, not the parents' objectives).

The mothers discussed a sense of being rendered invisible at the school, even when their actions conformed to the school's expectations of "good" parent involvement. Ofelia shared the following at one of our meetings: "Yo lo que he aprendido también, que si yo voy como voluntaria a ayudar en la escuela, ya sé que nadie me va a reconocer lo que yo estoy haciendo . . . Porque, yo ayudé mucho a [la directora], los sábados, a botar basura, he ido a la librería a organizar libros . . . Nunca me dijo, 'Gracias por tu ayuda, gracias porque tú me has ayudado'" (What I have also learned is that if I volunteer at the school, I know that nobody is going to recognize what I do . . . Because I helped the principal a lot, on Saturdays, to throw out trash, I've gone to the library to organize books . . . And [the principal] never said to me, "Thank you for your help, thank you because you have helped me").

Following this story of Ofelia's, Baudelia suggested that it was because they were seen as problem parents that their participation in the school was no longer recognized or appreciated. Here she articulated her analysis of why their participation was sidelined by the staff.

> *Baudelia:* Porque siempre estamos expresando francamente lo que no nos gusta, y tenemos el valor de decirlo, y no toda la gente tiene el valor. Entonces ya nosotros hace cuenta como que ya lo que nosotros pidamos, o expongamos, hace cuenta como que nos ignoran. Pero yo creo que nosotros tenemos derecho de seguir expresando lo que nosotros sentimos. Y yo siento que a mí se me han violado derechos como padre. Pero yo ya no estoy diciendo nada, pero ya que yo me apunté eso, ¡un día va a explotar! No, la verdad, es que llega un momento en que se cansa—
> *Ofelia:* No aguanta uno.
> *Baudelia:* Eso no es justo. Un día voy a decir, "Si usted no me escucha aquí, yo me voy a ir a otro lado para que me escuchen."

> *Baudelia:* Because we are always expressing frankly what we don't like, and we have the courage to say it, and not everyone has the courage. So it's like now whatever we ask for or express, it's like they ignore us. But I think we have the right to keep expressing what we feel. And I feel that my rights as a parent have been violated. But I don't say anything anymore, but ever since I noted that, one day it's going to explode! No, really, there comes a time when you get tired—
> *Ofelia:* You can't stand it anymore.
> *Baudelia:* It's not fair. One day I'm going to say, "If you don't listen to me here, I'm going to go somewhere else where they will listen to me."

These Friday debriefing sessions became a key element of our research, in which each mother's experience became the basis for group learning. Their growing sense that the framing of them as "problem parents" was legitimizing their exclusion gave rise to particular questions and research methods that would shed light on this process. Our group made a number of methodological decisions based on the desire to illuminate and disrupt the controlling image of the "problem parent." The first decision was to make the parents' first formal research activity at the school an individual interview with the principal. The mothers felt that Baudelia and Ofelia should conduct this interview as a pair. At first this decision surprised me, given the history of tension between the principal and Baudelia and Ofelia, but the mothers decided that it was precisely because of the conflict with Marie that Baudelia and Ofelia needed to interview her. They saw in this the opportunity to interact with Marie on terms other than those that had shaped their previous interactions, and to gain some credibility for themselves and their research.[1] The mothers were genuinely curious about how Marie viewed her role as principal and her relationship to parents, but they also hoped that the interview might change her image of them and improve their relationship. It was an early indication of how the role of researchers assumed symbolic importance in their quest to recast their identities at the school.

The second methodological decision the group made was to begin, as soon as possible, focus groups with parents. The mothers wanted to talk to as many parents as possible, and had already begun to do so informally. I suggested the focus group methodology as a way to expand the base of their informants and to collect systematically some of the information they had begun to gather piecemeal in casual conversations about how parents felt about the school. The more data they had from parents, I reminded them, the harder it would be for staff members to isolate them as antagonists. So we settled on parent focus groups as an opportunity to both get to know and record parents' stories and concerns, and to strengthen their collective voice as parents in the dialogue about parents' roles at the school. The mothers were particularly interested to learn from parents what roles they were playing in the school, what they understood about the school's vision and mission, and how they felt about the relationship between parents and teachers in the new small school. For parents who had been present in the school's planning phases, the mothers wanted to hear about their experience in organizing the school and the obstacles they had encountered. The parent focus groups were motivating to the Madres, then, both for the information they hoped to learn from them and for the ways this information could be used to transform controlling images of parents at the school.

"Los Padres Se Sienten Utilizados"

The mothers conducted three parent focus groups, with seven to eight parents each, after school on late fall afternoons. Hoping to record stories about parents' involvement in the organizing of the school, the Madres were disappointed. Many parents were unaware of the history and origins of the school, having joined the school that year after being chosen in the lottery, or, as described in the preceding chapter, being brought in by a teacher or the principal. These parents were also unaware of the new roles they were expected to play in the school. Amelia recalled, "Otra cosa que yo encontré fue que los padres no saben sobre sus derechos en la escuela. Eso es muy duro porque yo misma tampoco los sabía, hasta ahora que estoy en esta investigación me he estado enterando de nuestros derechos" (Another thing I learned was that the parents don't know their rights in the school. This is hard because I myself didn't know them either, until now that I'm working on this research, I'm finding out about our rights). Most parents the Madres talked to had not seen the school's proposal and were unaware of its contents. Although copies of the proposal in Spanish had been made available to all parents at the end of the planning year, newcomer parents who had not been at those planning meetings did not have access to those documents.

Founding parents and newcomer parents emerged as two distinct groups with contrasting relationships to the school. Newcomer parents, those who had not participated in community organizing or design team meetings before the school opened, expressed more positive views of the principal and the school's relationship to parents than those who had participated in organizing the school. In one focus group, Ofelia wrote, "the majority of [these] parents sympathize with the principal, I mean they feel in *confianza*, even though I think it is because for the majority, she is the one who helped them get their children into the school."[2] Newcomer parents who had been brought in by the principal or a teacher had no understanding of the politics that had shaped the school's history or the way parents had fought for a voice in the school. The Madres perceived that these parents were used strategically by school staff to defuse the claims of founding parents. Baudelia, in one of her analyses, articulated it this way:

Mi punto de vista es que actualmente estos padres que entraron de esta manera, se sienten tan agradecidos con la directora y maestros, que no quieren reconocer y apoyar los derechos de los demás padres. Es por eso que tal vez, puede verse cierta división entre los padres. Y se puede ver que estos padres son usados para lograr los intereses del personal.

My point of view is that currently these parents who got in this way feel so grateful to the principal and teachers that they don't want to recognize and support the rights of the other parents. It is for this reason maybe that a certain division among the parents exists. And you can see that these [newcomer] parents are used to achieve the interests of the staff.

Baudelia drew a direct connection between the existence of hand-picked parents in the school—the admissions "anomalies"—and the division among the parents that the staff exploited to silence some parents. Recall that Norma, the principal's appointed cochair of the School Site Council, was a newcomer parent. Handpicked newcomer parents were automatic allies of the principal and teachers in struggles with founding parents. Owing their presence in the school to the principal's or a teacher's good favor, the Madres believed, these parents were loyal to the staff and anxious to maintain their favor. Certainly, there were divisions among parents before the school opened. As we saw, some parents were always loyal to the principal, and the principal publicly rewarded them as model parents. In place of the school's good parent/bad parent paradigm, the mothers perceived the division among parents as being a division between those who wanted change and those who supported the status quo. In response to one mother's charge that the Madres were being "too negative," Carolina said, "She is the negative one because she doesn't want to make change!" What the Madres discovered in their research was that the principal and staff, by bringing people into the school in violation of the admissions criteria, had increased the pool of parents loyal to them and the status quo. The principal made use of these parents' loyalty to delegitimate the claims of "problem parents"—or parents who wanted change.

While newcomer parents were unaware of the school's history and were more positive about school–parent relations, founding parents were often disenchanted and disillusioned about the prospects for parent participation. Particularly revealing was the case of Samuel, a father who was selected for the school's English Language Advisory Committee (ELAC). After meeting Samuel in one of the focus groups, the Madres decided to interview him individually to learn more about his experiences with ELAC. Samuel, a hotel worker from El Salvador, had a daughter in fourth grade at UCS. He had participated in the meetings to help plan UCS, and when the new school opened, volunteered to serve on the ELAC committee as a way of staying involved. As Ofelia explained:

Nosotros queríamos entrevistarlo porque queríamos preguntarle cómo estaba en el comité, qué había aprendido, cómo le había parecido el comité de

ELAC, qué información iba a tener para los padres, pero nuestra sorpresa fue cuando lo fuimos a entrevistar nos dijo que nunca le habían llamado, que él estaba esperando por todo el tiempo que le llamaran pero que él nunca había recibido una llamada. Le preguntamos por qué no fue a la escuela a decir ¿por qué no le han llamado? Y él dijo, "Porque me da vergüenza." . . . Y él estaba triste porque nadie le había llamado y ya había pasado seis meses.

We wanted to interview him because we wanted to ask him what it was like on the committee, what he had learned, what he thought about ELAC, and what information he would have for the parents. But to our surprise, when we went to interview him he told us that they had never called him, that he was still waiting for all that time for them to call him, but he had never received a call. We asked him why he didn't go to the school to ask why they never called him. And he said because he felt ashamed . . . and he was sad, because nobody had called him and six months had passed.

For the Madres, Samuel's story affirmed their own experience as founding parents, and provided a sad counterpart to the stories of newcomer parents. Baudelia commented, "Conocí cómo él se siente al igual que nosotras" (I learned how he feels just like us). Ofelia wrote:

Esta entrevista me sirvió mucho para saber que no sólo yo me siento triste y desilucionada de cómo está trabajando la escuela U.C.S. Pude encontrar respuestas a algunas de mis preguntas, por ejemplo ¿me pregunto por qué no asisten padres a las juntas? Ahora tengo claro, como Samuel dijo, hay mucho entusiasmo pero no hay acción. Creo que los padres nos cansamos de escuchar, participar, ayudar, para que al final no veamos nada en concreto . . .

This interview helped me a lot to know that it's not just me that feels sad and disillusioned with how UCS is working. I could find answers to some of my questions, for example, I wonder, Why don't more parents come to the meetings? Now I know, like Samuel said, there's a lot of enthusiasm at the school but there's no action. I think that as parents we get tired of listening, participating, helping, just so that in the end we don't see anything concrete . . .

In Ofelia's analysis, the lack of parent participation at the school was a direct response to the school's failure to incorporate parent voice. "Por eso pienso que cada reunión que pasa hay menos padres" (That's why I think with each meeting there are fewer parents). Parents don't come, she reasoned, because they have already seen it is useless: "we get tired of listening." Samuel had told the Madres that he had stopped going to the parent meetings out of frustration. Ofelia described him as "ashamed" and "sad." As the Madres' reports often did, Ofelia's reflection contained a suggestion for what would improve the situation:

> Como resultado a esta investigación, me gustaría poder hacer reflexionar a la directora para que pidiera una disculpa a padres que han mostrado interés en ayudar y que ella no les dio importancia. Me gustaría volver a tener confianza y esperanza en que nos escuchen y que tomen en cuenta las opiniones de los padres.

> As an outcome of this research, I would like to make the principal reflect so that she would apologize to parents who have shown an interest in helping that she didn't acknowledge. I would like to once again have confidence and hope that they would listen to us and take into account parents' opinions.

In her summary of how parents viewed their role in the school, Ofelia wrote, "Los padres se sienten utilizados" (Parents feel used).

"We Haven't Had Autonomy in Any Way"

Two teacher focus groups provided the Madres the opportunity to ask teachers directly how they viewed the role of parents in the new school. The parent facilitators asked teachers what they thought about the relationship between teachers and parents and how they would like to see parents participate in the school. If we had any fears that teachers would exaggerate their expectations for parent involvement when speaking to parent researchers, those fears were quickly dispelled. The Madres were dismayed by the limited visions of parents' roles that teachers expressed. Many teachers said they had better communication with parents and increased knowledge of students' families as a result of the smaller class size. But when asked about their ideas for further parent involvement, teachers' imaginations seemed stunted. Most appalling to the Madres was the following response, from Helen:

> Well, I'd like parents to take more of a role in some of the bigger issues of the cleanliness of the school, I mean I'm not saying parents should clean

the school, but they should approach the district, approach whoever needs to be approached, beyond Marie [the principal], to help deal with some of those larger issues, because a lot of times the district will respond to parent pressure.

Helen revealed a view of parents that was both condescending and utilitarian. First, parents were expected to be concerned with aspects of the physical environment and facilities, rather than with the instructional program or other academic or social issues. Second, parents were expected to perform roles useful to the teachers that teachers couldn't or wouldn't fill themselves, such as procuring goods and services from the district. (Helen went on to suggest that parents pressure the district about why the school was not wired to the Internet.) Helen's view that the district would respond more to parent pressure than to teachers was common among teachers at UCS. The idea that it was the job of parents to exert political pressure on the district had strong roots in the Oakland movement, as we have seen. Now that they had procured the new small schools, parents were expected to lobby the district for the things teachers were still missing: adequate custodial services, technology, and so on. Teachers also hoped that parents would mobilize for more new small schools. As Janice said:

> I would really like to see the parents come out to support City Academy,[3] because if the parents are happy with what's happening here, then they need to fight for the next step, because I think Helen's right, the district will listen more to the parents than they'll listen to us.

Teachers were more comfortable thinking about parents engaging with the district than envisioning parents engaging at their own school. This was partly because many believed that parents were already "happy with what's happening here." Teachers told us that parents were more involved at UCS than they had been at Whitman Elementary School, citing higher attendance at Back-to-School Night, parent conferences, and parent meetings as evidence of greater parent interest and participation. They also expressed faith in the school's Leadership Team (School Site Council, of which Baudelia was cochair) as a way of ensuring parents' leadership roles in the school. As Susan said:

> One thing I think is really important that is also a big difference between where we've been before [is] the fact that we have parents who are actually

involved in the Leadership Team . . . Parent involvement on Leadership Team at Whitman was a joke. It was the parent center staff, they barely attended, they didn't really participate for whatever reason. I think the way that we designed the Leadership Team at this school is much more equitable.

Susan expressed no concern about the fact that some parent representatives on a body intended to be elected by parents had been appointed by the principal. Of course, not all teachers shared rosy views about parent involvement in the school. Some admitted that "we have a long way to go," and that there was a lack of trust between teachers and parents. Some suggested the need for a parent center as a way for parents to begin to feel at home in the school.

Beyond this, however, insight into teachers' limited views of parents can be found in their own ideas about professionalism and the autonomy that had been promised them as teachers in the reform. In teachers' views, their professional training and expertise should have earned them ownership of the school. As we will see, teachers' interpretations of "autonomy"— notably as the ability to carry out their professional expertise with minimal intervention—left little room for collaboration with parents. Even before the parents asked them what they understood by an "autonomous" school, teachers in both focus groups expressed frustration with the district for imposing restrictions on their autonomy. Teachers said that they had been lured by the promise of autonomy—over hiring, curriculum, budget, and enrollment—only to find that they would not get it, and they felt cheated. The following quotes reveal their sense that the district had violated their right, as professionals, to have control and ownership over their school.

"I don't think we've had autonomy really in any way," Susan said. Laurie put it this way: "The district is still not clear on what autonomy really means for the small autonomous schools. So they attempt some things, then take a few steps back." Tracy said, "It's not even that we have different understandings of autonomy, we just didn't have any autonomy." In her view, the district's behavior was a denial of their professionalism:

The biggest thing is we spent a year working two jobs creating this school, proving to them—they approved our proposal. We said, this is what we want to do, and this is why we know how to do it, and here's the research that supports it. And they're not trusting us to do that. They're forcing all these other things on us, which is just not autonomy.

Here Tracy explains teachers' right to autonomy based on their professional expertise: "this is why we know how to do it," and cites "research"—not parent participation or support—as granting them legitimacy. Similarly, Tanya explained that being autonomous was about "being professionals," choosing your own professional development and having control over the way you teach. Instead, teachers described having to attend mandated professional developments, having to work with staff assigned to the school who did not share their vision, and being required to incorporate elements of Open Court[4] into their teaching. Although they did not say so, the need to collaborate with parents may have been experienced as another restriction on their autonomy.

The Madres saw in the teachers' resentment around the lack of autonomy a parallel to their own frustration with the school. Teachers felt betrayed by the district, which refused to share power after promising teachers autonomy, in the same way parents felt betrayed by the school staff. Ofelia drew this analogy when explaining to the Madres the teachers' sarcasm about autonomy. In the English teachers focus group, when asked what they understood by "autonomy," the teachers had spontaneously burst into laughter. When Ofelia described this to the other parents in Madres Unidas, Carmen asked why the teachers would laugh at the word. Ofelia turned to her and said, "The same way I might laugh if you said 'social justice.' You know, like, '*What* justice?'" The mothers often talked about how UCS was supposed to be a "social-justice" school. With this, Ofelia effectively conveyed the pain and humor of a word that evoked broken promises.

Teachers were seemingly less aware of the parallel. They had always viewed parents as allies in their struggles with the district, so it is not surprising that they should channel parent involvement toward pressuring the district to provide more support. But while they were hyperaware of the power struggle going on between the district and the new small schools, they were closed to the recognition of the power play within their own school between teachers and parents. Parent involvement was described in a decisively power-neutral language: parents were either "more involved" than at Whitman, or perhaps not involved enough, but at no point were they betrayed, deceived, disillusioned, or used by the staff (words the Madres used to describe their experience).

Why were teachers unable to see within the walls of their school the relationship they so resented with the district? Why should parents' anger be appropriate at the district but not admissible within the school? The answer to these questions, I argue, can be traced to controlling images of parents that circulated in the small schools movement, which justified parents' continued subordination in school reform.

The Eleventh Commandment

On a cold Saturday in January, teachers from across the city gathered in the sanctuary of First Baptist Church for the keynote address of the annual small schools conference, convened by BACEE. The speaker, a renowned scholar of school reform from a nearby university, delivered a rousing address on the topic "10 Commandments for Small Schools." The ten commandments advised educators on aspects of curriculum, instruction, and school structure that research has shown make small schools successful. The speaker ended her address with quotes from Frederick Douglass and Langston Hughes and drew a standing ovation from the crowd. At the podium, Assistant Superintendent of School Reform José Morales took the microphone and told the audience he had an "eleventh commandment" to add: "Thou shalt remember thy community." The audience clapped obligingly, and Morales explained, "We need the community will to change Oakland Unified."

Morales's eleventh commandment reveals much about how parents and community were constructed by educators in the small schools movement. That "community" should enter the dialogue only as an afterthought, as an eleventh commandment, is significant. Morales's emphasis is also telling: "We need the community *will* to change Oakland Unified." The community holds the "political will" necessary to make change. Parents' power lies in their demands. Parents here are a group who should want and demand something different. As Morales told me in an interview, what made the Oakland small schools movement unique was that in Oakland the reform was "politically motivated," not "instructionally motivated." Parents are "indignant," he said, and "that's great."

The "indignant parent," so unwelcome at UCS, was praised as the "engine" of the reform. In the small schools movement, it was "angry parents" who had pushed the school board to pass the new small schools policy and forced officials to provide adequate facilities for the new schools. Parents' anger was recognized, welcomed, and even encouraged by OCCA organizers and reform leaders who sought crowds of parents at actions to leverage policy change. The following field notes taken at a local organizing committee meeting illustrate how anger was used strategically by OCCA organizers to prepare parents for their role in public actions.

> About 25 parents gathered in the cafeteria of the parish school. After the parents who had met with public officials reported on their meetings, Laura, an OCCA organizer, led the group in a discussion of the upcoming action. She began by asking the question, "¿Qué es una acción?" (What is an action?). Baudelia was one of the first to reply: "Pedir lo que necesitamos a los encargados que pueden hacer una solución, exigir que lo hagan" (To ask for what we need from the authorities who have the solution, and demand that they do it). Others followed with, "Es una manifestación, para exigir los cambios que necesitamos" (It's a demonstration, to demand the changes that we need). Laura affirmed this, saying "an action is to make change." When Laura asked, "What power do we have?" Baudelia replied, "¡La unión! ¡Voz y voto!" (Unity! Voice and vote!).
>
> Martha, another OCCA organizer, reviewed the Oakland schools map showing the disparities in size and achievement between the schools in the hills and the schools in the flats. She asked, "¿Es justo?" "No!" everyone cried. Then Laura did an exercise showing "Power respects power." "Who will we be inviting to the action who has the power to make decisions?" They listed the public officials they have been inviting: the mayor, the superintendent, city council members, school-board members. She wrote their names on the poster paper. "What power do they have?" They make decisions, and they have money. She told the parents, "The Oakland School District has $30 million to buy new facilities." Then, on another sheet, "What power do we have?" Baudelia cried out, "¡Voz!" But Laura waited for another answer. Others cried out, "¡Voto!" "¡La unión!" and finally someone said, "¡Gente!" and that's when Laura drew a whole bunch of stick figures standing together in the middle of the page. "Nosotros tenemos gente" (We have people).

In this meeting, parents are told that their power resides in their numbers: the crowd of stick figures is juxtaposed to the names of the public officials they will be confronting. And it is through numbers, and the "electoral threat" they represent, that OCCA achieves its victories.[5] OCCA organizers appeal to parents' anger at the injustices they are faced with— the Oakland schools map serves as the prompt for this—to encourage them to bring large numbers to the action. Anger at inequities is the basis on which parents can demand change.

There is no doubt that this training gives parents new confidence and skills and accomplishes significant political victories. The action for new small school sites, when it did happen several weeks later, was attended by the mayor, the superintendent, and prominent school-board and city council members, and gained commitments from these officials to open three new small schools in the Fruitvale-San Antonio neighborhood by the following school year. But in the context of the small schools movement, parents were taught that their role was to be one of many in an angry crowd demanding change. Their participation was directed to exert political pressure on the city and the school district, not to be involved in discussions of what kind of change was necessary or how it should be achieved: as Morales had told me, OCCA was the engine of the movement, but BACEE was the brains.

While parents packed auditoriums for public actions, they were notably scarce at Incubator meetings where teachers were being trained for their roles in the reform, and where the nuts and bolts of school design were being discussed. The Incubator, the primary vehicle for providing coaching and technical assistance to design teams as they planned their new small schools, played a major role in shaping how teachers perceived and related to parents. Consider the advice given to teachers in one Incubator session I observed in 2000, in a handout distributed by BACEE and titled "12 Ideas for Designing New Small Schools." The purpose of the "12 Design Ideas" was to introduce teachers to "what school reformers have learned over the past 20 years that can help you design a school that will be truly different." Parents appear in only one of the twelve design ideas, titled "Team Composition: Who is on your Design Team? Why are all voices needed?" This section contained the following clause:

> What is essential is that all [new small autonomous schools] be designed by the educators who hope to teach there, with support, input and advice from parents, students and others who care. *The educators who will teach in the school must have the responsibility for the design because they are the ones, day in and day out, who will make the school live and flourish. But the school can only succeed in partnership with the parents and the students.* (Emphasis added)

Teachers reading this could have interpreted it as official permission to sideline parent input. Teachers and aspiring new small school leaders were told directly that they had primary responsibility (and therefore authority)

Where does funding this? does fit into this?

in school design, and parents were there to "support" them. It was assumed that teachers know best what parents need.

The Design Ideas document advised teachers to incorporate current learning theory, current brain research, child-development theory and practice, and research on cultural and racial diversity, among other things, into their school vision. In none of these areas were parents authorities. Even "cultural and racial diversity," presumably the area where parents' experience would be relevant, was to be understood by research, removing it one step from parents' authority and experience. The implication that parents' needs were encompassed by "cultural, linguistic, and racial diversity," and that a body of research already existed to explain this, made parent participation on design teams all but unnecessary. And certainly, the exclusion of community needs from the coaching at Incubator meetings was made easier by the absence of parents at these meetings. Parents were often not invited to Incubator sessions, or, if they were, according to parents at Whitman, they were unable to attend because the meetings were held too late in the evening and no child care was provided.

Reformers and organizers gave many rationales for the lack of parent participation on small school design teams. Recall the retired elementary school teacher in chapter 2 who told us that parents probably wouldn't *want* to help with the writing of the school's proposal. Assumptions about what parents wanted, what they were capable of, and what they valued revealed two controlling images of parents in the small schools movement: the passive and submissive Latino parent, who deferred to teachers' authority and was uninterested in school design issues; and the angry and impatient parent, suitable for turning up at large actions, but not for engaging in a deeper discussion about reform. Both controlling images served educator self-interests in rationalizing a subordinate role for parents in reform.

Erica, a BACEE staff member told me, "I don't imagine that every parent is going to have the capacity to sit home at night with their computer and type up their educational theory." Like many reformers and organizers in the small schools movement, Erica had been a classroom teacher before joining BACEE, and her experience with parents as a teacher shaped her expectations of parent behavior in the small schools reform. "It's like developing a new culture for parents, too," she said. "It's having parents think differently about what they expect of teachers, specifically Latino parents who are, like, 'Whatever the teacher says is right.' You know, they're not like Baudelia, most of them, you know, most of my parents were, like,

'Whatever you say, *maestra!*'" Here, the active parent (Baudelia) is seen as an exception to the norm of passive, subservient Latino parents.

Rather than seeing patterns of passivity as an outcome of parents' experiences with school personnel, reformers saw these as reflecting cultural traits of Latino parents. There was no recognition that all parents, if given the opportunity, might have an interest in school design. A senior staff member at BACEE wrote in a memo to other small schools activists: "Often what parents really want is to be heard and considered. They may be less concerned with the details of design and more interested in making sure that the changes educators make will really address their issues. It is likely that leaders will emerge from the community who want to be active in planning reform while others will feel that that is the job of the school professionals. My advice here is to encourage participation and leadership but to keep an eye on process and on making sure that decisions about what you intend to do get distributed widely for comment." Here, the possibility is granted that there may be some exceptional parents who will be more active in planning reform, but not that all parents have the potential to become involved at this level. Patterns of parent involvement are accepted as a given, and not seen as something that educators have the power or responsibility to change.

The angry and impatient parents, while key figures in the small schools movement through their role at public actions, were not suitable for participating in long-term planning for school reform. "Parents are interested in immediacy, this school year," reformers often said. A senior staff member at BACEE told me that while policy makers think and plan for the long term—in two-, five-, or seven-year periods—community members want immediate gratification. It was easier to mobilize them for new resources or facilities than to involve them in planning a reform that might not take effect until after their child graduated from school. In fact, however, I met more than one parent who defied this assumption, organizing for new schools as a way to help their community.

Certainly, reformers and organizers had the desire to involve parents in new ways and were reflective about the challenges this posed. The small schools reform represented a new role for organizing, and the partners were only just beginning to grasp the implications of this. As OCCA's director said, "Part of what this small school stuff has done for us is brought parents to the table as different kinds of partners than they have been before," adding, "I don't know what this is gonna look like." Erica, from

BACEE, reflected, "As I become more and more involved in this, I realize that schools are not like other organizing efforts which involve getting a grocery store or speed bumps put in a neighborhood. The job of the organizer ends when the victory is gained in those arenas. But the work of creating a sustainable and strong school in many ways begins the day that the school opens its doors."

But in their efforts to involve parents as "different kinds of partners," reformers and organizers were limited by controlling images of which even they seemed unaware. Parents were constructed as fixed in time and unchanging, with needs that were readily explainable by education professionals: either too angry and impatient to get involved with the "details of design" or culturally incapable of seeing themselves as intellectual equals with teachers. While the Madres through their research at UCS identified patterns of parent participation as being shaped by the school, through teacher–parent interactions, the reformers' discourse about parents showed no awareness that parents' "nature" was at all socially constructed; that is, the very patterns of parent behavior that educators identified and described were institutionally produced, much like the patterns of student achievement that these educators aimed to change.

The Resignation

Early one morning in March, Baudelia called me to tell me that she had resigned from the School Site Council. It had been a dramatic week at UCS. On Monday, Baudelia submitted a letter of resignation to the principal and the members of the council. Within two days of Baudelia's resignation, Baudelia's cochair, Norma, had also resigned. Both the principal and Linda, Baudelia's daughter's teacher, had called Baudelia individually to plead with her. Linda wanted to call a meeting with Baudelia and the council to discuss Baudelia's reasons for resigning and what they could do about it. Baudelia told her she wouldn't meet with them without me and Martha, the OCCA organizer, also being present. So Baudelia was calling to invite me to the meeting and to talk to me about what she should say.

Baudelia's resignation letter read as follows:

Directora y Leadership Team:
   Através de este medio quiero informar a ustedes que apartir de hoy dejo de pertenecer a este comité. Mis razones son las siguientes:

-No estoy de acuerdo en la forma de organizar para trabajar.

-Falta de comunicación entre los miembros de este equipo.

-Hasta este momento desconozco mis funciones como miembro de este comité.

-He perdido algo que es muy importante para continuar: y esto es la confianza, aclarando este punto no es en general para todos los miembros de este comité.

-No quiero seguir siendo una persona que exige demasiado. No me gustaría que ustedes piensen que reacciono así porque he gastado cierta energía, sino al contrario porque me gustan las cosas claras, la verdad y la justicia.

Gracias,

Baudelia.

Principal and Leadership Team:

Through this communication I would like to inform you that as of today I no longer belong to this committee. My reasons are the following:

-I do not agree with the way the work is organized.

-Lack of communication between the members of this team.

-Up to this moment I do not know my functions as a member of this committee.

-I have lost something that is very important to continue, and that is trust, clarifying that this point is not meant in general for all members of the committee.

-I don't want to keep being a person who demands too much. I don't want you all to think that I act this way because I am worn out, but, on the contrary, because I like things to be clear, truthful, and just.

Thank you,

Baudelia.

Baudelia's last point indicates her understanding that she was being viewed as a difficult person, "a person who demands too much," by the other members of the committee, and her rejection of this identity. "I don't want you all to think that I act this way because I am worn out," she emphasized, again rejecting the image of the overworked founding parent. In submitting a formally written letter of resignation, Baudelia attempted to make her critique of the committee known to all.

Baudelia had many reasons for resigning, the most egregious of which was a recent incident when she had been asked by the principal to sign a blank form. It turned out the form was authorizing the budget, but Baudelia wasn't allowed to see what the items were. Marie had told her that they urgently needed to send it to the district, and Baudelia was essentially forced to sign. She had told Marie that was the first and last time she would ever sign "un papel en blanco." Then there was the fact that Marie never called her for planning meetings. Marie would meet privately with Norma and then tell everyone that the committee had met. Baudelia would find out after the fact, or sometimes hours before the meeting, from the OCCA organizer. Then she would show up, surprising Marie with her uninvited presence.

The Madres tried three times to interview Norma, Baudelia's cochair, about her experiences on the council and at the school. Each time, Norma made the appointment and then failed to show up. Not long after her resignation, the mothers heard that she had moved to a town in the Central Valley. We never got her story.

A week after the resignation, a group of teachers and parents assembled anxiously in the staff lunchroom to discuss Baudelia's reasons for resigning. The meeting, attended by five parents, five staff members, including the principal, and myself, revealed the staff's use of controlling images to censor Baudelia's critique. Baudelia addressed the group, explaining that she had the intention of working for the good of the school, and that she did not intend to offend anybody, but she had to be honest. From the start of the meeting, then, she took the opportunity to publicly name and deny the identity politics that would mark her as a person with bad intentions. She held a copy of her resignation letter, which everyone was to have read, and said she would be happy to further explain or answer questions about any of the points in the letter. The group asked her to go point by point, so she did.

When it came to explaining the "falta de confianza," or how Baudelia had lost trust in the team, Baudelia gave the example of how Marie had asked her to sign a blank form authorizing the budget. This appalled one of the parents, who said she would never have signed a blank form. Another parent suggested that Marie was probably feeling pressured and rushed, and because of the *confianza* she has with parents, thought she could get a signature from Baudelia without explaining everything. Nancy, the teacher sitting next to Marie, asked Marie if the form Baudelia had signed was really blank, and Marie confirmed that it was. Nancy raised her eyebrows and said, "Oh!" Marie did not apologize for asking Baudelia to sign a blank form. A little later in the meeting, she explained that the form was authorizing the allocation of the budget into three distinct funds so that the school could access it, but it wasn't designating particular expenditures. Linda said that she would like some commitment from Marie that this would never happen again, that nobody would be asked to sign a blank form for anything again, but Marie did not respond to this request.

The discussion continued. Baudelia explained that in general she felt that parents were not listened to at the school, that parents did not have a voice. She gave the example of how parent meetings were often not translated, making it difficult for parents like her to communicate with English-speaking parents. Marie asked for another example. Baudelia brought up the uniform policy: how parents had voted at a meeting, but the decision was disregarded. She then gave the example of the meeting when Marie had told parents that they were not allowed to switch their children from a bilingual to an English program or vice versa, because this was an "autonomous school."

After this, Nancy said, "These examples happened way back in September. Is there anything more recent?" However, Baudelia had started out with two recent examples: that she was not informed about Leadership Team meetings, and that she was forced to sign a blank form. Only when Marie asked her for more examples did she bring up the meetings from the past. Nancy's question seemed to imply that the recent examples Baudelia had started with weren't good enough.

Baudelia, unfazed, responded with another recent example of miscommunication to the parents. Here Nancy said to Baudelia, "You and Norma are cochairs. Why did Norma know about this and not you?" Her tone was distinctly accusatory. Her use of the present tense—"You and Norma *are* cochairs," rather than "*were* cochairs"—denied that Baudelia and Norma had both resigned. And her question placed blame on Baudelia for not knowing about something that Norma knew about, rather than inquiring why Marie would consistently inform Norma and not Baudelia. But nobody said anything. Baudelia then gave the example of the meeting when Norma had been forced to repeat everything Marie said, and said that she (Baudelia) would never do that. At this point, another parent defended the principal, saying that she was teaching Norma how to run a meeting. She said, "We don't have the leadership skills, we need help."

After some more discussion, Nancy addressed Baudelia, "We need to know: Are you going to resign or are you going to stay and help us work out these problems?" Each time Nancy spoke, her voice rang out across the table in a loud, confrontational tone. Her question implied that it was up to Baudelia to make a change, rather than up to the Leadership Team. I spoke up and said, "I don't think it's fair to put pressure on Baudelia to make a decision tonight. The purpose of this meeting was to discuss her concerns and reasons for resigning, and if anything the Leadership Team has a task now to decide how it is going to change."

Nancy responded, "We are going to change, we've all admitted there's a communication problem. The question is, is Baudelia going to come and be a part of the change or is she going to stay out and watch it happen?" The implication, "You're either with us or against us," invoked the good parent/bad parent normative apparatus to censor Baudelia's critique. If Baudelia was a "good parent," that is, cooperative and compliant, she would keep her position on the School Site Council. If she chose to maintain her resignation, it would be assumed that she had a bad attitude.

The message to the other parents present was that they too would be punished for speaking up, for critiquing the committee, for daring to resign. There was no inquiry into what had gone wrong on the committee that had marginalized Baudelia or what abuses of power had enabled the principal to force Baudelia's signature on a blank form. The one attempt, by Linda, to secure a commitment from Marie that this would not happen again was unsuccessful. The meeting was conducted as if Baudelia were on trial. I felt myself getting a stomachache, and remembered how Baudelia and Amelia always said they left parent meetings with a stomachache or a headache.

Baudelia, however, refused to be pressured. She told the group calmly that she always wanted to work with parents for the good of the school, but she didn't need a position on the council to do that. There are a lot of ways to work with parents, she said. (Before the meeting had started, she had spoken to me excitedly about her ideas for a parent center, and her recent visit to the Whitman School Parent Center.)

As we got up to leave, Linda asked her, "So you'll think about it and let us know your decision, right?" Baudelia uttered a very noncommittal "okay."

I drove Baudelia and her two daughters home, and we talked about the meeting. She said she felt better now that she had unloaded. But when I asked what she thought about keeping her position, she told me she was inclined not to. She was more interested in talking to me about the parent center. She spoke so fast about her visit to the center at Whitman that I almost couldn't keep up with her. When I dropped her and the children off in front of their apartment building, Baudelia was in good spirits. I drove away with renewed admiration for her, and a smile playing at my lips all the way home. If anyone at the school thought they had reined in her defiant spirit, they were sorely mistaken.

In this chapter I have attempted to show how professionals in the small schools movement made use of controlling images to limit the subject positions of parents and to punish parents who transgressed accepted roles. The "angry parent," while useful to reformers at a district-wide level, was threatening to professionals within the new small schools and was quickly condemned. The mothers in Madres Unidas, in their research meetings, were able to recognize and reflect on these dynamics and collectively fashion their resistance. Baudelia and Ofelia's meeting with school staff, and Baudelia's resignation from the School Site Council, were two early attempts of the mothers to "talk back" to the staff and reposition themselves as responsible parents. In the face of frustration and exclusion at the school, participation in Madres Unidas offered the mothers a new way to view themselves and to engage with the school. As I will argue in the next chapter, Ofelia's kitchen became a site of renewal and resistance.

5. Ofelia's Kitchen
A COUNTERSPACE FOR RESISTANCE

Es informal, pero para hacer todo el trabajo siempre estamos ya formalmente. O sea, es informal la manera de venir al trabajo, y tomamos café, a veces comida, pero el trabajo siempre es muy serio, y lo tomamos muy en serio.

It's informal, but to do all the work we're always here formally. I mean, our way of working is informal, we drink coffee, sometimes there's food, but the work is always very serious, and we take it very seriously.

—Carmen

In our young minds houses belonged to women, were their special domain, not as property, but as places where all that truly mattered in life took place.

—bell hooks, *Yearning*

Ofelia and her husband rented a spacious old house centrally located on one of Fruitvale's main avenues. Baudelia lived in an apartment building just across the street. Often, when I pulled up to park before our meeting, I would see Baudelia crossing the street with her three children, on her way to Ofelia's house. Carmen, Amelia, and Carolina also lived nearby. Amelia often walked to Ofelia's house with her son Ernesto, but when the weather was cold, she would ask for a ride with Carolina or me. Between 5 o'clock and 5:15 on Friday afternoons, all of us would converge on Ofelia's house. The children, happy to see each other, would run off to play outside in back, or, on dark winter evenings, in the children's room. We could hear the sounds of their playing throughout our meetings, and they were never afraid to come and ask for a drink or a snack. The mothers would get up to pour them a glass of juice, hand them a plate of cookies, or sometimes scold them if they came screaming through the kitchen. But this was all part of the rhythm of our meetings—soothing, comforting, like background music without which we would not have been able to work.

Although Ofelia had a comfortable living room, the mothers preferred to meet in the kitchen. The kitchen-table setting lent a relaxed and intimate tone to our meetings. We all had the sense of being welcomed into Ofelia's home, part of the family. As Baudelia said, "Yo me siento bien a gusto de estar en el grupo, porque siento que somos como una familia, o sea porque siento que todas nos entendemos" (I feel really at home in this group, because I feel like we're a family. I feel that we all understand each other). Meeting in the home allowed the mothers to be present in their wholeness: as mothers, whose children were playing nearby in the other room, and as friends, who cooked for each other, ate together, and shared stories of their personal experiences. It is in these ways, I argue, that Madres Unidas created a unique *mujerista* or Latina womanist space (Villenas 2005; Trinidad Galván 2006), based on the use of *testimonio* and relationships of *confianza* (trust) that enhanced their capacity to make change at their children's school.

Ruth Trinidad Galván (2006) explains:

A *mujerista* or Latina womanist vision . . . aims to uncover, share, and validate the diverse knowledge and experiences of Latinas in the United States and abroad. It takes a holistic approach to self that includes spirit and emotion, and recognizes our individual/communal struggles and efforts to name ourselves, record our history, and choose our own destiny. (172)

As they explored their personal and collective histories as parents in the new small school, the mothers in Ofelia's kitchen supported each other in naming and recording the experiences that had been suppressed, rejecting the controlling images that framed them as unworthy or "problem parents," and recasting themselves as concerned advocates for their families and community. Ofelia, our host, offered her home as an example of the resilience born of hard times, and illustrated with her life the spirit of defiance, generosity, and love that has been nurtured through struggle.

Ofelia

On her kitchen counter, Ofelia kept a votive candle to La Virgen de Guadalupe always burning.[1] Ofelia was a devotee of La Virgen de Guadalupe. She believed she had the Virgin Mother to thank for her current home. She once told me the story: when she was eighteen years old, new to this country, and pregnant, she lived with her mother-in-law for a year. Her husband was serving prison time for drug offenses. Ofelia remembers that year as the hardest in her life: alone, away from all her friends, separated from her husband (her mother-in-law would tell him when he called that Ofelia wasn't home), and with a mother-in-law who seemed to resent her presence. Ofelia prayed incessantly that she would be able to find her own place to live, and one night the Virgin of Guadalupe appeared to her in a dream, surrounded by a pool of water: "Don't worry," she told Ofelia. "Everything is going to work out." Ofelia awoke with a deep sense of peace. Soon after, a kindly neighbor told her that his rental house was becoming available. It was a Section 8 unit and, as a young mother, Ofelia would qualify. He helped Ofelia through the application process, and shortly after that, Ofelia moved in.

This was the home Ofelia now shared with her husband and two children, and where Madres Unidas met. If you shared Ofelia's faith, you might believe that the Virgin Mother presided over our meetings, blessing Ofelia's efforts to create the healing home she once lacked. If you were not spiritually inclined, you could see the votive candle as a visual reminder of help in hard times. In either case, the kitchen represented Ofelia's hard-won autonomy, a place where she was free from the control of her mother-in-law, her husband, and the bruising interactions with employers, social-service institutions, and her children's teachers. In the safety of her kitchen, Ofelia could articulate her hard-learned lessons and pass them on to her children. As she explained:

> Las experiencias que yo viví y he vivido han sido bien fuertes para mi edad, han sido duras, y esas experiencias me enseñaron a hablar, a defenderme, a no dejar que me tengan de menos o pensar que yo soy menos que otra persona . . . No importa si no tienes estudios, no importa dónde trabajes, importa quién eres tú, cómo eres tú, eres una persona honesta, eres una persona que respeta a las demás, eso es lo importante, no lo que tengas.

> The experiences that I've lived have been very strong for my age, they've been hard, and those experiences taught me to speak, to defend myself, to not let anyone depreciate me or think that I'm less than someone else . . . It doesn't matter if you're not educated, it doesn't matter where you work; what matters is who you are, how you are, you are an honest person, you are a person who respects others, that's what matters, not what you have.

Self-possessed and outspoken, Ofelia was a confident parent advocate who embraced the roles in Madres Unidas as a natural extension of her desire to "speak up." But she recognized that she wasn't always like this. She believed her experience as a young migrant from rural El Salvador to the sometimes mean streets of Oakland had shaped her ability to see clearly and be secure of herself.

Ofelia remembered her childhood home in El Salvador nostalgically, as a place where she had felt free and without fear, at least before the war. In her rural town of "pretty views, no pollution, and animals everywhere," all the neighbors knew each other, and she never had to worry about talking to strangers the way she worries about her children in Oakland. But she also remembered extreme financial hardship, and having to work at an early age. Her mother did washing and ironing for others and occasionally worked a farm nearby, but with her meager earnings and the money Ofelia's sister sent home from the United States, they had barely enough to get by. Ofelia helped out by carting water from the river for the washing and wood for cooking, as soon as she got home from school:

> No descansaba. Estaba siempre trabajando, pero es una cultura muy diferente porque allá uno no está renegando como, "Ay, ¿por qué me pones a trabajar tanto?" Es como sus padres lo crían a uno de esa forma y uno no pone excusas o no reniega. Como yo digo acá a mi hijo, "Recoge tu cuarto," y dice, "Ay, ¡ahorita no tengo ganas!" O, "ahorita no quiero, estoy jugando."

> I never rested. I was always working, but it's a very different culture there, because you would never complain, like, "Oh, why are you making me work so much?" It's like your parents raise you that way and you don't make excuses or protests. Like here I say to my son, "Clean up your room," and he says, "Aw, I don't feel like it!" Or, "I don't want to right now, I'm playing!"

Ofelia was very aware of the contrast between her childhood in El Salvador and her children's lives in Oakland. Her children enjoyed privilege where she had suffered want, but the respect for elders that was deeply ingrained in Ofelia from her upbringing in El Salvador was missing in the United States. This respect was especially to be extended to teachers: "Los maestros son como un papá para uno [allá], es un respeto muy grande para los maestros. Y aquí, no. Acá cuando yo llegué y fui a la escuela, ¡yo estaba impresionada! Estaba como, yo no lo podía creer, cómo tratan aquí a los maestros" (Teachers are like a parent to you [there], there is a very big respect for teachers. But not here. Here when I arrived and went to school, I was amazed! I was like, I couldn't believe it, how they treat teachers here).

Ofelia completed the eighth grade in El Salvador, and when she immigrated to the United States at the age of sixteen, she enrolled in a public high school in Oakland. The adjustment to an inner-city high school was difficult. She remembered being discriminated against as a Salvadoran in a majority-Mexican student body, and being shocked by the disrespect for teachers expressed by students. In spite of this atmosphere, she excelled in her studies and got A's in all subjects except English. She hoped to become a nurse, but circumstances would not allow her to finish school. Her oldest sister, who she was living with, told her she would need to help out with the rent. Ofelia looked for work in all the local stores, but without a Social Security card, nobody would hire her. "Entonces yo me sentía atrapada" (I felt trapped).

Ofelia married her husband, a neighbor of her sister's, in part as a way out of her troubles. He was older than she, legally in the country, and had a steady job. "Yo lo quería, yo sí me enamoré de él y todo, pero yo tenía otros planes para mí. Pero al mismo tiempo me sentía como presionada" (I loved him, I did fall in love with him and everything, but I had other plans for myself. But at the same time, I felt pressured). Within a year, Ofelia was pregnant with her first son. Hard times followed. She dropped out of school to take care of him after the eleventh grade. She moved in with her mother-in-law but was never accepted by her husband's family. Once again, she was at somebody else's mercy, and she longed for a place of her own.

Now in her own home with her husband and two children, and earning a decent income as a housecleaner in a wealthy San Francisco neighborhood, Ofelia has achieved many of the things she longed for as a teenager: financial stability, a safe, comfortable home, and enough income to send some home to her mother in El Salvador every month. The year after our research, she saved enough money to take her children to El Salvador for the first time to visit their grandmother. She wanted them to see where she came from:

> [Ellos] vieron cómo mi mamá vive, no vive en una casa preciosa, seguimos siendo pobres, somos pobres, pero siempre les digo, "Yo estoy bien orgullosa

de mi familia, de mi mamá, de dónde vivo, de lo que tenemos, ¡a mí nadie, nadie que tenga más, que tenga una casa preciosa o que tenga más que yo, me va a hacer sentir mal!"

They saw how my mom lives, she doesn't live in a gorgeous house, we are still poor, we're poor, but I've always told them, "I am very proud of my family, of my mom, of where I live, of what we have, and nobody, nobody who has more, who has a gorgeous house or has more than I do, is going to make me feel bad!"

Ofelia wanted to raise her children with the best of the values she learned as a child in El Salvador, but at the same time, her experiences had taught her that "being submissive" and "keeping quiet" were not always appropriate.

Te debes de quedar callada. Esa era la enseñanza de mi mamá para mí. Y ahora que soy adulta, yo sola he aprendido, que así no, ¡que esa forma no me gustó! De que todo el tiempo tienes que estar callada, siento que es al revéz, te debes de defender, y debes de luchar por lo que piensas y defender lo que piensas, y tienes el derecho a opinar y hacer decisiones . . . porque quedarse callado, no es bueno, para mí . . . esa enseñanza por ejemplo no me gustaría dársela a mis hijos . . .

Les enseño que se defiendan, si alguien les ofendió o les dijo algo que no les gustó, siempre les digo, "Sean seguros de lo que ustedes son. Sean seguros de lo que ustedes tienen, sean seguros de ustedes mismos."

You should keep quiet. That was my mother's teaching for me. And now that I'm an adult, on my own I have learned that it doesn't work, that I didn't like that way of being! That all the time you should keep quiet, I feel that it's the reverse: you should defend yourself, you should fight for what you think and defend what you think, and you have the right to have opinions and make decisions . . . Because keeping quiet, that's not good, for me . . . That teaching, for example, I would not like to pass on to my children . . .

I teach them to defend themselves, if somebody offended them or said something they didn't like, I always tell them, "Be sure of who you are. Be sure of what you have, be sure of yourselves."

Ofelia's teaching for her children may not be the same as her mother's teaching for her, but it was rooted in her mother's experience of poverty, and her own experience of battling and surviving poverty and discrimination—in Spanish, *sobrevivencia* (survival and beyond). As she said, "We're poor, but I've always told them, 'I am very proud of my family, of my mom.'" This experience has given her the strength to confront whatever new assaults she or her children might face:

> Siempre a mis hijos les enseño, [cuando me preguntan] "'Mami, ¿dónde trabajas? ¿Limpiando casas?" Es un trabajo con orgullo que yo hago. No me da pena decir que yo hago eso, porque es la forma que yo me gano la vida . . . Y así les enseño a mis hijos, que no deben de sentir mal, cualquier trabajo es honrado y respetado . . . Y soy una persona ahora de adulta muy segura de mí.

> I always teach my kids, [when they ask] "Mom, where do you work? Cleaning houses?" It's a job I do with pride. I'm not ashamed to say that I do that, because it's how I earn my living . . . And that's how I teach my kids, that they shouldn't feel bad, any work is honored and respected . . . And now, as an adult, I am very sure of myself.

In her child rearing and in her work for Madres Unidas and the school, Ofelia demonstrated the resilience and flexibility that U.S. third-world feminists have argued is a product of life lived on the margins and a unique resource for social change (Anzaldúa 1987; hooks 1990; Sandoval 2000). Ofelia directly translated her life-learned values of self-respect, cultural pride, and community into her work for the school. As she explained, "No nada más lucho por mis hijos, o nada más me defiendo yo, defiendo otros padres, les aconsejo, 'No tienen que hacer eso si no quieren.' O sea, he luchado no sólo por mis hijos, sino por todos los niños de la escuela" (I don't just struggle for my own children, I don't just defend myself, I defend other parents, I advise them, "You don't have to do that if you don't want to." I mean, I have struggled not just for my own children, but for all the children in the school). This spirit of determination and defiance also helped her confront controlling images of Latina motherhood from her husband and her children's teachers. Ofelia told us that when she first decided to take a job outside the home, her husband had opposed it. Whenever he felt that she was asserting too much control over her life, he would remind her that she had to stay with him because of her legal status (at the time, he was a legal resident, she was not). Finally, Ofelia had said to him, "If that's the only reason I'm with you, let's go to the lawyers and sign the divorce papers right now!" After that, he never brought it up again.

Ofelia was similarly undeterred by the negative reactions of some teachers to her and the other mothers' research at the school. As she explained, coming across teachers who were not supportive of the research or who said things that were difficult for her to hear was a valuable learning experience for her: "Eso a mí me ayudó a ser más fuerte, aprender a tratar a la gente" (That helped me to be stronger, to learn to deal with people). She also had a sharp critique for teachers' limited views of parents' capabilities: "No sólo porque ellas tienen poder o más estudios, pensar que los padres no podemos hacer cambios" (Just because they [teachers] have more power or more education doesn't mean we parents can't make changes).

Ofelia had learned from her life that it was not education and credentials that give one the ability to work for change, but one's own experience of hardship and *sobrevivencia,* and she reminded the Madres of this every week through her own example and efforts to affirm the other mothers' experiences. Her offering of her home and her hospitality for Madres Unidas was symbolic of her commitment to community uplift and self- and social transformation. I believe that in the context of the oppression the mothers experienced in their daily lives, Ofelia's kitchen became a sacred space: a place of healing, affirmation, and, in the words of bell hooks (1990), a site of resistance.

Creating Community and *Confianza*

Bell hooks (1990) has written about the significance of the homeplace for African American women, who consciously sought to create a space for "one's own" after working all day in the white community. "Throughout our history," she writes, "African-Americans have recognized the subversive value of homeplace, of having access to private space where we do not directly encounter white racist aggression" (47). Within the brutal reality of racial apartheid and domination, hooks writes, black women resisted by making homes where "we could restore to ourselves the dignity denied us on the outside in the public world" (42).

During the year that Madres Unidas met, three of the five mothers worked as *domésticas:* housecleaners and caretakers for white families. Latina immigrant women have largely replaced African American women in this growing low-wage sector of the economy (Hondagneu-Sotelo

2001). It is now more often than not Latina immigrant women who take multiple buses and trains to neighborhoods far from their own to service other people's homes. Sometimes, their own children are far away, left in the care of parents and relatives in their home countries (Hondagneu-Sotelo 2001; Hondagneu-Sotelo and Avila 2003). Other times, their children are in the United States, left in the care of white teachers at urban public schools. That the mothers in Madres Unidas returned from jobs in suburban homes and found time to attend endless meetings at their children's school indicates their refusal to give up their own homes, their refusal to leave the care of their children completely in the hands of others. Even if their participation at school meetings left them less time to attend to their children, it was an effort to shape their children's upbringing and the community in which they would grow up. As Ofelia explained, "We're all here because we care about the future of our children, and we want something better for them and for our community."

In Ofelia's kitchen, the mothers in Madres Unidas created a safe space where they could share stories, interrogate their experiences at the school, and find new ways of being in community that preserved their dignity and wholeness. Wholeness, in Latina feminist thought, acknowledges the need for personal healing and for the emotional, spiritual, and relational resources that Latina women draw on in their struggles against oppression (Trinidad Galván 2006). As Ruth Trinidad Galván explains, "A *mujerista* vision enlightens our understanding of pedagogies that encompass personal, collective, spiritual, and survival undertakings" (2006, 175). In this way, Latina feminist thought bears similarity to black feminist thought and other race-based feminisms born of life at "the intersecting oppressions of race, class, gender, and sexuality" (Collins 2000, 98). According to Patricia Hill Collins, African American women have long drawn upon "safe spaces," such as extended family, churches, and African American community groups, to strengthen their resistance to controlling images and "refashion themselves" after their own role models (ibid., 101). Ofelia's kitchen was such a space for Madres Unidas.

Unlike school meetings that excluded, silenced, and delegitimized the personal experiences of parents, Madres Unidas created a space that privileged personal experience as the foundation of its being. The beginning of every meeting was dedicated to open sharing and socializing over food. We took turns in pairs providing food for the group, and often feasted on homemade enchiladas, tamalitos, taquitos, tostadas, chiles rellenos, chile verde, and flan. The mothers discussed new jobs, child-care dilemmas, the high cost of health care, or family news. In late spring, Carmen went to El Salvador for the first time in seven years, to visit her son and mother. In the weeks before her trip, she shared her excitement and anxiety about return-ing to her home country. She told us that as result of her experience with Madres Unidas, she wanted to interview the director of her son's school there, and to visit the rural school she had attended as a girl. When she returned, she showed us pictures and told us about her experiences there. Several mothers testified that this personal sharing was what they appre-ciated most about the group. As Baudelia said, "Era bien bonito porque se había la confianza, compartíamos, conocíamos algo que no solamente conocíamos como una compañera de trabajo, sino que fue algo más, más familiar" (It was really nice because there was trust, we shared, we got to know each other not just as coworkers, but something more family-like). They emphasized the combination of learning, working, and personal shar-ing that made the group enjoyable to them, as Carmen said, "Drinking coffee and relaxing, and at the same time learning and sharing personal things from your home life, your kids, and learning a lot at the same time that you're relaxed."

But importantly, relationships of trust allowed the mothers to retell experiences they had had at the school and debrief painful and frustrating meetings in the company of supportive friends. In doing so, the Madres drew on the practice of *testimonio*, which has a long tradition in Latin American activism and has recently been revived by Chicana and Latina feminist scholars (Latina Feminist Group 2001; Delgado Bernal et al. 2006; Benmayor 1991). The Latina Feminist Group describes *testimonio* as a "crucial means of bearing witness and inscribing into history those lived realities that would otherwise succumb to the alchemy of erasure" (2001, 2). They note that historically, *testimonio* as a form of expression was born out of intense repression or struggle, in which the purpose of the story was less about disclosing a personal life than it was about creating a record of violence on whole communities (13). In this way, *testimonio* serves both personal and collective goals, and is explicitly connected to struggles for justice and liberation. Through *testimonio*, the mothers in Madres Unidas reaffirmed each other's experiences of injustice at their children's school and supported each other in acts of resistance.

If *testimonio* was the medium of sharing stories, *confianza* (a word that means both trust and confidence) created the conditions that made this possible. *Confianza* enabled mothers who were newly "coming to speech" (hooks 1989) to share their stories and draw strength from them. In one meeting in Ofelia's kitchen, Amelia described feeling scorned in a parent meeting at the school for raising a question that was critical of a new policy:

> Amelia reported that the school has instituted a "complaint box" for parents, and parents are to write their complaints or suggestions on a piece of paper and place them in the box, instead of bringing them up at the meeting. The mothers thought this unfair because: (1) it keeps them secret, so parents can't find out about other parents' complaints, and (2) how would they know that teachers were actually reading the complaints? Amelia explained that she had brought up the latter issue in the meeting, and she described a feeling of complete mortification as she raised the question, and all eyes turned to her. I was so proud of her for having spoken up! Another new rule she thought was unfair was that parents are to be limited to one question each at the meetings. (Field notes, November 30, 2001)

This particular example was poignant to me because it so clearly revealed Amelia's budding anger and awareness of the ways parents were being silenced by the school and her own coming to speech. Keeping parents' complaints secret in a "complaint box," and limiting them to one question each at parent meetings, was for the mothers a clear attempt by the staff to silence them. When Amelia attempted to break the silence, questioning teachers in front of parents about the fairness of the process, she was made to feel deeply embarrassed. She told us she turned bright red as she felt all the eyes in the room fixed on her. Retelling the event to the Madres around Ofelia's kitchen table, she drew on their support and solidarity to recover the dignity that was denied her at the time. In *confianza* her act of speaking up was transformed from an experience of shame to an act of resistance. "Moving from silence into speech is for the oppressed . . . a gesture of defiance that heals, that makes new life and new growth possible," writes bell hooks (1989, 9). Feminist scholars remind us that resistance is as much about personal healing and wholeness as it is about transforming structures of domination (Latina Feminist Group 2001; hooks 1989, 1990). We cannot hope to transform social structures without first transforming ourselves, without "remaking and reconstituting ourselves so that we can be radical" (hooks 1989, 32). I believe, as other scholars have suggested, that this transformation in the intimacy of Ofelia's home enabled more public forms of resistance (Villenas 2001; Scott 1990).

While the mothers said that meetings at the school frequently left them with headaches or stomachaches from the stress, they described our meetings in Ofelia's kitchen as leaving them confident, at peace, and energized. Ofelia explained:

> Para mí, esperaba cada viernes, "O, ya vamos a tener la junta," aunque ande corriendo de mi trabajo acá a la casa tener lista la cocina y todo, es algo que a mí me gusta, y si no nos juntamos más va a ser como bien extraño . . . Pues sí, no veníamos nada más a vernos, sino que a trabajar, pero el modo de que nosotros trabajábamos pues me sentía cómoda, a gusto. No sentía presión, no sentía como "¡Ay! ¡Ya llegó viernes otra vez!" ¿Verdad? O sea, me sentía con energía de seguir.

> For me, I looked forward to every Friday, "Oh, we're going to have the meeting," even though I would be running from my job to the house to get the kitchen ready and everything, it's something that I like, and if we ever stop meeting, it's going to feel really strange . . . Well, we didn't come just to see each other, we came to work, but the way in which we worked made me feel comfortable, at home. I didn't feel pressure, I didn't feel like "Oh! It's already Friday again!" You know? I felt energized to keep working.

Similarly, during one of our evaluation meetings, Carolina said, "Yo les doy las gracias a todas ustedes aquí, porque cada vez que yo vengo aquí a las reuniones me siento bien tranquila, relajada, en confianza" (I want to thank all of you here, because every time I come here to these meetings I feel really peaceful, relaxed, and in confidence). She explained to the group that when Ofelia invited her to join the group, she was going through a time of personal hardship:

> Y a la vez yo pensé que Dios me ayudó, porque en ese momento que tuve yo esa problema que ya me pasó, fue cuando ella me dijo de venir a la junta, entonces dije bueno, lo voy a hacer, no no más por el problema, sino por mi hijo y por mí misma, para mantenerme ocupada . . . Y para mí es muy importante también para aprender. Porque yo estaba entusiasmada de desenvolverme con las personas, porque nunca había hecho nada así.

And at the time I thought that God helped me, because it was at that moment when I had that problem that has now passed that [Ofelia] invited me to come to the meeting, so I said, well, I'm going to do it, not just because of my problem, but for my son and for myself, to keep myself busy . . . And for me it's very important also to learn. Because I was enthusiastic about getting involved with people, because I had never done anything like this before.

Carolina's story signals the importance of Madres Unidas as a support network, countering the isolation that the mothers felt before. These spaces are especially important for Latina immigrants, whose jobs often isolate them from traditional contexts for collective organizing, such as the workplace (Benmayor, Torruellas, and Juarbe 1997), and for whom even family and social ties are severely conditioned by structural constraints (Menjívar 2000). Amelia, who was a housecleaner in suburban Orinda, shared the following:

Bueno, yo les doy las gracias a todas ustedes por haberme tomado en cuenta en esta investigación que estamos haciendo. Y por tener amigas, porque yo las considero mis amigas, no tengo más amigas, sólo ustedes . . . Para mí es difícil también tener amigas, porque yo tengo dieciseis años viviendo aquí y nunca había tenido amigas, sólo "¡Buenas tardes! Hola, ¿cómo le va?" A Ofelia le tengo de conocer desde que los niños estaban en Kinder, pero nunca en una relación que estamos ahorita.

Well, I want to thank all of you for taking me into account for this research that we're doing. And for having friends, because I consider you my friends, I don't have any other friends, just you . . . For me it is difficult to make friends, because I've been living here for sixteen years and I've never had friends, just "Good afternoon! Hey, how's it going?" I've known Ofelia since our children started kindergarten, but never in a relationship like we have now.

In their daily lives as domestics or restaurant workers, and in parent meetings at the school, the mothers had too few opportunities to nurture personal relationships or their own needs for intellectual development and community service. In Madres Unidas, healing came not just from the being together—*convivencia*—but from the opportunity to develop their skills and apply them to new and meaningful work. As Ofelia said, "We didn't come just to see each other, we came to work"; and Carolina said, "For me it's very important also to learn." In one of her earliest reflections, Amelia wrote, "Para mí fue una experiencia ser anotadora, porque uno tiene que tener rapidez para escribir, y yo no tengo rapidez, pero sin embargo me siento útil y necesito tener más experiencia" (For me it was an experience to be the note taker, because you have to be able to write fast, and I can't write fast; however, I feel useful and I need to have more experience). This reflection signaled both the challenge and the power the role of note taker held for a woman who was not accustomed to writing in her daily life. Being in a position of writing helped Amelia to see herself in a new way ("I feel useful").

The planning of the focus groups and interviews became the most exciting meetings for the mothers. In contrast to the impotence they often felt at parent meetings, the process of collectively coming up with questions to ask in the focus groups and preparing for the role of interviewer allowed them to experience their own agency. All of the mothers participated eagerly in brainstorming questions and discussing their meaning, and praised each other's suggestions. As the following excerpt from my field notes shows, the energy in the room was palpable:

> At the end of the meeting, I asked them how they were feeling. Amelia, Carolina, and Carmen all responded, "¡Feliz!" I was most struck by Amelia's enthusiasm, since she is the one who often seems the least sure of her abilities and of what to contribute. But she volunteered to be primary facilitator for one of the parent focus groups! "We're learning," she kept saying, and Carmen, too: "We're going to learn." At the beginning, during our first few meetings, Carmen and Amelia used to say that they felt inferior because Baudelia "has studied" and she's so competent in this. They don't say that anymore. They say, "We're learning." I knew Baudelia and Ofelia were happy, because they had been participating eagerly throughout. Baudelia at one point exclaimed, clapping her hands together, "I can't wait!" at the prospect of doing the focus groups. And at the beginning . . . Baudelia had told me, "You have really lifted our spirits [Nos has levantado el ánimo.] You really listen to us, and you give us a chance that nobody else has." (Field notes, November 2, 2001)

While Baudelia observed that my role as a "listener" was critical in affirming the mothers' right to speak and be heard, she also played a key role in encouraging the mothers who were less confident in their research abilities to participate equally. Baudelia often came to our meetings prepared with a list of questions or ideas (she said they should do this as "homework"), but she never dominated the discussion. She would read one or two questions from her list, then wait for others to contribute. The atmosphere of mutual support and trust, or *confianza*, made the learning of new skills—a risk for many of the mothers who had had limited or negative schooling experiences—possible. Ofelia commented, "Porque somos un grupo que trabajamos con mucha confianza, que podíamos decir en qué estábamos mal o qué podíamos mejorar, y eso para mí ha sido algo muy bonito, porque en confianza uno se puede decir las cosas" (Because we are a group that works with much *confianza*, we could tell each other what we were doing wrong or how we could improve, and that for me has been really neat, because in confidence you could say things). The following excerpts from my field notes reveal some of the ways mutual affirmation and support were enacted in the group:

> [One] issue we discussed was that the parents in the focus group were too eager to list their complaints—seemingly under the impression that we work for the school and have the ability to make the changes they suggested. We talked about how we should explain in the introduction of the focus groups that we don't work for the school and don't have the authority to change a lot of things. How should we explain this? The mothers wanted to know. They thought it would be rude to say, "We aren't here to resolve your problems." Amelia suggested that we say, "We can't guarantee" that we will resolve the problems they identify, but that we would "bring them to light." She said it so professionally that everyone clapped for her! She said she hoped she would remember how she had said it when it was the real thing! I realize that we often clap for each other when someone has a good idea or says something well. It is a spontaneous expression of support and enthusiasm. (Field notes, November 17, 2001)

> We had a lesson on note taking and writing up interviews and observations. I read some of their own notes/reflections out loud, to emphasize what I thought was good and so they could see what the others had written.

Everybody praised each other's observations. Baudelia was especially encouraging to Carmen and Amelia. (Field notes, December 7, 2001)

As the mothers ventured into the new territory of research—interviewing, observing, videotaping, and writing—and were affirmed by each other in their new roles, their confidence in their abilities grew. As I will show in further detail in chapter 6, engaging in collective research transformed their individual fears and self-doubts—the wounds of past experiences—into social critique and resistance. But if conducting research provided the mothers with new knowledge and perspectives and bolstered their confidence as intellectual actors, their transformation into critical agents was ultimately made possible by activating their own ways of being in community—what I am referring to as Latina womanist values of wholeness, *confianza*, *convivencia*, and *testimonio*—to heal and reimagine themselves.

Oftentimes, humor became a source of healing, as the mothers poked fun at the very things that caused them pain. Laughter—genuine shoulder-shaking, tear-making, stomach-squeezing laughter—abounded around Ofelia's kitchen table. The mothers laughed at themselves, at me, at each other, at the principal, and at teachers. On occasion, they broke into spontaneous role play, acting out scenes between the principal or teachers and parents that had occurred at the school, collapsing into giggles at their exaggerated renditions of the principal's behavior.

Rosario Carrillo (2006) writes that "humor casero mujerista" or womanist humor of the home is one way in which Latina women refigure the terms of their existence and transgress relations of inequality in their everyday lives. Describing the comedic skits and humorous language of six Latina bakery workers who formed a union, Carrillo argues that their humor subverts negative and hurtful images of them and "transforms Latinas into decisive speaking subjects with self-determination" (190). Like the Latina bakery workers, the mothers in Madres Unidas, through their humorous parodies of school staff, enacted "exemplary, counter, educative ways of creating meaningful, resilient, and joyous lives—indeed ways of interacting, behaving, speaking, believing, and thinking that can transgress inequitable social relations based on class, race and gender" (ibid., 193).

A range of scholars from neo-Marxist to Chicana/Latina feminist have taught us to look beyond the formal, public, and explicit scripts to these informal, private, and "hidden" expressions of resistance to domination among the marginalized (Scott 1990; Luykx 1996, 1999; Villenas 2006b; Delgado Bernal et al. 2006). James Scott (1990), writing about slaves in the antebellum South, argues that "neither everyday forms of resistance nor the occasional insurrection can be understood without reference to the sequestered social sites at which such resistance can be nurtured and given meaning" (20). In his analysis of "hidden transcripts," what happened between slaves in "those offstage speeches, gestures, and practices" contained insights into power relations between dominant and subordinate groups. While members of subordinate groups might maintain a mask of deference and compliance in the presence of power holders, what Scott calls the "public transcript," what they do among themselves contains the seeds of a "sharply dissonant political culture" (18).

It is the private speeches, rituals, jokes, and gossip among subordinates, shared in the relative safety of friendship, that nurture and make possible public acts of resistance. Rebellion, or social change, in this analysis are brought about not by exceptional leaders or charismatic people, but by "charismatic acts" of ordinary people sustained by the informal rituals of the hidden transcript. Scott uses the example of Mrs. Poyser, a tenant farmer in George Eliot's *Adam Bede*, who dares to speak back to the ruthless squire. "Mrs. Poyser was not a charismatic character," Scott writes, "but she undertook a charismatic act. Understanding that charismatic act, and many others like it . . . depends upon appreciating how her gesture represented a shared hidden transcript that no one as yet had the courage to declare in the teeth of power" (20).

Seen in this light, Amelia's speaking up in the parent meeting, described earlier in this chapter, and Baudelia's and Ofelia's confronting the principal in chapter 4, were charismatic acts animated and sustained by the shared hidden transcript of Ofelia's kitchen: a hidden transcript shaped by the *mujerista* values of *confianza* and *convivencia*. As an intimate social space where mothers could come together "offstage," away from the school, Madres Unidas provided "the social and normative basis for practical forms of resistance" (ibid.). And there is other evidence that the transformative process begun in Ofelia's kitchen translated into public acts of resistance at the school.

One of the earliest experiences Madres Unidas analyzed was that of Baudelia, who had been elected chair of the School Site Council and then publicly warned by the principal to "change her attitude." The other mothers, who had been present at the meeting, expressed their outrage at the principal's *falta de respeto* (lack of respect) toward Baudelia and voiced their support and solidarity with her. As related in chapter 4, they encouraged Baudelia to serve as chair of the council in spite of her misgivings, because they believed the council needed someone like her. Throughout the year, Baudelia brought her experiences on the School Site Council to Ofelia's kitchen table, where they became part of the group's *testimonio*. She shared how the principal failed to inform of her of a key meeting with a city council member, to which other School Site Council members were invited, and how the principal had forced her to sign a blank form authorizing the budget, without letting her see the figures. With each *testimonio*, the mothers affirmed Baudelia's anger as a rightful response to injustice. As the Latina Feminist Group (2001) asserts, "We reclaim *testimonio* as a tool for Latinas to theorize oppression, resistance, and subjectivity" (19).

Madres Unidas enabled Baudelia to persevere on the council in the face of much difficulty, and finally, supported her in resigning with dignity when the list of offenses became too much to tolerate. In one meeting, she read aloud the letter of resignation she had written for the principal and members of the council. The letter, itself a *testimonio*, listed her reasons for resigning, and ended as follows: "I don't want to keep being a person who demands too much. I don't want you all to think I react this way because I am worn out, but, on the contrary, because I like things to be clear, truthful, and just" (my translation). With her last point, Baudelia revealed her understanding that she was being viewed as a difficult person, "a person who demands too much," by the other members of the committee, and her rejection of this identity. The very act of writing the letter was a form of "counterstorytelling" (Solorzano and Yosso 2001; Villenas 2001), disrupting the dominant story she knew was likely to circulate about her resignation, and making public her own critique of the committee.

The response of Madres Unidas to Baudelia's experience on the School Site Council (SSC) illustrates the use of Ofelia's kitchen as a counterspace, a space to critique negative images of the mothers' roles at the school and nurture supportive relationships.[2] While school staff, reformers, and organizers condemned the mothers' anger as disruptive, Madres Unidas, through *testimonio*, affirmed anger as a healthy alternative to the self-blame and hurt that their school experiences would have otherwise inflicted—a necessary response to the politics of exclusion. As critical race theorists Solorzano and Yosso write, "It is often our anger that fuels our spirit, gives voice and direction to the silence, and provides the energy to go on" (2001,

483). Within counterspaces, as people of color realize they are not alone in their experiences, feelings of demoralization and self-doubt are replaced by anger and collective outrage at injustice; anger is affirmed as a first step toward transformative action. Feminist and critical race scholars have documented the importance of these spaces in nurturing resilience for urban youth of color (Pastor, McCormick, and Fine 2007; López and Lechuga 2007; Torre et al. 2007); African American college students (Solorzano, Ceja, and Yosso 2000); Chicano/a and Latino/a undergraduate students (Yosso 2006); and Chicana/o graduate students (Solorzano and Yosso 2001).

Michelle Fine, reporting on her work with high school students of color conducting participatory research on educational inequality, quotes an African American principal who maintained that even if the youths' research changed nothing, "at least they'll know they're not crazy."[3] Similarly, the mothers in Madres Unidas who left meetings at the school wondering if they were crazy, or if they really were the "negative" and difficult parents school staff painted them to be, were affirmed in their views of reality by the other mothers in Ofelia's kitchen. We may never know or be able to measure the transformative effects of this profoundly personal shift, but for some Latina women, the experience is like "oxygen" (Yosso 2006). Baudelia often said our Friday meetings were "like therapy." She explains: "Para mí me ha servido este grupo, y yo creo que a todas, porque los problemas que tenemos en la escuela, venimos y los desahogamos" (For me, and I think for all of us, this group has helped, because the problems we have at school, we come [here] and unload them). As the mothers reflected on what was most valuable about the group, in taped evaluation sessions midway through and at the end of the year, the theme of *confianza* surfaced with meanings more nuanced than trust or closeness. *Confianza* was a condition that made possible a clear-eyed and honest discussion of reality, a slicing through of the distortions and evasions that plagued social relations at the school, to face difficult truths. As Baudelia had written in her letter of resignation to the SSC, she wanted to be known as someone who liked things to be "clear, truthful, and just."

When I asked the group how you could build *confianza*, I received the following responses: "El ser sincera, la sinceridad, la honestidad y el ser directo" (Being sincere, sincerity, honesty, and being direct). "El respeto" (Respect). "Respetar, hablar con la sinceridad, ser directas, y honestidad (Respect, speak with sincerity, be direct, and honest). "Sinceridad. Ser sincero, decir lo que le molesta a uno, lo que le gusta, hablar sinceramente, decir, 'a mí no me gustó . . .'" (Sincerity. Be sincere, say what bothers you, what you like, talk openly, say, "I didn't like . . ."). Importantly for all of them, *confianza* was not built on false pretenses of getting along or avoiding conflict: it came with the open expression of one's opinions and experiences, as long as these were voiced with respect. Reflecting, Baudelia summed it up this way:

> Confianza es, con aquella persona que puedo ser yo misma, con la que yo me puedo expresar, puedo hablar, puedo decir sin temor alguno . . . Sé que esta persona me va a respetar, sé que esta persona, allí va a quedar mi comentario, y no va a salir fuera de este lugar. Que esta persona me puede entender, que esta persona no me va a juzgar. Es donde yo puedo ser yo misma.

> *Confianza* is, with that person with whom I can be myself, with whom I can express myself, I can talk, I can speak without any fear . . . I know that this person is going to respect me, I know that this person will keep my comments to herself, that my words won't leave this place. That this person can understand me, that this person is not going to judge me. It's where I can be myself.

Here Baudelia speaks to the need for self-definition, highlighting the importance of a place "where I can be myself." Too often at their children's school, the mothers' identities were defined by others, in ways that fractured and distorted their sense of selves. In Ofelia's kitchen, they could recover their wholeness, and exercise and develop those parts of themselves that were not given expression at the school. This, writes bell hooks, is the essence of resistance. Hooks quotes Vietnamese Buddhist monk Thich Nhat Hahn: "I think that communities of resistance should be places where people can return to themselves more easily, where the conditions are such that they can heal themselves and recover their wholeness" (cited in hooks 1990, 43).

In many ways, the experience in Ofelia's kitchen was a process of politicization, of coming to consciousness, in Paulo Freire's terms (1970/2005), where consciousness combines the naming of one's personal experience of oppression with a critical understanding of the material conditions— especially structures of domination—that shape that experience. This process is not an easy one. As bell hooks writes, "true politicization—coming to critical consciousness—is a difficult, trying process, one that demands that we give up set ways of thinking and being, that we shift our paradigms, that we open ourselves to the unknown" (1989, 25). Inés Hernández Avila, a Native American scholar and poet, describes the process this way: "Each discovery adds more light to the path, allowing us to see and be with others in solidarity. Each piece of sifted information helps us figure out the puzzles, personally, collectively, globally. Once begun, there is no turning back. To forsake consciousness is to forsake being human" (2001, 300).

I end this chapter with an image of the mothers, laughing around Ofelia's kitchen table. They are writing down questions to ask in a focus group, laughing at each other's wording and miswording. Their faces are radiant with confidence. During the year that we met, I often wished the teachers could see them as they were in Ofelia's kitchen. "If only this part of them could be seen at the school." But better now than never. Better here than nowhere. I think of a line from Inés Hernández Avila: "As we heal, we tenderly regather ourselves in our totality as physical, emotional, intellectual, spiritual, creative beings" (2001, 301).

6. *En Confianza*
LESSONS FOR EDUCATORS ON WORKING FOR CHANGE WITH IMMIGRANT PARENTS

On a sunny spring day in a leafy annex of the university campus, a conference room fills with professors and graduate students, and a few community members from local nonprofit organizations, who have come to hear about parent participatory research in new small schools. Sitting behind a long table at the front of the room, with water glasses and filled pitchers in front of them, Amelia, Baudelia, and Carmen are dressed in their best formal attire. Baudelia looks elegant in a black suit, her hair pinned fashionably behind her head. Amelia is wearing a pretty lavender sweater, and, for perhaps only the second time since I have known her, has applied makeup. Carmen is wearing a pressed white blouse and pearl earrings. Looking at them waiting for their presentation to begin, one would never know that they have never done this before.

An hour and a half later, we emerge into the sunshine outside, laughing and congratulating each other on our performance. Relieved that it is over, and elated at their accomplishment, the mothers tease each other about the painful moments of preparation and rehearsing. They excitedly recount humorous or tense moments in the presentation—a minor slipup, laughter from the audience at their video, Baudelia's dramatic hand gestures—like actors reveling backstage after a show. Tonight, they will be at home with their families, presiding over rituals of homework, dinner, bath, and bedtime, and life will resume pretty much as it has been. But something is different. Even as they put their children to bed, the mothers cradle new images of themselves in their minds. They see themselves in the conference room as speakers, professionals, experts; and they nurse the memory like a precious secret.

"At first it was horrible" ("al principio era horrible"), recalled Carmen later, about the lead-up to their first presentation:

Yo tenía mucho temor desde que empezamos acá la práctica, era para mí era como que ¡oy!, como que yo me iba a desmayar, me temblaban las piernas, yo pensaba que realmente no iba a poder. Pero por pensar en que tú creíste en nosotros . . . Entonces si tú dices que sí, más yo tengo que poner mi esfuerzo. Pues yo digo si tú crees en mí, ¿cómo yo no voy a creer en mí misma? Entonces por eso es que yo hacía y he tratado de superarme.

I was so afraid from the time we started practicing [in Ofelia's house], it was like *¡Oy!* Like I was going to faint. My legs shook, and I thought that I really was not going to be able to do it. But to think that you [Andrea] believed in us . . . So, if you say I can, I've got to put in my effort. I said if you believe in me, how am I not to believe in myself? So, that's why I did it and I've tried to overcome my fears.

For Carmen, the fact of somebody else believing in her was important in triggering her own self-confidence, in giving her the will to "put in my effort." Once she made the effort, however, the experience of presenting successfully made her realize that she had the abilities within herself. As she explained: "Y después, cuando ya acabó la conferencia, ¡uy! era como dije yo, si ahora yo pude hacer esto, ¡ya puedo hacer más! Y sentí también como que éramos bien importantes todas, porque habíamos ido a la universidad" (And afterwards, when the conference was over, wow! It was like I said, if I could do that, now I can do *more*! And I also felt that we were all very important, because we had gone to the university).

The experience of presenting at the university, at a conference on the topic Popular Education and Participatory Research, was transformative for the Madres. Initially reticent and uncertain of their abilities, they had prepared painstakingly. They had never participated in a conference before, and, with the exception of Baudelia, who had given testimony at OCCA actions, none of them had public speaking experience. They were particularly worried about how they would field questions from the audience. What if people ask us questions we can't answer? they asked me. My attempts to reassure them seemed useless, and our first and only rehearsal, in Ofelia's living room, dissolved in chaos. I began to wonder if it was really such a good idea to ask them to do something that seemed to only add stress to their already stressful lives. But on that spring morning, encouraged by the warmth of a supportive audience, the mothers relaxed into the personalities I knew them to be and delivered their presentations with grace and flair.

By the time they invited questions from the audience—the part they had worried about beforehand—the mothers seemed to be positively enjoying themselves. Rather than catching them off guard, the questions allowed them to exhibit their leadership and expertise, and they relished the opportunity. Carmen, who had claimed to be "only a housewife," became an authority on how to conduct interviews with parents, while Amelia, who had also worried she would faint, was indulging in telling humorous stories from her experience as a researcher. The more the audience laughed, the more stories the mothers would dig up, as if finally realizing what rich experience they had.

Our first presentation together revealed several lessons about the products of participatory research and the hard-won changes Madres Unidas achieved that will be the focus of this chapter. In their efforts to take their research public, and to use their new knowledge to make change, Madres Unidas publicly challenged controlling of images of Latina mothers that sought to limit their roles in reform and enacted new identities as experts, advocates, and agents of change. But in order to be seen differently by their children's teachers and other professionals, the mothers first had to *see themselves* differently. Creating change at their children's school and beyond depended on a transformation that was as much personal as political, and illustrated the third-world feminist insight that in order to transform social structures, we must first transform ourselves (hooks 1989).[1] As Carmen's story testifies, her newly developed self-image as something more than "a housewife" came hand in hand with an increased capacity to intervene effectively in the public world—speaking at conferences, and later, opening and running a parent center at the school—and none of these changes came without a struggle. Professionals, I learned—whether teachers, organizers, reformers, or university researchers—had a key role to play in this transformation. They could support it, sometimes as simply as by providing a respectful audience for the new researchers. Or they could obstruct it, by refusing to recognize the mothers as change agents. But once the struggle was under way, they could never fully stop it. In the remainder of this chapter, I describe how the mothers sought to educate professionals at their children's school about parents' needs, insights, and values, and how they used their own stories of change to make change possible for others. I end with a series of lessons for educators on working for change with immigrant parents.

"If They Were Interested, They Would Have Come"

The day after our conference presentation at the university, Baudelia, Carmen, Amelia, and I make our way through the crowded hallways of a local public high school, where another conference is under way. The event is the annual Small Schools Conference, sponsored by BACEE and OCCA, and the people bustling to and fro are teachers, parents, and reformers interested in new small schools. The mothers and I find our way to our assigned classroom, where we are to present in a workshop session called "The Parent Experience." That this is their second conference presentation and the locale seems considerably less formal than the university helps put the mothers at ease. They greet Martha, the OCCA organizer, and some other parents outside our classroom.

Two doors down from our classroom, I spot Marie, the principal, and several teachers from UCS waiting for another workshop to begin. I pop in to say hello, and to find out if they know that Madres Unidas is presenting down the hallway. There had been a room change at the last minute, and many people did not receive the program insert indicating the correct room for our workshop. But it turns out the teachers intend to be where they are, and they show only a vague and polite interest in hearing that the Madres are presenting two doors down. A man dressed formally in a suit stands at the front of the room, holding handouts, clearly the presenter. I ask the teachers which workshop this is and Yvonne tells me, "Paradoxes of School Change."

In the weeks before our two conference presentations, Madres Unidas spent hours poring over our data, selecting and analyzing the most important themes, and debating how to present sensitive and controversial findings to an audience that might include their children's teachers. The issue of how to take our findings public was of some anxiety to the Madres and myself, and also of considerable political importance to UCS's staff and reform partners. I had already been cautioned on more than one occasion by BACEE and OCCA staff to avoid publicly naming the conflicts at UCS because of the fragility of the new small schools and the larger reform movement. Two weeks before the small schools conference, I met with Martha, from OCCA, at a café to discuss our workshop presentation, which was also to include OCCA parents from two other small schools. During that meeting, I shared my concerns with Martha that many of the

Madres' findings touched on areas of conflict between teachers and parents, and risked offending the UCS teachers. Martha was thoughtful and asked for examples of some of the things that might cause controversy. We discussed at length the issue of the student selection process and the violations that the Madres had discovered. In the end, Martha said it was important to name the conflicts, because, in her words, "it is their [the parents'] community." Since this workshop was on the parent experience in starting new small schools, it was important for teachers to hear from the parents about the effects of their actions on the community.

But on that Saturday as we gathered in the classroom of Bridgemont High, the small group of people in the audience were mostly parents. Although we had been informed that all of UCS's teachers were attending the conference, and we had informed them about our workshop, not one of them came to hear Madres Unidas. Carmen, Baudelia, and Amelia (Ofelia was recovering from surgery) engaged in an informal discussion with other parents, which Martha facilitated.

As we walked to the car afterwards, the mothers expressed their dismay that the teachers had not come to their presentation. Amelia was the first to comment on it. She told us, "Si ellas me preguntan cómo nos fue, yo les voy a decir que si les interesaba, hubieran venido" (If they ask me how it went, I'm going to tell them that if they were interested, they would have come). In her view, the teachers' failure to show up revealed a lack of interest in the parents' work. Baudelia, too, thought it was inexcusable that not a single teacher had cared to come. Wouldn't they want to hear what the parents were saying about their school? she wondered.

I wondered, too. I had hoped that the Madres' presenting in a professional venue such as the small schools conference—one that was recognized and respected by the teachers, as evidenced by their attendance at the last small schools conference—would elevate their status in the school and lend credibility to their work among teachers. Perhaps the teachers' refusal to come to their workshop was a refusal to grant them that credibility, a refusal to view them as professionals. Or perhaps the teachers didn't want to hear what the parents had to say, because they were afraid of facing their conflicts. More likely than not, the teachers suspected that there would be nothing new in the Madres' presentation: that it would be the same griping they had been hearing Monday through Friday for the past several months. Why should they listen to it on a Saturday when they had come to a professional conference to hear something new, something they could learn from?

Although our small schools conference presentation failed to attract the attention of UCS teachers, it helped to develop the Madres' public speaking confidence, and their awareness that their roles as "experts" would not be easily recognized by their children's teachers. Even when they spoke in a professional venue that was respected by the teachers, their presentation was not chosen by a single teacher as worth attending. "If they were interested," as Amelia said, "they would have come."

"I Don't Want Another Tostada Meeting"

While those of us who are based in the university often debate whether and how to use our research to promote change, for Madres Unidas, making change was the purpose of undertaking research on their children's school. As they said repeatedly, they hoped that their research would help correct problems at the school and enable the school to fulfill its promise of change. Throughout our research, the Madres demonstrated the seamless relationship between research and action that is at the heart of participatory research, but nowhere was this more evident than in the planning of our research products.

The concern about how to address the problems they identified emerged early in the research when Carmen observed that her first parent focus group had been "almost all complaints." In her reflection after the focus group, she had written, "This really worries me, because we're going to bring the problems to light, but we can't resolve them right now." While the mothers were heartened by stories they heard indicating that the school was making a difference in the lives of some children, they were troubled by the continuing pattern of excluding parent voice, and they felt a personal responsibility to the parents who shared stories of pain and exclusion. As they debriefed, analyzed, and shared stories in Ofelia's kitchen, the question was always raised, "What can we *do* about this?"

The Madres decided on two main action items intended to change the relationship between teachers and parents at the school. The first was a presentation to the school staff of their research process and findings, at the end of the school year. If teachers would not come to their public presentations, they would bring their presentation to them. The second was the opening of a parent center at the new small school. As products of their research, both the presentation and the parent center assumed special significance for the mothers as expressions of their transformation and their aspirations for the school and their children. Through both products, the Madres attempted to extend the practices of *testiminio* and *confianza*, key to their own transformation, from the intimacy of Ofelia's kitchen to the school and to establish new forms of community in the school. Their efforts to carry out these actions, and the responses of professionals, reveal the obstacles Latina mothers face and the unique strategies they deploy in their pursuit of social justice.

In planning the presentation for their children's teachers, the Madres faced a challenge professional social-science researchers rarely undertake: that of sharing their findings with their research subjects, face-to-face, along with their critical analysis. As Baudelia reflected in our video, "Yo creo que a veces el riesgo de hacer una investigación es que la gente no entiende cuál es el objetivo de que nosotros estemos allí, o no entiende, puede malinterpretarse nuestra investigación. Puede ser que digan, 'Están tratando de buscar lo malo nada más'" (I think that sometimes the risk of doing research is that people don't understand what our objective is, why we are there, they don't understand, or they can misinterpret our research. They can say, "They're just out to find the bad and nothing else"). The charge that the mothers were only out to find the negative—central to the controlling image of the "angry parent"—had resurfaced with a vengeance as word got out of their upcoming presentation to the staff.

Martha from OCCA had met with me to share her concern that Madres Unidas were "too far ahead" of the rest of the parents and would isolate themselves in the school. She was particularly concerned about the anger the mothers expressed at parent meetings, which she felt was alienating them from teachers and other parents. Amelia especially, Martha told me, was "too angry," and was becoming difficult to listen to. Martha wanted me to work with Madres Unidas to encourage them to talk to other parents. Although the censorship of anger was a well-established pattern at UCS, as discussed in chapter 4, I was a bit surprised to hear this critique coming from OCCA, given the role of parent anger at OCCA actions. I told Martha that from my perspective, Amelia's anger represented a new and promising confidence, considering that she never used to speak up at all. But Martha was worried that if our presentation to the staff took an angry tone, it might do more to divide the parents and close down discussion at the school. I agreed, and told her that this was a serious concern of the mothers.

Madres Unidas wanted nothing more than for their research to be a positive force for change at the school, to stimulate dialogue and reflection that would break through the impasse of the past year. As Baudelia explained, "Nuestro objetivo siempre fue descubrir para mejorar, para hacer planes de acciones, para ver de qué manera pudiéramos mejorar y de evitar lo malo que estaba sucediendo" (Our objective was always to discover in order to improve, to make action plans, to see how we might improve and avoid the bad things that were happening). But Martha's urging me to discipline the Madres was revealing of several factors that shaped professionals' responses to our research. The first was their tendency to hold me responsible for the actions of Madres Unidas at the school, thereby denying the Madres any agency or legitimacy in their own right. Like the principal's request for me to work with the Madres after the infamous "tostada meeting," Martha expressed her concern to me with Amelia's "excessive" anger, as if I could or should do something about this. Amelia's anger, or Angry Amelia, was a problem. Presumably, she was a problem that I, as another professional, could help solve. But in no instance was she someone whose anger deserved to be confronted. Martha's warning about the mothers' anger also revealed the common pattern of professionals assuming negative intentions. Why was the assumption that the mothers wanted to divide or hurt the school? Couldn't the Madres be angry because they wanted the best for the school and their children? And while there were certainly some parents who disapproved of the mothers' outspoken habits and preferred to stay silent in parent meetings, why was their behavior not seen as worrisome?

Finally, Martha's concerns revealed professionals' commitment to defending organizational interests that could not accommodate any agenda for change apart from their own. Martha wanted me to go about things as an organizer would, encouraging the mothers to talk to other parents (apparently, the focus groups and interviews and daily conversations they had with parents were not sufficient) and channel their energy collectively in a public action at the school or district. While participatory research empowers participants to take action—in whatever form they choose—to address the problems they identify, organizing trains participants to build a movement.[2] In the planning of our presentation to the UCS staff, it became increasingly clear that Martha did not understand or support participatory research, and would try to assert an organizing agenda on the Madres' presentation.

We also received advice about our presentation from two BACEE school coaches, or "school change facilitators," who worked with the school. Their task was "to work with leaders in the school community to articulate their vision for a high achieving and equitable school" and to support leaders in implementing this vision.[3] The two BACEE coaches were part of a "Support Providers Team" that met with the principal every two weeks. At the principal's invitation, I had participated in these meetings on two or three occasions, but the coaches had never met the Madres, and, as I soon discovered, they understood very little about our work.

Madres Unidas knew about the presence of BACEE in the school and believed that we needed the support of BACEE and OCCA to pull off a successful presentation to the staff. So, in mid-April we scheduled a meeting with the two BACEE coaches and Martha from OCCA, to discuss our research findings and enlist their help in preparing our presentation. This was the Madres' first attempt to work with the school's reform partners to counter controlling images that circulated at the school and speak "the truth" about their experience.

We met at Ofelia's house on a weekday evening. Carolina and Carmen, who had a new job at a nursing home, had both had to get excused from work in order to be there. Ofelia and Amelia had made child-care arrangements so that we could meet uninterrupted. The meeting lasted nearly three hours and contained much rich discussion. Here, I will highlight those aspects that illustrate the coaching agendas of BACEE and OCCA for the Madres' presentation. I will also show how the Madres utilized the meeting for their own ends: to strengthen their own professional credibility and to project an image of themselves that challenged what the professionals wanted for them. In this way they both appropriated and subverted the professionals' agendas for their own purposes.

To all of our surprise, Martha had arrived with Lucia, an OCCA parent organizer from another school, and offered no introductions or explanation for why she was there. The mothers later fumed that Lucia's presence and behavior in the meeting were inappropriate, and that she had been brought specifically to challenge Baudelia's role in the school. Indeed, as the Madres explained our research process and major findings to the coaches, Lucia would repeatedly jump in to argue with the findings, singling out Baudelia for questioning and debate. Baudelia explained that these were just some examples, and that we could go on forever, but we wanted their advice on how we could present them in a positive way to the school. She said we also had some positive findings to share. Then Martha said, "I would like to hear something positive right now." I suggested the case of Sr. Romero, a single father raising three daughters on his own, and Carmen volunteered his story: how this father has received special attention and care from the staff. Lucia asked loudly, "Can that really be the only positive thing you've found in all this research?" "No!" we all said.

Baudelia immediately listed a series of positive findings (we had prepared this list at a previous meeting, and she had it in front of her), including positive commentaries about the teachers, better treatment from the office staff, and more. But Lucia persisted, lecturing Baudelia about the need to talk to more parents, telling her, "Tu liderazgo ha bajado" (Your leadership has dropped). Baudelia explained that we have focused on the negative in this meeting because that is what we need the most help with. She said it was never our intention to hurt the school or anyone in the school, that they wanted what's best for the children. "What can we do so that these problems don't continue?" she asked. Here Baudelia reminded the guests that we had invited them specifically to help us figure out how to address the negative findings in a constructive way. And she reminded them that the mothers' ultimate interest was in seeing these problems solved.

Cynthia, from BACEE, then addressed the group, asking, "What kind of feedback do you want from us right now?" I translated for the parents, and Ofelia immediately responded, in careful English: "How did you *feel* listening to all of this?"

There was a momentary pause, as if the question had caught Cynthia by surprise. Then she responded, saying she had two things to say. First: "I am very proud of you" for doing all of this work and for "caring so much about your kids." Her voice broke and she stopped, wiping tears from her eyes. The room was silent, and she composed herself and continued. "I hear your sadness and frustration, and that hurts." She said the tragedy was that everybody in the school came together because they wanted to help the kids, so what went wrong? Baudelia and Ofelia nodded, but Amelia asked for translation, so I translated. Cynthia then said that she also heard the teachers' voice on the other side of her head, and she could imagine what they would say, that they have worked so hard, and so on.

Cynthia said that when she heard the Madres as a teacher, she got defensive. She pointed out the places where teachers could critique our research: the parents should be careful about adding their personal experience to the research, making it clear when they're talking about something that happened to them or something they learned from an interview. She counseled parents to separate their personal experiences from the research, and to depersonalize the presentation. In this way, Cynthia affirmed the positivist paradigm that holds personal experiences as less valid than "objective" data, the very paradigm participatory research was meant to dismantle (Park 1993; Gaventa 1993). Cynthia gave several more pointers, saying that the Madres should start with the warm feedback, the things the teachers do well. Thank the teachers for their efforts, and thank them for listening to what you have to say. Since Madres Unidas didn't have a trusting relationship with the teachers, they had to be careful how they phrased things. Using humorous examples, Cynthia explained the importance of framing critique as questions. The mothers listened attentively, laughing and nodding in agreement. They welcomed any advice that would help them be heard by the teachers.

At certain points, however, Cynthia's coaching strayed from stylistic suggestions for the presentation and challenged their analysis. For example, when the mothers discussed how the principal had betrayed the parents' trust, Cynthia defended her, saying she "is a Latina principal with an almost entirely white staff." We had discussed this issue before, and the parents felt the bizarreness of a situation in which the label of "Latina" was used to protect the principal from their own—Latina mothers'—critique. In the discussion that ensued, Cynthia revealed her refusal to accept the mothers' analysis, offering her own interpretive lens, which flatly denied the reality of the mothers' experience at the school.

Cynthia said that the Madres should have three outcomes in mind for the presentation: (1) to bridge the gap with the other parents, (2) to visualize what the school would look like in an ideal world, and (3) to create a vision that has student achievement at the center. The need to honestly communicate the parents' pain and the truth of the history they had uncovered was not included in this vision. In fact, the coaches urged the Madres not to dwell on "the past," but to look forward, toward the future. This reflected BACEE's coaching agenda for schools. In a private meeting with me, Cynthia had emphasized the need to be "objective," telling me she did not take sides in "adult politics and squabbles," because the only thing that mattered was student achievement. In this way, the coaches urged the

Madres to be team players, for the sake of community. They encouraged a sanitized presentation that would protect the staff (and the partners) from personal stress and public embarrassment.

The Madres were not discouraged by this advice. On the contrary, they embraced much of the coaching as useful in their struggle to represent themselves as positive, credible researchers, and they eagerly added the new wisdom to their repository of professional skills and capacities. As Ofelia reflected later, "Nos ayudó mucho juntarnos con BACEE. Los consejos que nos daban eran impresionante. ¡Yo de ellos aprendí un montón!" (It really helped us to meet with BACEE. The advice they gave us was impressive. I learned a lot from them!). As we will see, they incorporated the advice they saw as helpful, and ignored the rest.

Between the first meeting with the coaches and our presentation at the school, we lost two members of our group. Carmen went to El Salvador for three weeks to visit her mother and son, amid much excitement. On a sadder note, Carolina was hospitalized after a sudden illness. Although she recovered, she remained under the care of family members in a neighboring city and never rejoined our group. We missed her greatly. As we prepared for the presentation, we were a small, sad, and somewhat subdued group.

The coaches had asked for one more meeting with the Madres to prepare the agenda for the presentation, and they wanted the principal to be present. They thought it was important for her to know as much as possible about the presentation beforehand. When I told this to the Madres, Baudelia remarked, "Yo siento que ellos apoyan a Ms. Campos" (I feel that [the coaches] support [the principal]). Indeed, while the BACEE coaches officially maintained a neutral position in the school, they met regularly with the principal and with the staff, but never with parents. The Madres were apprehensive about including the principal in the meeting to approve our agenda. As we talked about it, they arrived at a firm resolve to maintain control of the presentation, regardless of what the coaches or the principal said. We decided to begin the presentation with a discussion of *confianza*, in which we would explain to the staff the meaning of the word for us and what it had allowed us as a group to accomplish, and invite them into *confianza*. It was only in *confianza* that the truth could be spoken, and if *confianza* did not exist, then the mothers would try to create it. *Confianza*, then, became the key that enabled the mothers to maintain control: to be themselves, as Baudelia had once said, and to hold on to their own goals for the presentation.

At the start of the meeting with Marie, each person shared her hopes and fears for the upcoming presentation. Baudelia said she hoped the presentation would bring *confianza*, and that teachers and parents would be able to work openly together. Amelia hoped parents and teachers would be able to understand the problem, and work together in *confianza*. Ofelia hoped the presentation would help everyone "learn from our mistakes," and "learn to recognize our mistakes." Her fear, she said, was simple: "La verdad duele" (The truth hurts).

Marie's fear was expressed by invoking a previous painful event. She said, "I don't want another tostada meeting." Her reference to the infamous meeting at Ofelia's house that had left two teachers in tears indexed the tensions simmering below the surface that threatened to boil over if the forbidden subjects were broached. It was an implicit warning to the Madres that the teachers would not hear them if they approached matters as they had in the past.

As we moved forward to discuss the agenda, I had expected our biggest opposition to come from Marie. Instead, it came from Martha. We were discussing how to involve the teachers in planning our next steps, when Martha suddenly exploded. "What do you mean, 'next steps'? Isn't this research *over*?" She directed her outrage at me, yelling in English and Spanish that she had been waiting patiently for this to finish so that Baudelia could come back to organizing. She said we had promised that this would not become an "organization," but it looked like we were becoming one. "Madres Unidas sounds like an organization!" she cried. And she told us that none of us would be there if it weren't for OCCA. Martha's outburst reflected her belief that the Madres' research was a distraction from the "real" (legitimate) change-work of organizing. It may also have reflected the belief that the mothers, apart from OCCA, were not capable of making change.

I told Martha that any future steps would be taken in consultation with OCCA, but for now, it wasn't fair to rob the mothers of the opportunity to plan a productive presentation (what Martha had claimed to want). In the silence that followed, only Ofelia dared to speak up. She addressed Martha directly, saying that this wasn't a competition, and reminding her that they all wanted unity in the school community. Furthermore, she said,

"We don't care what name we work under, whether it's BACEE or OCCA or Madres Unidas, we just want to help our children's school!" Her reminder was a poignant critique of the organizational politics that tried to stifle their work for change.

We received two final cautions in the remainder of the meeting. The first, from Marie, warned that we should expect questions from the teachers about why we had not involved any non-Latina mothers on the team. As a group of Spanish-speaking mothers, Madres Unidas did not reflect the school as a whole, she said, and teachers would want to know why we didn't include any Chinese, African American, or Bosnian parents on the team.[4] Madres Unidas had already seen how the claims of diversity and integration could become grounds to exclude Latino parents. Now, at the moment when they began to assert their collective voice, the Madres were told that a solely Spanish-speaking parent voice was not welcome. They were expected to produce an integrated parent voice or no voice at all.

The final caution came from Cynthia, one of the BACEE coaches. She told us that teachers should not be expected to sit quietly through a one-hour presentation, and suggested that the Madres build in pauses to give the teachers a chance to respond. We discussed this as a group later, and decided against it. We opted instead for a structured discussion after the presentation. We all believed that if we let the teachers talk before the parents were finished, we would never get through the presentation. Furthermore, I remarked, parents were regularly expected to sit quietly through hour-long meetings at the school, during parent meetings when the staff talked at them. Why was it too much to expect teachers to listen to parents?

Armed with the advice of many coaches, the stories of all the parents, students, and teachers they had interviewed, and their own determination to be heard, Madres Unidas prepared to tell the truth to their children's teachers.

The Presentation

At the end of the school day, on a warm afternoon in late May, the classrooms are empty of children, chairs stacked on tables, with the exception of one. In that room, Ofelia, Baudelia, and Amelia, dressed elegantly in spring clothes, are hurriedly preparing for the arrival of their children's teachers. They have arranged a lavish spread of food on one table: vegetables and dip, fruit salad, taquitos, crackers and cheese, bottles of juice and soda (in case the teachers want caffeine). The TV and VCR are set up at the front of the room, ready to show the Madres' video.

As the Madres finish arranging, the teachers begin entering the room, in twos, threes. They are exhausted after a long day and survey the room anxiously, as if trying to deduce what this meeting will expect from them. Several of them light up at the sight of food, and exclaim gratefully to the Madres as they help themselves to plates of snacks. But the room is quieter than usual as the teachers take their seats, and it's hard to know who is more anxious about this presentation: the parents or the teachers. They have never come together in this way before. Amelia, Ofelia, and Baudelia take their places at the front of the room and resolutely draw up their professional selves. This is the moment they have been waiting for.

"I sort of felt this sense of anxiety," recalled Yvonne, a bilingual teacher, later. "Not a lot, just a little bit, sort of, 'Oh, what are they going to tell us?' 'Cause we knew there had been miscommunications and mistakes that we had made and—we felt like there were better ways to get off to a year at a new school. So I was sort of feeling like, hmmm, so here's the other perspective, what are they going to tell us?" But the anxiety dissipated as she watched the presentation. "I remember feeling after the presentation so incredibly appreciative of all the work that they did . . . I just remember feeling, my God, that's the most incredible thing that's happened at the school this year!"

As Yvonne's story testifies, the Madres' approach succeeded in earning the teachers' respect and support for their process. Despite the advice they had received from BACEE to "depersonalize" the presentation, the mothers were convinced that they had to speak from the heart, that the only way to communicate these difficult truths was to make it clear how much they cared about them. They structured the presentation in a way that would allow the teachers to see and experience some of the emotion that they as parents had felt during the research. At my suggestion, they selected some of their personal reflections to read aloud to the teachers after presenting the "data" around each theme. These written reflections were powerful and eloquent testimonies about why the research mattered to them. Importantly, they introduced their testimonies by explaining the *confianza* in Madres Unidas that had nurtured these reflections, and inviting the staff to enter into their *confianza*. They shared with the staff about their process in Ofelia's kitchen, describing the food and the jokes and the learning experiences they had shared as new researchers.

The Madres showed video clips, summarized the findings, and shared their reflections around several different themes, including the advantages of a small school, dedicated teachers, the different perspectives between teachers and parents on the founding of the school, the selection of students, autonomy, and parent voice. Following the BACEE coaches' advice to start with positive findings, or "warm feedback," they clustered heartwarming stories from students and parents at the front of the presentation. Teachers laughed and cooed at video of their students explaining class projects. When the Madres arrived at points of conflict between teachers and parents, teachers listened to the Madres' reflections with rapt attention. The mothers ended with a discussion of obstacles and their reflections on the research process. They then passed out a list of questions for reflection and discussion (see Appendix), and asked the teachers to break into small groups to discuss the questions. The room buzzed with conversation as teachers discussed the questions, and when the Madres called the group back together, some groups were reluctant to stop talking.

The opportunity to see parents in a new light was powerful for many teachers. As Susan testified later, "I was just like, wow. They're so awesome—I've never had the opportunity to see this person in this light. Maybe she goes around in her personal life all the time like this, but I've never seen her this way and that was really fun for me." Laurie, a bilingual teacher, told the Madres after the presentation, "I'm so impressed with your questions. We teachers have many of the same questions." Linda said, "I'm glad you haven't lost so much *confianza* that you don't want to keep working with us." And she added, "When can we meet again to discuss next steps? I know you have lots of ideas for what to do, and we want to hear them."

Teachers testified that they appreciated the opportunity, so rare in their daily lives, to see things from the parents' perspective. As Rachel said, "I think that we get really involved in what we're doing as teachers, that there's always the danger of becoming a separate entity from the parents and to become very isolated and to have this kind of insulated perspective . . . so I think it's really important and healthy for us as a school to have a chance always to listen to what the parents are seeing." Some insights were surprising. Susan remarked, "I learned from that meeting that . . . the group of moms had a perspective about how the enrollment process was conducted that may have been different from the teachers' perspective. And there were some issues there that I wasn't aware were still so present in the minds of the parents." As Yvonne said, "It was a really good lesson for us . . . to get some feedback, but also just to see what they've been doing without us."

The mothers' presentation revealed that parents could be and were very different outside of the school, and had ways of being in community that the school could learn from. Teachers testified that they were moved by the mothers' courage and honesty. As Laurie told me later in an interview:

> I was really impressed with their honesty . . . the honesty with which they presented what they had found. They touched on issues that people—staff in general—have been dancing around but not willing to confront . . . And I was thinking, "I wish the staff would learn to do this the way this group of mothers has."

The Madres provided a model and a forum for engaging in this kind of conversation, Yvonne observed: "I think that format, especially having parents in that role, has really helped, at least for some of the staff to be able to talk about some things that don't have a venue at this point." Similarly, Rachel remarked, "There were some difficult conversations that came out of it, but it was presented in such a positive framework and it really felt like the mothers were being very honest with us and were framing things in a way that was very constructive and would . . . move this school forward." Perhaps most surprising to the Madres, Marie, the principal, thanked the parents for their honesty, and wondered how we could make it possible for more parents to engage in this research.

Madres Unidas had succeeded in bringing the *confianza* they developed in Ofelia's kitchen—based on sincerity, honesty, and respect—to their presentation at the school. Ruth Trinidad Galván (2006) writes, "Good pedagogy, like everyday living, consists of making present our entire selves" (173). In being present in their wholeness, exposing the intellectual, emotional, relational, and spiritual foundations of their work together, the Madres modeled a *mujerista* approach to learning and community at their children's school.

Only one voice of disapproval marred the mothers' presentation. It was Martha's. She argued that "the role of organizing didn't come out in the presentation," and that OCCA was not mentioned enough. "The danger of not recognizing the role of organizing," she said, "is that you need power to make change, and OCCA is a powerful organization." This was the clearest statement of her belief that parents were incapable of making change without OCCA. Now, voiced in the angry tone that it was, it communicated the message to the parents that "you're either with us or you're against us." As one of the mothers observed later, "That sounds like a threat." The mothers later pondered why OCCA was so unwilling to recognize their research, suspecting that perhaps it was "envidia" (envy). But in the euphoria after the presentation, and the excitement of having won the support of the teachers to push forward with their ideas, the mothers were not long deterred.

A Second Home for Parents

On a cold January morning, Amelia is on duty at the parent center. The classroom has now been fully outfitted, and looks bright and cheerful. New, colorful rugs cover the floors, and festive *papel picado*, Mexican paper decorations, are hung around the room. Three Latina mothers come in to have a cup of coffee and "warm up." The coffeemaker, Amelia tells me, remains on with coffee brewed, so parents can come in any time they want and have a cup of coffee. The mothers sit down at one of the big, round tables with their coffee and pastries, talking and laughing. They are talking about the latest parent workshop from the People's Clinic. Then Angela, another mother, comes in with her toddler son, joking that she didn't expect to find anyone here and she had come to change his diaper! She sets him up on one of the rugs and changes his diaper while participating in the conversation. About the workshop discussions she says, "Es bueno cuando uno puede salir de la rutina" (It's good to get out of one's routine). Then she asks the other mothers to watch her son while she goes to the bathroom.

The parent center, which had been a fantasy of the Madres from our earliest meetings, became real in the fall of 2002. When I observed this scene at the school more than a year after we had finished our research, I couldn't help noticing how *at home* Amelia, and the other mothers, appeared. It struck me that this was one of their primary goals for the parent center. As Ofelia explained, "El Centro de Padres era un sueño de todos nosotros, del grupo Madres Unidas . . . porque vemos que un Centro de Padres es como un lugar donde los padres se sientan a gustos" (The parent center was a dream of all of ours, of the group Madres Unidas . . . because we see that a parent center is a place where parents feel at home). In a grant proposal they wrote collectively, the Madres articulated the center's goals this way:

> Our goal is for parents to be heard and feel part of the school, creating a family atmosphere where all families receive support . . . since one of our purposes is to orient, assist, involve, and motivate the parents, so that they participate actively in the school, and for the Parent Center *to be a second home for them.* (Emphasis added)

Plans for the parent center began immediately after the Madres' presentation to the staff, when Linda and two other bilingual teachers volunteered to join the Madres on a committee to form and oversee the center. The group met throughout the summer and opened the center that fall in half of a resource classroom. Most encouragingly, they convinced the staff to designate space for the parent center in the plans for the new building, so, when the school moved into its beautiful new facilities in January 2004, the center had a classroom of its own.

The parent center had the twin goals of bringing parents into the school by offering them support and services, on the one hand, and training and development, on the other. First and foremost, it was a place for parents to drop in at any time, chat with other parents, and receive assistance and support in a variety of areas. With Carmen, Amelia, and Ofelia as its first volunteers, the center offered drop-in counseling, food and clothing, referrals to community and public services, and, in collaboration with local agencies, an impressive array of workshops on topics including domestic violence, immigration, and early childhood education. The Madres used their research skills to canvass local agencies and inquire about the services they provided, bringing these services to the school wherever possible. They continually surveyed parents at the school about what kinds of workshops they would like. As Amelia explained, "Los padres dicen como qué clase de taller quieren recibir. Y si está en nuestra alcance buscar el taller, lo buscamos para traer" (The parents tell us what kind of workshops they want. And if it's within our reach to find it, we find it to bring to the school).

For Carmen and Amelia, who embraced the tasks of running the center with uncharacteristic fervor, the parent center signified newfound community and a place to try out new leadership roles in the school. Neither

of them would call themselves "leaders" when asked, and would empha-
size that they were still learning. Amelia would use the phrases "Me voy
superando mi temor" (I'm overcoming my fears) and "Sigo adelante"
(I keep moving forward) to explain that her journey was still in progress.
The parent center was important precisely because it enabled them to learn
and grow even as they helped others, and to see themselves as people who
were changing and "moving forward."

Carmen

For most of the year that Madres Unidas met, Carmen claimed she couldn't
write. It had been so long since she had been in school, she said, that her
brain had gotten rusty. Her written reflections after research activities were
short, but almost always packed with insightful observations and critique.
Then, at the end of the year, she surprised me by handing me her autobiography, a stream-of-consciousness story of her life, ending with a nostalgic
poem.[5] We were putting together a grant application for the parent center, and the assignment was for each of them to write their "bios." Carmen
produced an autobiography. She said she hadn't realized how interesting
her life was until she wrote that, and she appreciated the opportunity to tell
her story. The telling of one's personal story can be a cathartic experience
for many immigrant women (Hurtig 2005, 2008; Benmayor, Torruellas, and
Juarbe 1997; Benmayor 1991). For Carmen, it was a chance to reflect on
how far she had come since she left her hometown in El Salvador and to
realize how strong the pull of "home" still was. She wrote: "I am 34 years
old, I have two children, one thirteen and the other four, and I have my
husband who has always supported me, and I feel fulfilled as a mother, wife,
and woman. Only, I feel a lot of nostalgia and melancholy for my country."[6]

Carmen was born in a small town in the department of Cuscatlán, El
Salvador, the fourth of five children (Ofelia was the fifth). Her autobiography is a story of interrupted schooling and sacrifices to support her family,
who struggled to survive in the absence of a father. The lines of gender are
deeply drawn in Carmen's story: after being abandoned by their father, the
girls of the family had to work at an early age to support their mother and
allow their brothers to go to school. Carmen left school after fifth grade so
that her older brother could finish school. When she later had the opportunity to return to school, this same brother opposed it. "Everyone at home

agreed that I should go back to school, except my brother," she writes. "He said that to be a housewife I didn't need to go to school, and that women are only good for having kids, washing and ironing." However, Carmen did return to school and completed ninth grade in El Salvador.

When Carmen was nineteen she emigrated to the United States "against my will," to join her older sister, Alicia, who was already working in Oakland. The family depended on Alicia's remittances, and their mother decided Carmen needed to help take care of Alicia's daughter. Once again, the needs of the family came before her own dreams. Carmen writes, "I always thought I wanted to be a teacher or a nurse, I never wanted to travel." Once in the United States, she met her husband, took care of her niece, and had two children of her own. She tried to learn English, but this was difficult. "I went to three different schools," she writes, "but all I could think about was returning to my country, so I think that's why I didn't learn very much."

Education figures prominently in Carmen's story. First, she remembers that it was denied her in El Salvador because she was a girl, and she had to struggle to achieve it through the ninth grade. Once in the United States, she volunteered in her niece's classroom, and later in her son's, every day for a total of eleven years. Presumably, she enjoyed working in the classroom because she had wanted to be a teacher as a child. When she came to Madres Unidas, then, Carmen brought vast educational experience, although her own formal schooling was limited. She also tried to return to school when her first son was nine—"I thought I could finally do something for myself"—when she was surprised by her second pregnancy. "This time I felt trapped by my own children."

What emerges from her story is a hunger for learning and for opportunities to develop herself personally and professionally. Carmen often mentioned the importance of schooling in our Friday meetings, as something she felt she had missed out on. She greatly admired Baudelia's eloquence and writing skills and often said this was where she could tell that Baudelia "had studied." In the beginning, Carmen would use her lack of schooling as a disclaimer, claiming not to be able to do some things. When we prepared for our first conference presentation, extremely apprehensive and unsure of her ability to speak in public, she said to me apologetically, "Nosotras somos amas de casa, eso es lo que hacemos. Lo único que yo sé hacer sin nadie que me diga es cuidar a mi hijo" (We are housewives, that's what we do. The only thing I know how to do without anyone telling me how is to take care of my son). At these times, Carmen seemed to revert to notions of womanhood her brother in El Salvador had upheld. But gradually, she transformed her limited educational experience from a personal liability into an opportunity for growth and change. When presented with new tasks that challenged her abilities, she would say, "I'm learning," and "I'm going to learn."

Carmen incorporated new skills with the enthusiasm of one who has waited her whole life to learn, and capitalized on her experience with Madres Unidas to expand in all areas of her life. When she went to El Salvador in April, she decided she wanted to interview the principal of her son's school there, and the principal of the rural school she had attended as a girl. She asked me to go over her interview questions with her before she left. Her research skills were clearly valuable to her beyond the scope of our study at UCS. The year after our research, she and Ofelia were elected to serve as parent representatives on the hiring committee to select three new teachers for the following year. They received a special training at the district on how to interview candidates. Afterwards, Carmen told me that her experience with Madres Unidas had prepared her for this. When they instructed her on interview techniques, such as making eye contact with the interviewee, she felt proud because, she said, "I already knew that!"

For Carmen, Madres Unidas helped her realize "it's never too late to learn," and she could still achieve her girlhood dream of going back to school and getting a job she loved. For most of the year we met, Carmen worked as a housecleaner. Then, in the spring, she enrolled in a nursing program and was certified as a nurse's assistant, and obtained a full-time job at a convalescent home. She found the courage, confidence, and perseverance to finally go after her dream, and she told me she directly attributed this career change to Madres Unidas:

> Al estar viniendo a las juntas [de Madres Unidas] y saber de que uno todavía puede luchar, puede estudiar, este siempre yo quise ser una maestra o una enfermera, pero uno siempre quiere pero no hace nada. Entonces cuando yo empecé a venir a las juntas, volví otra vez a sentarme donde uno tiene que estar leyendo, y después vino la oportunidad de que yo fuera a la escuela, y entonces otra vez vino el temor de que las clases eran en inglés y que no iba a poder, y me acordé de lo que tú dijiste, que ¡uno sí puede si uno lucha!

Entonces por eso es que yo siento también que esto me sirvió para yo ir a la escuela y ahora soy asistente de enfermería.

Coming to the meetings [with Madres Unidas] and realizing that you can still struggle, you can study, I always wanted to be a teacher or a nurse, but one always wants to and doesn't do anything. So, then when I started coming to the meetings, I was once again in a setting where you had to be reading, and then the opportunity came for me to go back to school, and again came the fear that the classes were in English and I wasn't going to be able to, [but] I remembered what you said, that you can if you try! So that's why I feel that this helped me to go back to school and now I am a nurse's assistant.

Once timid and afraid of talking to other parents, by the end of the year Carmen was a recognized parent leader. When Madres Unidas opened the parent center, Carmen was one of its key advocates. Carmen and Amelia organized the center's first parent workshop series, on domestic violence prevention, in collaboration with a community health clinic. As a member of the parent committee overseeing the center, Carmen reported back to the staff and to other parents in general meetings on the affairs of the center. Carmen was also elected vice president of the school's English Language Advisory Committee (ELAC), finally convened a year after the Madres discovered Samuel's disheartening story.[7] (Her sister, Ofelia, was elected secretary.)

In many ways, Carmen's experience with Madres Unidas challenged her image of herself as a "normal mother" ("una madre normal") and housewife ("ama de casa"). As she reflected, "I have gotten more courage, I'm not so afraid of people anymore! [Laughs] Because, before I could barely stand up from my seat to talk! . . . I used to think I would never be able to do many of the things that I've done now [in this research], I felt that I would never be able to do them" (taped interview, June 14, 2002). But her achievements must also be seen as part of her lifelong struggle to educate herself, and to reconcile the needs of her family with her own need for personal development and fulfillment. Being involved at UCS, through the parent center and Madres Unidas, enabled Carmen to support her son's education at the same time that she educated herself: bringing in parent workshops that allowed other parents (and herself) the kind of learning she craved.

Amelia

Like Carmen, Amelia began the year with Madres Unidas unsure of her ability to contribute or do "research." One of the oldest members of the group, Amelia had been in the United States for sixteen years when we started our research, and later told us she had not developed a single friendship. Often incredibly homesick, she spent the years cleaning houses, raising her children, but not, she said, participating in her children's school: "A mí me invitaban a juntas en [Whitman Elementary School], yo no iba a las juntas. No me llamaban la atención, porque se habla de lo mismo y de lo mismo . . . Mejor me quedaba en la casa con mis hijos, ayudándoles con la tarea" (They invited me to the meetings at Whitman, I didn't go. I wasn't interested, because they talk about the same things over and over . . . I'd rather stay home with my children and help them with their homework). Amelia was one of the mothers whose transformation through Madres Unidas was the most dramatic, in the sense that it was most visibly apparent to everyone, including herself.

Amelia grew up in a small town in the western part of Guatemala, and, like Carmen and Ofelia, had nostalgic memories of a close-knit community: "Allí vivíamos, en un pueblito muy bonito, muy tranquilo, todos nos conocíamos, todos los vecinos. Y estábamos muy contentos" (We lived there, in a pretty little town [that was] very peaceful, we all knew each other, all the neighbors. And we were very happy). Her father was absent most of her childhood: first serving prison time for public drunkenness, and later away in the United States. As a result, Amelia started working at a young age to help her mother out: "Toda mi vida he trabajado" (All my life I have worked). "Mi mamá nos hacía arroz en leche, hacía tortillas a mano para salirlas a vender, y [yo] salía a vender con mis canastos de bananas, tamales, pan, todo" (My mom made us rice pudding, she made tortillas by hand for us to sell, and I went out to sell with my baskets of bananas, tamales, bread, everything).

The theme of sacrificing for the family, so prominent in Carmen's story, was also central in Amelia's life. Amelia pitched in to allow her two older brothers to go to school in the capital. But Amelia also went to school. As she announced proudly at the beginning of our interview, "Antes de venir a los Estados Unidos, yo en Guatemala estudiaba" (Before coming to the United States, I studied in Guatemala). Amelia completed secondary school and one year of Magisterio (the course of study for a teacher's certificate in Guatemala after high school) to become a teacher, before dropping out to work full-time in her hometown. Then, at the age of twenty, she was enlisted by her family to emigrate to the United States. It was not her choice to go, but the family had already paid the *coyote* (smuggler of undocumented immigrants). Her sister was to have gone, and at the last minute ran away with her boyfriend. In order not to lose the money, Amelia was sent in her place.

Amelia now lives in an apartment in Fruitvale with her husband, from the same town in Guatemala, and their two children. She sends money— the money that she makes cleaning houses in Orinda—home to her mother every month. "Por eso yo sigo trabajando para seguirla ayudando a ella. Porque la necesidad que ella ha pasado, y no quiero que siga pasando la necesidad" (That's why I keep working, to keep helping her. Because of the need she has experienced, and I don't want her to keep facing need).

Amelia stepped into the role of researcher with some anxiety, but her reflections after her first research activities show how she embraced each opportunity to learn new skills: "Para mí fue una experiencia ser anotadora, porque uno tiene que tener rapidez para escribir, y yo no tengo rapidez, pero sin embargo me siento útil y necesito tener más experiencia" (For me it was an experience being note taker, because you have to be able to write fast, and I can't write fast. However, I feel useful and I need to have more experience). A year later, Amelia was a recognized parent leader at her son's school. Ofelia was amazed at the transformation she saw in Amelia and her sister through their work at the parent center:

> Lo que más me impresiona a mí en lo personal es que ellas dos eran las mas calladas del grupo, las que menos opiniones o ideas tenían, decían que no podían . . . y ahora yo he visto que increíblemente ellas dos son las que han formado los talleres, han buscado la información, han hecho las llamadas a los padres, y ahora ellas son bien famosas, ya las reconocen en toda la escuela, siempre andan preguntando por ellas . . . y me siento bien orgullosa de ellas.

> What most impresses me personally is that the two of them were the most quiet in the group, the ones who had the fewest opinions and ideas, they would say that they couldn't . . . And now I have seen that, incredibly, the two of them are the ones who have organized the workshops, have sought the information, have made the phone calls to the parents. And now they

are really famous, and they are recognized throughout the school, people always ask for them . . . I feel very proud of them.

As Amelia explains it, she has found new friends and new motivation through her work in Madres Unidas:

La verdad, yo no tenía amigas. Yo sólo miraba las personas, "Buenos días, Adiós," nada más. No eran mis amigas, eran unas personas que miraba en la escuela diario. En cambio, con esta junta de Madres Unidas, tengo amigas que de veras no pensaba tenerlas. Si no hubiera participado, hubiera seguida lo mismo. Pero sí, por eso le doy gracias a Dios y al grupo que me dio la oportunidad, porque tengo amigas y tengo ahora como comunicarme con los demás padres.

The truth is, I didn't have friends. I just looked at people—"Good morning, Good-bye," nothing more. They weren't my friends, they were people I saw at school every day. In contrast, with this group Madres Unidas, I have friends I never thought I would have. If I hadn't participated, I would have continued as I was. But yes, for that I give thanks to God and to the group that gave me this opportunity, because I have friends and now I have a way to communicate with the other parents.

For Amelia, organizing the parent workshops was a way to take what she had gained from Madres Unidas to other parents: new friends, a community, a chance to learn, and motivation to participate in the school. As she said, the workshops are making a big difference, because more parents attend the workshops than the parent meetings. When I asked why, she said it was because they learn useful things and they get a chance to talk about issues that are important to them. That doesn't happen at the school's parent meetings, she said:

[Los padres] quieren sacar lo que está pasando con su niño o con algún miembro del personal de la escuela y no pueden. Tienen que poner su queja en una caja y no decirla frente de todo el público, y yo creo que un padre debe dar su opinión allí, ¡no meterla en una caja sin saber si la van a leer o la van a tirar a la basura!

[Parents] want to express what is happening with their child or with some member of the staff at the school and they can't [at the meetings]. They have to put their complaint in a box, and not say it in front of everyone. And I think that a parent should give their opinion there, not stick it in a box without knowing if it will be read or thrown in the trash!

In contrast, the parent workshops gave parents the opportunity to share very personal stories, and through this, to build *confianza*. Amelia said:

Cuando hacen testimonios, porque ha habido muchos testimonios de las madres que están aquí, nos están dando su confianza, ellas, y lo que se dice en el grupo de nosotros en el taller, no sale para afuera. Porque ella nos está dando la confianza en decirnos lo que ha pasado, con su esposo o con sus familiares, entonces por eso es un ambiente muy personal, y estamos como en familia. Digamos nos estamos abriendo, nos estamos diciendo lo que hemos pasado, y estamos confiando uno al otro.

When they give testimonies, because a lot of mothers there have given their testimonies, they're giving us their *confianza*, and what is said in that group in the workshop doesn't leave the room. Because she is giving us her *confianza* by telling us what she's been through, with her husband or her family, so it's a very personal atmosphere, and we're like a family. We're opening up, we're telling each other what we've been through, and we're trusting each other.

Confianza, and a sense of community, was something Amelia felt had been missing from the school for too long. During our research, she expressed frustration with teachers who did not return her greeting when they saw her on the schoolyard. Although she said relationships had improved with some teachers after the Madres' presentation, there was still much work to be done: "Hay maestros que no lo saludan a uno, lo ven, y yo creo que si estamos en una escuela pequeña, es para dar los buenos días, buenas tardes, adiós, que le vaya bien, ¿cómo está? Y eso no pasa con algunas maestras. Son muy poquitas las que de veras saludan a los padres" (There are [still] teachers who don't greet you, they see you, and I think if we're in a small school, it's to exchange "Good morning," "Good afternoon," "Good-bye," "How are you?" And that doesn't happen with some teachers. There are very few who really greet parents). For Amelia, a small school should have the sense of community she enjoyed in her small town growing up, where "you get home and you go around to your neighbors." With the parent workshops, that was starting to happen, at least among the parents. "Nos estamos conociendo mejor, y ya nos saludamos con alegría, no como antes" (We're getting to know each other better, and now we greet each other with joy, not like before).

Amelia discovered that it was possible to create community at the school, and she enjoyed being one of the people who could make this change happen. Her sense of her own transformation motivated her to encourage other parents: if she could do it, anyone could. "Ya no me da temor hablar" (I'm not afraid to talk anymore). She used her role in the workshops to invite parents to come to the other meetings: "Aprovecho y les digo, 'Vengan a la junta, va a estar muy interesante,' los motivo para que vengan. Ya que yo no tenía esa motivación antes, ahora sí la tengo y se las digo a los padres que asistan a los talleres" (I take advantage and I tell them, "Come to the meeting, it's going to be really interesting"; I motivate them to come. Since I didn't have that motivation before, and now I do have it, I pass it on to the parents who come to the workshops).

Making Space for Change

Even before the parent center moved into its own designated classroom in the school's spacious new building, its existence had a visible impact on the school. As Rachel, a teacher, testified a few months after it opened, "I see a lot of parents, not only the parents that are involved in the parent center, but a lot more parents becoming involved, and I think a lot of that can be attributed to the fact that there's a space and a place for that to happen." Critical to its impact, however, was the *kind* of space the Madres created, unlike any other at the school. Based on their experience in Ofelia's kitchen, the mothers created in the parent center a *mujerista*-inspired counterspace where parents who struggled with the multiple indignities of life at the interstices of racism, sexism, classism, and xenophobia could support each other in naming their experiences and interrogating the structures that worked to marginalize them.

In one workshop I observed, the sixth in the series organized by Amelia and Carmen on domestic violence prevention, more than twenty mothers engaged in intense discussion about gender roles in the media, in children's toys, and in marriage. The facilitator from the People's Clinic raised questions that encouraged the mothers to think critically, and they jumped at the chance. Later, a twenty-seven-year-old mother of four shared how she had developed the courage to confront her abusive, alcoholic husband. Forty minutes after the workshop was scheduled to end, no mother wanted to leave. The workshop series had achieved what the school's parent meetings had been unable to: allowing parents to make present their entire selves.

Central to the function of counterspaces is the ability to collectively dissect controlling images of one's group and fashion alternative selves (López and Lechuga 2007; Solorzano, Ceja, and Yosso 2000). In the workshop series on domestic violence, the women were not just supporting each other in sharing their experiences; they were critically analyzing controlling images of Latina women that keep them in subordinate roles. This is a key step in the process of *conscientization* (Freire 1970) or politicization (hooks 1989), where coming to critical consciousness involves connecting one's personal experience to larger social structures—especially structures of domination—that shape that experience. Through the planning of the parent center, Carmen, Amelia, and Ofelia, along with the three teachers who supported them, opened a space where these kinds of conversations could flourish. The following conversation I recorded during a parent center planning meeting shows the mothers connecting their situation at the school with a statewide anti-immigrant discourse. The discussion began with a teacher, Linda, explaining that she was going to a school-board meeting that night to protest proposed budget cuts:

Linda: Cada vez están recortando más y más, y luego el estado también ha cortado dinero.

Ofelia: El Gray Davis, ¿verdad? Dijo que iba a cortar.

Linda: Entonces el distrito tiene deficit.

Ofelia: Yo digo, ¿cómo es posible que el estado, el gobierno o quien sea, corte dinero al educación, a lo más importante para los niños? ¡Y tenga dinero para cosas como armas, bombas atómicas, las cárceles!

Carmen: ¡Y mantener tantos en la cárcel!

Ofelia: Yo digo eso es como no me cabe en mi cabeza, no sé cómo entenderlos a ellos, digo yo, ¿por qué será así? Tal vez habrá una razón que yo no entienda, ¿verdad? Digo yo. No sé, porque yo no entiendo.

Dyrness: Es una buena pregunta.

Linda: Bueno, para los que tienen el poder es más conveniente tener la gente sin educación.

Ofelia: ¿Verdad? Sin saber.

Carmen: Oh, sí.

Dyrness: Ellos sólo quieren sus ganancias.

Ofelia: Es todo, ¿verdad? ¡No les interesa la educación de nuestros hijos, pues! ¡Y eso es triste!

Carmen: Y también yo oyo porque California también sólo hay inmigrantes y que por eso también ya no quieren como, que ya parece que sólo hay centroamericanos y por eso también a la gente no le importa que uno se educa.

Ofelia: Siempre dicen que California es uno de los estados que tiene más inmigrantes que cualquier otro estado. Pero también eso no les da derecho a quitarlos la educación a los hijos, ¿verdad? ¡Los niños son los más, el futuro de este mismo país!

Amelia: Pero los inmigrantes somos los que pagamos taxes, y eso no se da cuenta.

Ofelia: Regresan dinero.

[Voz de Laurie]: Hacen un trabajo duro.

Ofelia: Y son los que hacen los trabajos que nadie quiere hacer, como a los inmigrantes no le ven al trabajo, ¿verdad? Lo hacen.

Linda: They keep cutting more and more, and then the state is also cutting funds.

Ofelia: [Governor] Gray Davis, right? He said he was going to make cuts.

Linda: So the district has a deficit.

Ofelia: I ask, how is it possible that the state, or the government or whoever, could cut money for education, the most important thing for the children? And have money for things like weapons, atom bombs, and jails!

Carmen: And keep so many in jail!

Ofelia: I say that is like something that doesn't fit in my head, I don't know how to understand them, I ask, how come it's this way? There must be a reason that I don't get, right? That's what I say. I don't know, because I don't understand.

Dyrness [from behind camera]: It's a good question.

Linda: Well, for those who have the power it's more convenient to keep the people uneducated.

Ofelia: Right? [To keep people] not knowing.

Carmen: Oh, yes.

Dyrness: They just want their profits.

Ofelia: That's it, right? They're not interested in the education of our children! And that is sad!

Carmen: And I have also heard that because in California there are only immigrants they don't want to, that because it seems like there are only Central Americans [here], that's why people don't care if we're educated.

Ofelia: They always say that California is one of the states that has the most immigrants. But that doesn't give them the right to take away the education of our children, does it? The children are the most, the future of this very country!

Amelia: But we immigrants are the ones who pay taxes, and that is not noticed.

Ofelia: They return money [to the economy].

[Voice of Laurie, another teacher]: They do a tough job.

Ofelia: And they are the ones who do the jobs that nobody else wants to do, you know, immigrants aren't afraid of work, right? They do it.

When Ofelia questioned how the state could be cutting funds for education, Carmen suggested that it was because "there are only immigrants" in the public schools. The mothers were very aware of the rising fear and hostility toward California's growing immigrant population. Although immigrants did not, in fact, make up a majority of public school students in 2002, their numbers had already provoked several anti-immigrant measures, including most notably Proposition 187, passed in 1994, which sought to deny public schooling and other benefits to undocumented immigrant children. New census figures released in 2002 heralded a future of a Latino majority, showing that Latinos accounted for a majority of births in the state and would be the majority of children entering kindergarten in 2006.[8] In this conversation, while Ofelia defended their children's right to an education because they "are the future of this very country," Amelia also pointed out that immigrants pay taxes, which nobody recognizes. Together with the teachers, they rejected the image of immigrants as a burden on the economy and social services and affirmed them as hard workers who add to the economy and fill needed roles. This conversation, in the casual setting of the parent center, brought together the teachers' activism with the parents' life experiences, engaging both groups as equals in a shared critique of California politics.

Another function of the parent center, then, was to build *confianza* between parents and teachers, at least among the teachers who participated in the center. In the spring of the center's first year, the mothers organized a teacher appreciation luncheon. Using some of their grant money, they staged a formal affair complete with flowers and speeches for the teachers. Amelia, with Ofelia translating, offered her thanks to the teachers: "For the patience and dedication that you have had with the children, not only the children who are doing well academically, but also those who are below grade level. And for the parents who have had problems here in the school and you have been here to support them. We are proud to have teachers like you." Ofelia said, "Today I want to thank you because I can go to work and enjoy peace of mind [knowing my children are well cared for]." As I watched the teachers come forward to receive their flowers and hug the mothers, parents and teachers beaming, I thought about what a long way they had come from the tostada meeting some two years earlier. As Rachel, a bilingual teacher, said of the parent center, "It's a huge milestone in our growth as a school and our communication with parents."

Like all communities, the parent center was socially constructed, its meaning and boundaries continually negotiated by all those who had a stake in it. Arguments arose even among the Madres about what should be the center's primary focus. Baudelia, one of the center's earliest propo- nents, was full of ideas and ambitions, and typed out endless work plans and vision statements using the vocabulary of a seasoned social worker. At times she grew frustrated with the slow pace of change, arguing that giv- ing away clothes would do nothing to change parents' roles in the school. She was concerned that the parent center would become primarily a service center, doling out handouts, and wanted to make sure it would be a venue for parents' organizing and training. In the end, Baudelia took her skills elsewhere, accepting a full-time job as a social worker for a local federally funded family-service agency. The job was a major step forward in her ca- reer, allowing her some of the professional autonomy she had enjoyed in Mexico. Although it left her no time to volunteer at the school, the parent center and Madres Unidas benefited greatly from Baudelia's ideas and sug- gestions. Baudelia's imprint was clearly visible in the work that the other Madres took forward.

It was fitting that the parent center did not have one primary purpose or predefined set of tasks, for, as an expression of the Madres' transforma- tion, its value was in protecting a space for change, a place to enact new ways of being parents in the school. As a second home for parents, the par- ent center was a site of *becoming* and *belonging* whose outcomes could never be predicted or controlled. The testimonies of Carmen and Amelia, and of all the mothers, suggest some important lessons for professional educators and reformers. First, parents, like teachers and students, deserve to be seen as people in progress, capable of being something tomorrow that they weren't today. If some parents have grave doubts about their ability to contribute, as Carmen and Amelia did initially, their doubts must be understood in the context of their life experience as people who have been denied educational opportunities, or scarred by their interactions with educational institutions, not as a sign of their "culture" or innate passive nature. What is clear from the stories of all of the mothers is the yearning for opportunities to grow and develop themselves personally, intellectually, emotionally—the quest for wholeness—and the desire to use their skills meaningfully for the benefit of others. To change and to make change, as Freire saw it, is the ultimate vocation of all human beings, and in this light the mothers are no different from human beings everywhere. But as women whose quests for fulfillment have been so long denied, they must also contend with the internalized notion—ingrained in their girlhood and reinforced in everyday interactions with more powerful others—that they do not deserve wholeness. For this reason, Carmen said, as a "normal mother," "I used to think I would never be able to do many of the things that I've done now." For these mothers, the journey toward self-realization and social change involves unlearning many of the lessons they have been taught about their roles, and critically analyzing the structures that have unjustly limited their development and participation in society. Schools could provide spaces for this to happen. But the vast majority of parent involvement programs and parent education programs—teaching parents to participate in the school in scripted ways according to the school's agenda—miss the mark (see Hurtig and Dyrness, forthcoming).

Educators as Allies or Gatekeepers?

Educators who care about the development and participation of immigrant parents should support spaces where parents can meet their own goals of self-realization and transformation. This involves a second important lesson for professionals, which is that they sometimes may need to get out of the way. The experience of Madres Unidas shows that a significant barrier, if not the most significant barrier, to the participation of immigrant parents in school reform is the stubborn, trained inability of professionals to recognize these parents as change agents. First, educators err when they make assumptions or generalizations about parents' inability or unwillingness to participate based on observed patterns of behavior that are actually co-constructed, produced in hostile institutional contexts. Second, professionals stand in the way when their commitment to institutional interests, credentials, and norms blinds them to other ways of achieving change or silences the experiences of those whom they most mean to serve. This is as true for community organizers as it is for school administrators and teachers. Professionals stand in the way when they refuse to hear parent critique or when they condemn parents who voice critique as "too angry." They stand in the way when they attempt to set the terms of parent participation in limiting ways—requiring parents to divert their concerns to a "complaint box," or limiting parents to three questions to a meeting. There is no need to repeat the numerous examples here.

It is equally clear that professionals can play a supportive role in parents' transformative process. Each time professionals provided a respectful audience for the mothers—whether at conferences, in the presentation to the school staff, or in small parent center meetings—parents were affirmed in their critique and in the development of their identities as experts, advocates, and change agents. The three bilingual teachers who approached the mothers after their presentation asking, "How can we work with you? What can we do?" opened the way to a fruitful collaboration that resulted in the creation of the parent center. These teachers listened to the mothers, let them take the lead in the plans they proposed, and offered their support however they could. When professionals offered coaching and advice that answered the parents' own questions—as opposed to steering them toward a predefined institutional vision—or provided the opportunity for parents to explore their own questions, parents were strengthened in their development as effective actors. The lesson for professionals is simple: listen, learn, support, and follow. Professionals need not only to listen to parents' perspectives and critique of their children's schooling, but also to learn from parents' ways of being in community.

In striving to create the conditions necessary for growth and change at the school, Madres Unidas modeled the forms of community that nurtured them outside the school: relationships based on *confianza* (trust) that allowed each person to bring her whole self, and the sharing of personal stories. Trusting relationships were at the heart of everything we did as a group, and made possible each new leap of faith. Without *confianza*, there was no change. When presenting their research, the mothers invited the teachers into their *confianza*, saying, "We trust you enough to tell you what we've learned, and how you've hurt us. You have to trust us enough to listen." The mothers trusted the power of their stories to convey what everyday interactions in the school could not.

In seeking to create schools that dynamize community change, educators should ask how they can provide safe spaces for parents to be with their stories (Villenas 2005). They should acknowledge that parents come to them scarred and wounded, but not defeated. How can schools foster the conditions that support immigrant parents' own processes of growth, healing, and self-determination? How can they provide the space for parents to redefine their identities and develop their skills as agents of change? I am aware that these questions may sound utopian in the current climate of standards, regulation, and high-stakes testing. Some will ask, How can schools already overburdened be expected to also meet parents' needs for self-realization? But I am convinced that the lessons of Madres Unidas call not for an expansion of schools' work, but for a redefinition of this work. When teachers at UCS interpreted the call for greater collaboration with parents as "more meetings," the mothers countered that they didn't want more meetings, only a different *kind* of meeting. Perhaps part of the reason educators are so exhausted is that their professional template for working with parents precludes the kind of authentic conversations and relationships that would nourish their work for change; so that urban educators are, in effect, trying to combat the effects of large-scale processes of economic disinvestment and decline, dislocation, social exclusion, and inequality on their own with the limited resources of their profession.[9] To the extent that new relationships with immigrant parents and other urban parents unleash a creative resource for change, inviting parents to share their struggles and their dreams for themselves and their children could offer solutions to the failure of purpose in education. As immigrant parents bring their journeys into the school, and use the school's resources to understand and overcome the structural barriers that limit their and their children's lives, they lead the way for teachers to connect education to purposes of social renewal and social justice. Madres Unidas, through their research, their presentation to the staff, and the parent center, struggled to see themselves differently and *to be seen* differently by school staff. In the process of contesting the controlling images that sought to exclude them, they discovered that they were capable of more than even they expected.

Extranjera   *por Carmen*

En resumen, yo soy una extranjera
Más de tantos que habemos aquí
En este gran país.
Salí de mi pueblo un día hace tiempo
Ya pensando volver.
Llevaba una maleta vieja y en el corazón
Toda mi niñez.
Igual que un ave viajera yo tuve que emigrar
Buscando una vida nueva.
Llegué a un país lejano que me dio calor y porvenir.
Me enamoré de un muchacho que me dio su amor
Y soy feliz.
Pero al pensar en mi tierra
Tengo ganas de llorar, y quiero volver a allá.

¡Extranjera! Aún me grita el corazón
Cuando suena una guitarra o alguien
Canta una canción de mi país
Y no lo puedo evitar.
Después llegaron los hijos
Tuve que luchar y hacerlos crecer
Y así pasaron los años sin dejarme ya
Poder volver.
Pero el alma aunque calle vuelve a recordar,
Cuando era niña en mi tierra.

¡Extranjera! Te sientes en la piel
Cuando me hablan de la tierra
Que una vez me vio nacer
Lejos de aquí.

Foreigner   *by Carmen*

In summary, I am a foreigner
Like many in this great country.
I left my hometown long ago
Thinking I would be back.
I carried an old suitcase
And my childhood in my heart.
Like a migrating bird, I had to fly away
In search of a new life.
I arrived in a faraway country that gave me warmth and a future.
I fell in love with a boy who gave me his love
And I'm happy!
But when I think of my country
I want to cry, and I want to go back there.

Foreigner! My heart still cries to me
When I hear a guitar or someone
Singing a song from my country
And I can't help it.
Then came the children
I had to struggle to raise them
And in this way the years passed
Without letting me go back.
But the soul, though it falls quiet
It remembers again
When I was a girl in my country.

Foreigner! You feel it in your skin
When they talk to me about the land
That one day saw me born
Far from here.

Conclusion

PARTICIPATORY RESEARCH AND THE POLITICS OF SOCIAL CHANGE

We have been working since the beginning toward a vision of positive change.

—Baudelia

Just because [teachers] have more power or more education doesn't mean we parents can't make changes.

—Ofelia

I return to the questions I opened this book with: How do low-income Latina housewives and low-wage workers come to think of themselves as agents of change, as partners in movements for social and educational justice? What capacities do they animate in their struggles for change? And a further question, of interest to academics aligned with people in struggle: what research processes and practices might support and expand these capacities, and thereby contribute to social change? In recent years, the fields of anthropology and education have seen a resurgence of interest in engaged and activist research, research that explicitly aims to support social-change efforts. While anthropologists throughout history have sought to use anthropological research for social-justice purposes—from the antiracism of Boas to the feminist movements of the 1960s and 1970s—the past ten years have seen a more widespread and concerted movement among students, academics, and practicing anthropologists to reclaim public engagement as the core of the discipline's mission.[1] The inauguration of the "Public Anthropology Reviews" section of the flagship journal of the American Anthropological Association in 2010 recognizes new forms of scholarship that broaden and redefine the audience for anthropological work, the methods of knowledge production, and its goals, in an effort to deepen the discipline's public impact. A recent edited volume on activist scholarship supported by the Social Science Research Council (Hale

2008) reflects, and calls for, increased institutional support for this work. In education, growing numbers of scholars seek openly to lend their research to the efforts of underserved communities to achieve greater educational equity and justice, and call for others to do the same.[2] In 2007, the Council on Anthropology and Education voted to revise its bylaws to reflect its commitment to advancing "anti-oppressive, socially equitable, and racially just outcomes to educational problems through research using anthropological perspectives, theories, methods and findings."[3]

It has become increasingly recognized that engaged research—openly political, change-oriented research—is both theoretically defensible and at times ethically necessary (Speed 2006; Hale 2006; Hernández-Castillo 2006; Lipman 2005; Scheper-Hughes 1995). But this new commitment, in turn, generates thorny questions and challenges for researchers who find themselves torn between competing loyalties. Not the least of these questions is, who is to define the desirable changes research should promote when there is friction and disagreement within the communities we aim to support? What to do when the changes themselves provoke conflict with other actors wearing the mantle of progressive social change? In short, what does it mean to align oneself with a political struggle, a social movement, or an organized group when these entities are fractured with their own politics and inequalities?

In this Conclusion, I reflect on some of these challenges in light of the experience of Madres Unidas and attempt to extract some lessons for activist researchers in anthropology and education. I begin by distinguishing participatory research as a method from other models of activist research by highlighting differences in the role of the researcher, the construction of knowledge, and the kinds of changes that each model seeks to promote. Participatory research, as a model that elevates uncredentialed, unelected community members to the status of researchers and change agents, runs the risk of conflicting with many powerful institutional players—policy makers, reformers, community organizers, and university researchers—who have traditionally maintained the right to lobby for change. I argue that these conflicts and the politics they reflect offer activist researchers new theoretical insights, as well as new possibilities for supporting social change processes. Using the experience of Madres Unidas, I submit that participatory research among the least powerful actors is uniquely suited to uncovering and disrupting relations of domination and inequality within social movements and expanding the capacities of the least powerful actors to enact change in their own right. A Latina feminist lens helps illuminate and explain the kinds of changes such research promotes and their contribution to larger social-change processes. No doubt other changes are possible, and this discussion is in no way meant to endorse one model of engaged research over another. Rather, I hope to fill what I see as a gap in the literature on activist research in which social change is defined rather narrowly as policy change, and to highlight other kinds of changes that play equally important roles in the quest for a more just and humane social order.

Activist Research and the Everyday

While the terms "activist research" and "participatory research" have been used in different ways to mean many different things, some recent writings on activist research together reveal a policy-oriented model of activist research, which I contrast with participatory research processes. In the policy-oriented activist research model, researchers lend their research *products* and expertise to the service of marginalized groups seeking specific, winnable policy changes. Participatory research, by contrast, emphasizes a democratic research *process* that aims to transform relationships between "researcher" and "subjects" and expand the capacity of participants to make changes in their own lives and communities. The two models differ in who does the research, what is considered appropriate to research (what counts as knowledge), and the goals or hoped-for outcomes of the research.

Anthropologist Charles Hale (2006) defines activist research as "a method through which we affirm a political alignment with an organized group of people in struggle and allow dialogue with them to shape each phase of the research process, from conception of the research topic to data collection to verification and dissemination of the results" (97). He distinguishes this from cultural critique, the most common form of politically engaged anthropology, in which anthropologists incorporate into their writing an awareness and critique of power relations, but leave their field methods basically unchanged. The main difference he sees between the two is in loyalty: while cultural critique is loyal to the academy, and produces products meaningful primarily to an academic audience, activist research has "dual political commitments" to "the space of critical scholarly production" *and* to an organized group in struggle (104). There is an inherent tension between these loyalties that, in Hale's view, produces vibrancy and theoretical innovation.[4]

For Hale, cultural critique is a luxury of the academic, and is at times at odds with the demands of an organized group in struggle. Drawing on his work in support of indigenous land rights in Nicaragua, he argues that disenfranchised communities who are seeking new rights from the state will have little tolerance for cultural critiques produced by well-meaning ethnographers. They need, instead, an objective and infallible social science in order to advance their interests in the public sphere. Accordingly, he suggests that activist researchers more willingly embrace positivist research methodologies in the service of marginalized groups, even as they subject these methods to critique. In his research, research products including computer-generated, geo-referenced maps representing the territories indigenous communities claimed as their own, ethnographies showing the basis for these claims, and expert testimony in the Inter-American Human Rights Court were the key tools in the struggle for indigenous land rights.

Hale's work is emblematic of a growing trend in activist research in which the researcher plays the role of mediator or broker between disadvantaged community groups and legal bodies such as legislatures, school boards, and human rights courts, and tailors his or her research products to these powerful governing bodies. In an example of this from education, Pauline Lipman (2005) and her university colleagues produced maps showing the intersection of gentrification patterns and school closings in Chicago to aid African American community organizations in their efforts to fight school closings in their neighborhoods. In both Lipman's and Hale's work, researchers put specialized knowledge to work in the service of organized groups in struggle. The conditions of knowledge production—what counts as research and who does the research—are not changed. Indeed, there is a growing willingness among activist researchers to capitulate to reigning definitions of knowledge in order to advance the interests of powerless groups in the policy realm.[5] Wrestling with Audre Lorde's famous dictum, "The Master's Tools will never dismantle the Master's house," Hale concludes, "ultimately, there may be no way to begin casting off the Master's tools of our trade, except by putting them to use in radically alternative ways" (2006, 112). This conclusion precludes the possibility of activist research that draws upon the forms of knowledge production utilized by everyday people in the struggle for social change.

Another typology of collaborative research illustrates this trend. Foley and Valenzuela (2005) describe a continuum of activist research from least to most direct involvement in political action, offering their own work as case studies representing opposite ends of the continuum. On one end, Foley writes cultural critiques and attempts to make them more collaborative, accessible, and politically useful by involving community members in their editing and revising, among other things. Foley focuses his innovation on textual strategies that affect the final research product, while not significantly redefining the research process. At the other end of the continuum, Valenzuela became directly involved in the legislative process in Texas in an attempt to influence educational policy for Latino students. Drawing on her own expertise and research on Latino students, she helped author a bill for a more just assessment approach, based on multiple measures of academic performance, as an alternative to the state's standardized test. In this case, community members were not involved in shaping the research process or product, but Valenzuela worked to defend their interests in the legislative realm.

Foley and Valenzuela assert that "the most politically active form of action anthropology emphasizes direct involvement in political movements, court cases, and aggressive organizing activities," of which Valenzuela's work is a prime example (2005, 224). However, even in this model of activist research, it is the researcher's knowledge production that is key to the change process, not that of community members. This continuum of activist research, even at its most politically active end, maintains a separation of roles between "expert" researcher and community members who must rely on this (others') expertise in their struggles for change.

In all of these examples of activist research, the possibilities for change come not from how research is conducted but from how it is used, and knowledge production remains firmly in the hands of the expert researcher. As Hale says, anthropologists allied with people in struggle must "generate the kinds of knowledge *they ask* and *need us to produce*" (2006, 115, emphasis added). The underlying assumption that research, or knowledge production, is separate from action for change prevents us from seeing other possibilities in activist research: how "ordinary" people also produce knowledge that is useful in struggles for change, and how the research *process* itself could be an important arena for making change.

Although activist anthropology for public policy plays a vital role in the struggle for social justice, a wide range of feminist scholarship cautions against the presumption that public policy channels are the best way to enact democratic social change, or that social movements themselves are always democratic. Feminist scholars have critiqued the focus on legalism represented in this model of activist research (see Brown and Halley 2002; Brown 1995; Speed 2006). In focusing on short-term legal goals, these scholars point out, activist researchers may neglect to examine the ways their own scholarly production might reinforce structures and discourses of domination. Jennifer Bickham Mendez (2008) specifically questions the tendency of activist scholars "to frame information in order to make it more palatable to decision makers," arguing that such a move sacrifices the "counterhegemonic potential of subjugated ways of knowing" (148). In her critique of rights-based activism, feminist political theorist Wendy Brown (1995) raises the concern that, in seeking redress or recognition from the state, leftist activists (and, by extension, activist scholars aligned with them) reinforce the power of the state over all other realms of social relations where inequality is reproduced. If we believe that only the state has the power to make necessary changes (through the distribution of rights and resources), we neglect the way power operates in everyday life, and we do nothing to expand the capacity of ordinary citizens to confront relations of power and domination in their own lives.

Participatory research responds to these critiques, as well as other critiques of positivist social-science research methodologies, by radically altering who does the research and what counts as research, as well as to what purposes research is put. In contrast to the researcher-as-broker between the powerless and the powerful, participatory research, in the words of Budd Hall (1993), "attempts to put the less powerful at the centre of the knowledge creation process; to move people and their daily lived experiences of struggle and survival from the margins of epistemology to the centre" (15). Although uses of participatory research have also been plagued by conceptual fuzziness, Budd Hall's definition highlights key features that most uses of the term have in common: the participation of nonexpert, less powerful people as researchers, and a focus on everyday life as the starting point for all research and action for change. Similarly, Peter Park (1993) defines participatory research as "a means of putting research capabilities in the hands of deprived and disenfranchised people so that they can transform their lives for themselves" (1). Participatory research originated in the global South as a challenge to Western models of development and research that were seen as contributing to colonization, and remains much more well known outside the United States (Nabudere 2008; Hernández-

Castillo 2006). The earliest network of researchers to assemble from Latin America, Africa, and Asia in 1977 defined participatory research as "a research process in which the community participates in the analysis of its own reality in order to promote a social transformation for the benefit of the participants, who are the oppressed" (Francisco Vio Grossi, cited in Nabudere 2008, 67).

While participatory research shares the goal of social change with policy-oriented models of activist research, it defines change more broadly (or more specifically, perhaps) to include anything that participants need to change in order to realize their full humanity. In the long term, participatory research seeks both personal and structural transformation (Maguire 1993, 157). In the short term, it "presents people as researchers in pursuit of answers to questions of daily struggle and survival" (Hall 1993, 17). Reason and Bradbury (2001) write, "A primary purpose of action research is to produce practical knowledge that is useful to people in the everyday conduct of their lives" (2).

But the focus on "practical knowledge" or "daily survival" should not be taken to exclude the possibility for critical analysis. On the contrary, a closer look at the tenets of participatory research, informed by the perspectives of U.S. third-world feminist theorists, illustrates how everyday survival and cultural critique are linked in the struggle for full humanization. Participatory research is closely linked to processes of conscientization *(conscientização)* articulated by Brazilian educator Paulo Freire (1970/2005) in which a chief goal is the development of a critical conciousness in order to transform reality. Participatory research dissolves the distinctions between expert researcher and oppressed community members and between theoretical reflection and action for change, posing research and action as two parts of the same process, praxis, for social change (Fals-Borda and Rahman 1991; Nabudere 2008). As participants develop critical awareness of the historical and material conditions that limit their lives, they are moved to change them. Returning to Charles Hale's distinction between activist research and cultural critique, it may be true that disenfranchised community members have little need for cultural critiques written by ethnographers. But they can and do practice their own cultural critique, and participatory research views this as an essential step in the struggle for liberation.

Cultural critique is not the luxury of the privileged, or those who have no immediate need for change. According to U.S. third-world feminist and de-colonial theory, it is an act of survival on the margins of society. Chela Sandoval (2000) gives the example of the concept of "split consciousness" articulated by third-world thinkers such as W. E. B. DuBois, Frantz Fanon, Audre Lorde, Gloria Anzaldúa, and others. These thinkers, she explains, "see what they do as they do it from the dominant viewpoint as well as from their own, shuttling between realities, their identities reformatting out of another, third site" (85). This "third site," key to U.S. third-world feminist thinking, is "an interstitial site out of which new, undecidable forms of being and original theories and practices for emancipation are produced" (ibid). In this analysis, the movement between realities and perspectives— movement of thought, perception, and being—"is recognized as fundamental to advancing survival" (ibid). Freire, too, recognized the "duality" of the oppressed, who bear within themselves at once the identity of the oppressed and their oppressors (1970/2005, 48). For Freire, this was fraught with the possibility of false consciousness, the idea that the oppressed may so internalize their domination that they cannot see any other way of being, unless it is to mimic their oppressors. Freire and other third-world thinkers warn against the romantic notion that the oppressed will *always* critique or resist domination.[6] However, because it is only through critical consciousness that they can overcome the contradiction of their divided selves, cultural critique is the ultimate vocation of the oppressed.

The contribution of U.S. third-world feminist theory is not to suggest that marginalized people are inherently radical, but that the margins can be a space for radical resistance (hooks 1990), that the experience of marginalization generates a unique and privileged knowledge base for activism. As the stories of Ofelia, Carmen, and Amelia show, the quest for healing and wholeness, for self-realization, necessarily entailed critiquing and dismantling the structures in their everyday lives that sought to define them as less than. As they did so, they led the way for teachers to create change at the school. Bringing a third-world feminist perspective to bear on participatory research processes helps us understand the creative and critical capacities that have enabled women of color to survive over the centuries, the tools with which they have sought their own liberation, as tools in the struggle for social change, given, as Audre Lorde once wrote, "we were never meant to survive" (Lorde 1978, 31).

Participatory research thus shares the insight with third-world feminism that the tools oppressed people use to survive and overcome the limitations imposed on them are the best tools with which to wage the struggle for social transformation, because, for the oppressed, survival—*sobrevivencia* in Latina feminist thought (Trinidad Galván 2006)—and transformation are merged in the struggle for full humanization. Ruth Trinidad Galván writes, "*La sobrevivencia* is what lies ahead and beneath plain victimry, our ability to *saciar* (satiate) our hopes and dreams in creative and joyful ways" (2006, 163). Expanding on this concept, Sofia Villenas (2006a) defines it as the "will to act and intervene in the world with simultaneous joy, tragedy, tradition and innovation" (660). This insight also allows the fusion of inquiry and action, of critique and activism, what Charles Hale and so many others see as diametrically opposed, as complementary elements of *sobrevivencia*. For Freire, these processes respond to core human drives: "Human existence cannot be silent . . . To exist, humanly, is to name the world, to change it" (1970/2005, 88). The ability of the oppressed to think and do for themselves is critical to Freire's analysis of *conscientization*, which poses critical thinking as a fundamental right of all human beings. This is why, for Freire, the oppressed must lead the struggle for their own liberation, because it is only in critically analyzing and acting on their reality that they become fully human. "Any situation in which some individuals prevent others from engaging in the process of inquiry is one of violence," he writes. "To alienate human beings from their own decision-making is to change them into objects" (85).

With this in mind, I can reflect on the ways in which Madres Unidas made use of cultural critique as a key element of their transformation and intervention at their children's school, and the insights this afforded me, the academic researcher, that would have been unavailable to me as a lone ethnographer. To be sure, the mothers in Madres Unidas did not need to conduct research in order to develop a critique of the role of parents in the reform: they had a rich critique already from their own experience. What Madres Unidas provided was the opportunity to deepen and extend this critique by providing a venue for being together, a counterspace, in which they could collectively explore their experiences, inquire into the experiences of other parents, and analyze these experiences together in light of broader patterns at the school. I brought a set of research methodologies and tools for analysis that helped them sharpen and systematize their inquiry, which they welcomed. As Baudelia wrote, "He aprendido muchas técnicas y métodos de investigación que anteriormente ignoraba, y ahora forman parte de mi conocimiento y experiencia" (I've learned many research techniques and methods that I never knew before, that now form part of my knowledge and experience). Later, she reflected that "research" also lent credibility to their experience: "Una de las funciones de la investigación es que es científica. O sea, que no es una suposición. Que tú puedes decir, ésta es la verdad porque tengo los datos, puedo demostrar lo que yo estoy diciendo" (One of the functions of research is that it is scientific. That is, it's not a supposition. You can say, this is the truth because I have the data, I can prove what I'm saying). So, in addition to deepening their critique, the process of research lent legitimacy to their critique and allowed it to be heard at their children's school and beyond.

But to what extent was their critique their own, and not due to my influence? I am often asked this question when I present on our work at academic conferences, and certainly other professionals in the small schools movement believed that the Madres' critique and resulting actions at the school were my responsibility. Professionals so often want to know, "How much could they have really done without you?" By way of answering this question, I can offer what *I* could not have done or learned without *them*. And in this recognition I am not alone among activist researchers; as Hale writes in the introduction of his new volume, "whatever we contribute, as activist scholars, to struggles with which we are aligned, we are apt to learn much more from these struggles" (2008, 22).

Deconstructing Community, Social Justice, and Autonomy in the New Small Autonomous Schools

Cultural critique, according to Charles Hale (2006), consists of "the energetic deconstruction of powerful ideas, institutions, and practices" that affect the lives of subordinated peoples (102). As a doctoral student enrolled in courses in anthropology and seminars called "Sociocultural Critique of Education," I certainly brought this critical lens to my fieldwork in the small schools movement and was highly sensitized to relations of power between teachers and parents at Whitman Elementary School. However, collaborating with the women who formed Madres Unidas brought me down avenues of critique I could never have imagined as a lone ethnographer. As I have argued throughout this book, contesting controlling images of Latina mothers that rationalized their subordinate roles in reform was at the heart of Madres Unidas' process, and the mothers were naturally highly attuned to these images. Owing to their social location, they were also uniquely poised to deconstruct other "powerful ideas" in the small schools movement, such as "community," "social justice," and "autonomy."

The teachers at Whitman Elementary School planned to create a "community school" with a "social-justice theme" even before they brought parents into the conversation. But it was the mothers in Madres Unidas who raised the questions "What does it mean to be a 'community school'?" and "Who do we mean by 'community'?" The most obvious example of interrogating the concept of community was the Madres' decision, initiated by Baudelia, to interview parents of children who did not get into the new school, to learn their perspective on the school's founding and the student selection process. This was something that quite simply would never have occurred to me to do, because I did not know these parents and was unaware of their exclusion. Nor, as we have seen, were teachers aware of these parents. Baudelia, as a member of the community who had worked closely with some of these parents during the early phases of organizing, was acutely aware of their absence in the new school and chose to invite their critique by granting them interviews, at great risk to herself, because she realized they might find her to blame for their exclusion. As Baudelia explained one of these interviews in a conference presentation, "Yo dejé que ella se desahogara, porque yo me sentía culpable, me sentía muy mal" (I let her vent, because I felt guilty, I felt very bad). These interviews, as we have seen, were pivotal in the Madres' developing critical consciousness.

This example of a research activity that emerged organically from the mothers' unique social location illustrates the potential of research to contribute to positive change *and* yield critical insights into social processes that would have been otherwise inaccessible to an outside researcher. Baudelia's explaining that she let the mother *desahogarse*, or unburden herself, indicates her awareness that the opportunity to share their experience of exclusion could be healing for these parents, a form of *testimonio*. The word *desahogarse* has connotations of recovering or feeling better, after one has unloaded. Of course, the Madres also took action on these testimonies by inquiring about the waiting list and advocating for parent participation in future admissions decisions. The perspective of the excluded parents made all of us aware of the consequences the school's admissions decisions and mistakes had on the community, consequences that were felt unequally by parents and teachers and, as the Madres informed teachers in their presentation, "brought resentment to the community, to the people who organized the meetings, and resentment to the school." The findings underscored the harm in definitions of "community" that did not take into account historical relationships among parents and neighbors in the school community.

The school's professed "social-justice" focus also raised questions for the mothers and invited their critique. As described in chapter 2, in early conversations with teachers about the new small school, Baudelia did not understand what they meant by "social justice" and questioned them about it. When they responded with an answer that did not satisfy her, she had asked, "But aren't we also going to talk about *us*, about what *we* think, about what *we* want for those children?" With this question, Baudelia challenged a conception of social justice that did not take into account parents' experiences of injustice or their own hopes and dreams for their children. Madres Unidas would continue to critique the concept of "social justice" throughout their research. During one group conversation I tape-recorded midway through the year, Baudelia expressed hope that their research could hold the school accountable to its social-justice goals, specifically by recognizing the mistakes they had made that had harmed parents and the community. "Hablan de justicia social, ¡qué se haga!" (They talk about social justice, they should practice it!), she exclaimed. Ofelia drew laughs from the group when she responded, "Yo creo que el error de ellas fue también poner tanto, hacer énfasis en tanto en la justicia social, ¡y no la implementan en nada!" (I think that [the teachers'] mistake was to put so much emphasis on social justice, when they don't implement it anywhere!" Agreeing, Carmen said, "Mejor no dijeran de esto" (It would have been better for them not to say it).

Conversations like this, expressing the mothers' running critique of "powerful ideas," led to research activities to further explore these ideas, which yielded surprising insights. The Madres decided to explore the social-justice theme with students. In the two student focus groups, they asked students if their teachers had talked to them about social justice, and what they understood by the term. These conversations were particularly poignant and revealing. In both student focus groups, students at first claimed not to know what "social justice" was. The question on social justice drew blank looks, shaking heads, and questions of "What's that?" from the children. But with some prodding and coaxing from the parent-facilitators, and help from each other, students gradually revealed a complex and insightful understanding of the term. In the bilingual student focus group, talk of Cesar Chavez was a springboard to a discussion about rights, and students linked social justice to the efforts of oppressed people to defend their rights. Through learning about people like Cesar Chavez and Martin Luther King Jr., students were learning that the actions of people could change the world. One student explained, "Those men [Chavez and King] tried to do something with the community that was fair, something wasn't right and they tried to correct it." Following this discussion, the students were asked whether they had a better understanding of "social justice" now, and they all responded that they did. After reflecting a bit, one boy said, "Pienso que es que personas tienen derechos, cada persona tiene derecho de hacer lo que él quiere hacer, si quiere decir, eres un niño inteligente, y tú no te dejan hablar, la gente no va a saber las cosas bonitas o buenas que estás diciendo" (I think it's that people have rights, each person has the right to do what he wants, and if [for example], you're an intelligent boy and they never let you talk, people are never going to know the beautiful and good things you have to say). In her reflection on the student focus group, which she shared with the teachers, Ofelia wrote, "Esta entrevista me hizo pensar diferente, hoy me siento, contenta pienso positivamente. Hoy siento que todos los sacrificios que como padres hemos hecho para lograr esta escuela ha valido la pena . . . Mi mayor satisfacción es ver a estos niños contentos" (This interview made me think differently, now I feel happy, I think positively. Now I feel that all the sacrifices that we as parents made to achieve this school were worth it . . . My greatest satisfaction is to see these children happy).

This is an example of a case when the mothers' critique led them to inquiry that brought them closer to the teachers' understanding of a powerful idea, thereby countering the charge of reformers and some teachers that the mothers' critique was wholly disruptive. On the contrary, I argue that participatory research, in enabling the mothers to explore their critique, contributed to the democratization of school-reform discourses and rendered meaningful the powerful ideas and practices of educators that had otherwise excluded parents. Nowhere was this more apparent than in the exploration of the concept of "autonomous schools."

The official name of the policy passed by the Oakland School Board was the "New Small Autonomous Schools" policy, and this term was baffling to many parents. "Autonomy" was a powerful idea that became salient in the daily life of the school and that the mothers interrogated through their research. As Ofelia observed in our end-of-year group evaluation, when recalling their most striking findings, "Descubrimos que la mayoría de los padres no sabía qué es una escuela autónoma, no sabían el significado de autónoma" (We discovered that the majority of parents didn't know what an autonomous school was, they didn't know the meaning of autonomous).

Here the other mothers cut in, laughing: "¡Ni nosotras sabíamos!" (Neither did we!), and Ofelia agreed, "¡Ni nosotras mismas! ¡Lo aprendimos!" (We ourselves didn't know! We learned it). When the mothers discovered that "autonomy" was a politically loaded term that could be used against them, as when the principal told parents they would no longer have the right to transfer their child from an English-only to a bilingual program or vice versa because this was an "autonomous school" (described in chapter 4), they decided to explore it in their interviews.

When the Madres asked parents in the focus groups what they understood by *autonomy*, they were often met with blank stares. The following excerpt from a focus group illustrates some of the confusion around the word:

> *Amelia:* ¿Ustedes como padres saben que esta escuela es autónoma?
> [Silencio]
> *Jessica:* ¿Qué será eso? [Risa]
> *Teresa:* Específicamente, ¿qué es autónoma, porque muchos no sabemos?
> *Baudelia:* ¿Nadie puede explicar ni tiene una idea . . . ?
> *Maria:* Algo relacionado con la universidad.
> *Angela:* No, ¡eso es la Universidad Autónoma de México! [Risa de todos] A eso le suena.

> *Amelia:* Do you as parents know that this is an autonomous school?
> [Silence]
> *Jessica:* What is that? [Laughter]
> *Teresa:* Specifically, what is autonomy, because many of us don't know?
> *Baudelia:* Nobody can explain, or has an idea . . . ?
> *Maria:* Something to do with the university.
> *Angela:* No, that's the Autonomous University of Mexico! [Laughter from the group] That's what it sounds like!

In this same meeting, the parents went on to offer their ideas that autonomy implied freedom and more rights for parents. One mother said, "Puede uno trabajar aquí como entre familia" (You can work like you're among family here). Others suggested, "Tiene uno más derechos" (You have more rights) and "Los padres tienen el derecho de opinar y de expresarse" (Parents have the right to express their opinions). Often, parents would insist that Baudelia or the facilitator explain the meaning of autonomy to the group. Baudelia, always careful to explain that this was just her understanding of the term and not necessarily the right answer, would offer an example of one way UCS was autonomous. In this way, discussion of the term provided an opportunity for collective reflection and self-education.

The discussion of autonomy in the teacher focus groups provided a revealing counterpoint. As explained in chapter 4, the issue of autonomy came up in both teacher focus groups before the parents asked about it. In the English teachers focus group, when asked what they understood by "autonomy," the teachers had spontaneously burst into laughter. Teachers' feelings around "autonomy"—chiefly, their resentment that they did not have any—gave the mothers valuable insight into teachers' views of their roles in the school and their expectations of the reform that might have rationalized the exclusion of parents. The promise of autonomy, we learned, constructed teachers as entitled to control over school design by virtue of their professional expertise, and parents, by extension, were problematic infringements on this autonomy.

At the end of the year, as part of our group evaluation process, I asked the mothers to write out their answers to a series of questions about the research, which we then discussed together in a videotaped group evaluation. One of these questions asked them to explain what they now understood by "autonomous school," and whether they thought UCS was one. Their responses revealed how far their thinking had come. Amelia wrote, "Yo entiendo que una escuela autónoma es cuando toman sus propias decisiones aunque pertenecen al distrito pero el distrito les ofreció ser una escuela autónoma. UCS no lo es porque las maestras se sienten traicionadas o burladas por el distrito" (I understand that an autonomous school is when they make their own decisions even though they belong to the district, but the district offered them to be an autonomous school. UCS is not because the teachers feel betrayed or mocked by the district). Ofelia wrote, "Entiendo que son padres, maestros y directora trabajando juntos. UCS no creo que sería un modelo de autonomía, puesto que a los padres en muchas ocasiones no estamos enterados de lo que pasa o se hace" (I understand that it is parents, teachers, and the principal working together. I don't think UCS would be a model of autonomy, given that parents in many cases are not aware of what happens or what is done). More cutting still, Carmen wrote, "Creo que ya he aprendido lo que significa esta palabra. Pienso la UCS es autónoma sólo en lo que más les conviene, no cumplen todo lo que la palabra encierra" (I think I have finally learned what this word means. I think UCS is autonomous only in how it benefits them, they don't fulfill everything that the word encompasses).

There is no doubt that participatory research enabled the mothers to deconstruct powerful ideas in the small schools movement and to identify how these ideas were often used to exclude, rather than include, the very people the movement was meant to serve. This illustrates the role of Madres Unidas as a counterspace, a place to interrogate dominant representations of "parents," "community," and "social justice" in the reform and support alternative interpretations based on the lived experiences of Latina mothers. It may be that the greatest contribution of this methodology to the theory of activist research lies in exposing the risks of any movement or method that depends on some people (professionals) representing the interests of others (in this case, Latino parents and families) in the struggle for change. No one was better positioned to interrogate the construction of "community" and "parents" by educators in the small schools movement than the parents themselves, the ones who were being framed and depicted in Incubator meetings and teachers' lounges and School Site Councils and positioned strategically in public actions to leverage policy change, and in whose name these new small schools were claiming to stake out a better future. As long as the reproduction of power unfolds in the construction and dissemination of controlling images, as well as in the stately halls of policy making, contesting these images will be at the heart of the struggle for social change.

Confronting Relations of Domination and Inequality within Social Movements: Participatory Research as "Nuisance"

If cultural critique by professional ethnographers is of little use to marginalized groups advancing their interests in the public sphere, cultural critique by marginalized groups may be of even less use to professional reformers and organizers advancing their interests in the public sphere. As Madres Unidas began to take their critique public, and to use their new knowledge to make change at their children's school, the group began to encounter its most serious opposition from organizational leaders in the small schools movement, who communicated to us in multiple ways that our research threatened the success of the reform. And here activist researchers must face an inconvenient truth about participatory research: it may not be welcome within the social movements we aim to support. This realization was surprisingly slow to dawn on me. As an idealistic graduate student, I had begun my fieldwork convinced that my research could be useful to both Latino parents and the organizational leaders of the movement whose endorsement I sought. Well into my research and steeped in the power politics between the partners in the reform, I stubbornly continued to believe that we were working for the same goals and that organizational leaders would eventually embrace Madres Unidas' work. My reluctance to recognize the gravity of the conflict we faced or its real causes caused me undue stress and prevented me from gaining some important insights into the politics of social-change movements.

It is critical for activist researchers to recognize that even the most progressive social movements can and do reproduce patriarchy, racism, and other structures of social inequality (hooks 1989; Naples 2003). To the extent that our thinking about activist research is limited to the tensions between academia and activism, between the demands of scholarship and the demands of action, we neglect to examine the delicate politics *within* communities and activist movements, and may find ourselves walking into a land mine. As Bickham Mendez (2008) observes, "Communities and organizations are not homogenous, nor are they free from internal conflict, power struggles and contradictions" (153). Ethnographers seeking to lend our work to the interests of disenfranchised groups need to be attentive to these power struggles, and sensitive to the multiple ways our work might intersect with, reproduce, or disrupt them. What this means for our alliances may be different for each researcher, and is ultimately a personal, moral decision. At the very least, this recognition cautions against activist ethnography that uncritically engages only the most powerful actors in social-change movements: community organizers, reform leaders, district and school administrators. Had I continued as a single ethnographer, accountable primarily to movement leaders rather than to the Latina mothers who allowed me into their *confianza*, I would have missed the "hidden transcripts" of resistance (Scott 1990) that animated and sustained the mothers' engagement in the reform, and my ethnography might have unwittingly contributed to their silencing. Because I made the decision to join with the mothers, and to facilitate whatever inquiry and action they wanted to undertake to improve their understanding and position in the reform, I came face-to-face with the barriers they encounter in their own efforts for change.

In the first year of my research, when I engaged in more traditional ethnographic fieldwork—the lone researcher observing and describing—organizational leaders embraced my research enthusiastically (in the case of BACEE) and tentatively (in the case of OCCA). But once I began working closely with the Madres as coresearchers, the protests from organizational leaders grew loud and frequent. In addition to the occasions described in this book were many other conversations with BACEE and OCCA staff in which I found myself "disciplined"—chastised, warned, or lectured—by senior organizational staff who felt that my work (or the work of the Madres, which was still seen as my work) was interfering with theirs. When Madres Unidas voiced their critique of exclusionary politics at the school, the partners told me that anything negative we exposed would be used to blame the new small schools movement and could potentially bring it down. When Madres Unidas made an arrangement with teachers to open a parent center at their school, organizational leaders told me that we had "crossed the line" from research to implementation and were "setting them [the parents] up for failure" because they didn't have the resources or the know-how for long-term sustainability. We should focus on research, they said then, and leave the reform to the experts.

I began to see a parallel in the reactions that Madres Unidas drew from the school staff and the rebukes I drew from the organizational partners. In both cases, the powerful actors questioned the right and ability of uncredentialed, less powerful actors to enact change, and suggested that such undisciplined and uncoordinated efforts for change would imperil the larger reform currently being carefully directed by their expertise. Further, in both cases, they questioned our intentions and framed us as troublemakers. In multiple ways, organizers and reform leaders communicated the message to Madres Unidas that the success of the reform depended on forming a unified front in which there was no room for conflict or critique. They had come this far by delivering a single message to the public, loud and clear. Inequality was the problem; new small schools were the solution. To point out inequality *in* the new small schools, at a time when the future of the new small schools was still uncertain, was unacceptable. If we could not produce a research report highlighting successes in the new small schools, our findings were not welcome.

And what of these concerns? Are they not legitimate? It is certainly true that policy channels have shamefully little tolerance for nuance in the implementation of reforms, and that conservative forces are too ready to seize on any negative findings to eliminate programs for the poor: bilingual education is a case in point (see Crawford 2000; Faltis and Hudelson 1998). But here is where it becomes important to distinguish between policy and other kinds of changes that research can and should promote. If my end goal was to protect the new small autonomous schools policy and ensure the resources for its full implementation, I might have done well to listen to the partners and redirect my research to meet their goals. This is the policy-oriented model of activist research that holds such currency in anthropology and education today. But for this to come at the cost of silencing the mothers' critique—asking them to tolerate their oppression, to deny their full humanity for the sake of greater policy victories—is a trade-off that should make us all think twice.

Bell hooks writes, "Domination is not just a subject for radical discourse, for books. It is about pain . . . Even before the words, we remember the pain" (1989, 4). Looking back on our discussions around Ofelia's kitchen table, I can say that the mothers were suffering physical and emotional pain. Several times as they described their experience at the school they were at the point of tears. At times the frustration and desperation were so great that the pain became physical, as when Amelia and Baudelia complained of headaches or stomachaches that they would develop during meetings at the school or in interactions with school staff. If nothing else, our Friday meetings were a healing balm, a chance for the mothers to realize "they're not crazy." From a Latina feminist perspective, this personal healing is integral to the struggle for social change. A Latina feminist or *mujerista* lens places importance on the means of achieving change, and highlights the need for a research process that supports womanist ways of being in community, based on wholeness and *confianza*. Valuing wholeness means acknowledging the need for healing and for relationships that support our emotional, spiritual, and mental well-being as prerequisites for collective action.

Ultimately, I believe that the changes that Madres Unidas made possible contributed more to further the goals of democratic participation and community empowerment—stated aims of the small schools movement—than they hurt them. While OCCA organizers claimed that the Madres were sowing conflict at the school and alienating other parents, the mothers' expanded leadership roles in the school after our research ended suggest just the opposite: that they held considerable respect and moral authority among other parents. Near the end of our research, Ofelia was elected to the School Site Council, and the following year she was elected president (succeeding Baudelia, who had completed her term). Ofelia and Carmen were both selected to serve on the school's English Language Advisory Committee, and both also served as parent representatives on a hiring committee to hire new teachers for the school. Amelia continued to be a volunteer coordinator for the parent center for the year following our research.

All of the mothers testified that the skills they acquired through the research served them well in their continued quest to develop themselves personally, professionally, and intellectually. Baudelia, eloquent as usual, expressed her gratitude in this way: "Yo creo que los conocimientos es el único que podemos decir, 'Esto es mío.' Porque el dinero se acaba. Los papeles se van. Pero lo único que me queda es el conocimiento y esto es lo único que yo puedo decir, 'Es mío'" (I think that knowledge is the only thing that we can say, "This is mine." Because money runs out. Papers disappear. But all that I'm left with is knowledge, and that's the only thing that I can say, "It's mine"). Ofelia wrote, "Aprendí muchísimo. Porque ahora puedo entender mejor a las demás personas. Aprendí a escuchar diferentes opiniones, a no enojarme tanto cuando alguien hablaba y yo no estaba de acuerdo. Aprendí a reconocer algunos de mis errores" (I learned so much. Because now I can understand other people better. I learned to listen to different opinions, to not get so angry when I didn't agree with someone. I learned to recognize some of my own mistakes). Surely these new learnings contributed positively to the building of community at UCS. As we have seen, Carmen and Amelia dedicated themselves to helping other parents with new motivation and the empathy that can only come from having recently made the leap from isolation to engagement, from fear to confidence, and from self-doubt to social critique.

Through Madres Unidas, low-income Latina immigrant mothers were able to claim a place for themselves at their children's school and in so doing assert their right to belong. They rejected the school's terms for their involvement and defended their right to implement their own vision of community. It should come as no surprise that the new roles they carved out for themselves challenged some educators' expectations for parent involvement in the new small schools or provoked disapproval from other "experts" in reform. What Madres Unidas sought was the right to define their own identities and participate in their children's school from a place of wholeness, agency, and self-determination. Had the conditions existed for this before, a movement for new small schools would have never been necessary.

In its potential to unearth oppressive formulations of power and identity that stand in the way of full humanization, participatory research offers its greatest insights into social change. Participatory research contributes to the conditions that allow marginalized people to express and act upon their social critique and claim their own subjectivity. In this way, the same processes that garner new theoretical insights about relations of domination and inequality are the processes that also contest these relations. The Madres' understanding of their research best explains this double-edged sword. As Carmen wrote in an end-of-year reflection,

> Por lo que hemos encontrado en la investigación de UCS puede haber beneficios y ventajas para los niños, los maestros y toda la comunidad, siempre y cuando se haga un plan de acción . . . Para los maestros: El que nosotros estemos bastante involucrados en las cosas de la escuela es más apollo para ellos, los que lo quieran ver de ese modo, o si no también puede ser un estorbo.

> From what we have learned in our research on UCS there can be benefits and advantages for the children, the teachers, and the whole community, if and when there is an action plan . . . For the teachers, the fact that we are considerably involved in the matters of the school is more support for them, those who wish to see it that way, or if not, it could also be a nuisance.

Carmen's assertion that their research could be seen as a "nuisance" by some teachers reveals her awareness of the inevitable presence of conflict in this method: any change is necessarily a disruption, or an obstruction, of the way things were. This "double consciousness"—her ability to consider at once the perspectives of disapproving teachers and her own, and to navigate between and around them—is a fundamental feature of the Madres' resilience, or *sobrevivencia*, in the ongoing struggle for parents' rights in the school.

The experience of Madres Unidas suggests not that we glorify or uncritically endorse popular knowledge (see Nabudere 2008, 67), for the Madres needed participatory research to unlearn much of what they had learned about their roles as Latina mothers, but rather that the perceptions and experiences of subjugated peoples form a privileged starting point for both analysis of and action against injustice. It is only when the least powerful actors shape their own roles in reform that the imprisoning contours of the roles others have assigned to them are laid bare. Ofelia, reflecting on her new position on the School Site Council, expressed this best:

> Para mí estar en el SSC no ha sido fácil. Me he enfrentado a muchas cosas que no me gustan. Siento que la escuela, el SSC, utiliza a los padres, no les da voz, los utiliza, sólo porque en el distrito les exigen que el comité debe tener padres . . . La escuela a lo mejor piensa que los padres no tenemos ideas, o no sé qué es el problema, pero no quieren escuchar la voz de los padres, quieren hacer lo que ellos dicen, como ellos dicen, y yo pienso que están en un error . . . No sólo porque ellas tienen poder o más estudios, pensar que los padres no podemos hacer cambios.

> For me, being on the SSC has not been easy. I have confronted many things I don't like. I feel that the school, the SSC, uses parents, it doesn't give them voice, it uses them, just because the district requires the committee to have parents on it . . . The school probably thinks that parents don't have ideas, or I don't know what the problem is. But they don't want to hear the voice of the parents, they want to do what *they* say, how they say it, and I think they're making a mistake . . . Just because [the teachers] have power or more education doesn't mean we parents can't make changes.

With this testimony, Ofelia expressed both her critique of the roles prescribed for parents by teachers and the idea that teachers have a privileged claim to change processes because of their professional status or training.

The notion that low-income, uncredentialed, and unskilled (not to mention non-English-speaking, noncitizen, racially brown, immigrant) women could have an equal claim to shaping processes of school and community change that affect their lives defies the perceived wisdom of our knowledge society (Gaventa 1993), and not surprisingly provokes consternation from professionals who have traditionally controlled these processes: people who, in Ofelia's words, "want to do what *they* say, how they say it." Nowhere was this more apparent than in our meeting with the principal and coaches at UCS, described in chapter 6, when Martha burst out: "Isn't this research *over*?" This was quite possibly the most upsetting experience of my research. I felt that the Madres and I had worked hard to cultivate positive relationships with the principal, the BACEE coaches, and OCCA, and that we were finally working in collaboration. With Martha's outburst of accusations, all of that seemed shattered. Martha shouted at me about the parents as if they weren't there. I felt personally humiliated, as if I had lost face, as if it was *my* face (or my ego) that was at stake! Although I managed to continue the meeting calmly, I felt afterwards that I was ready to give up. I told myself I would never sit through another meeting like that one, or endure being yelled at in that way, again.

But one by one I debriefed with each of the mothers who had been present. Amelia told me her head started hurting so badly during the meeting that she couldn't think straight. She got a headache, she said, because she was so angry. Each of the three mothers expressed similar feelings of shock and helplessness. Baudelia, who called me at home later that night, wanted to apologize for not having been able to speak up to Martha in the meeting. She said she felt like someone had dumped a bucket of cold water over her and she was too stunned to reply. It was in talking to Baudelia and the other mothers that I realized I couldn't walk away. If the anger and hurt that I felt was crippling, the pain was much more theirs. And they could not walk away.

In spite of all the roadblocks, as the preceding chapter detailed, we went on to have a successful presentation at the school, which was an empowering experience for Madres Unidas. The warmth with which the presentation was received by the staff was gratifying and validating to all of us. But our shared experience of being attacked beforehand taught me an important lesson. If I stayed, it was not because I could ever claim that my work (or our work) was making a difference. It was not because I could win the approval of OCCA or anyone else whose approval mattered. My role was simply to *be with* the mothers in struggle—to hear them out, back them up, and share in some of the pain they experienced so that they would have a little more strength and wholeness for their journey. Activist research is, finally, an exercise in solidarity. And in solidarity with the Madres, I realized something they knew all along: the struggle for change is not undertaken for recognition or rewards, or because it feels good; it is a like-it-or-not necessity. You do it because you have no other choice. And then, your faith and your relationships with your *compañeras* see you through. In her kitchen one winter afternoon, as she taught me how to make *chile verde* and I recorded our conversation, Ofelia ended her interview with these words: "Y seguimos todavía . . . aunque a veces nos sentimos que ya no podemos más, pero seguimos adelante. Nosotras seguimos adelante" (We continue still . . . even though sometimes we feel we just can't go on anymore, we keep going. We keep going).

Appendix
QUESTIONS FOR REFLECTION BY MADRES UNIDAS

These questions were prepared by Madres Unidas for the teachers at UCS to discuss during the research presentation. The order and grouping of the questions is the order in which they were presented to the teachers. For more information on the questions, see chapter 6.

Selection of Students (Admissions)

What are the consequences of leaving out some families? How does this affect our community?

What suggestions do you have for the selection of students for next year?

How do you plan on doing the selection of students for next year?

How would we describe our school to say that it's a "community school"? What does it mean to be a community school?

What are the advantages and disadvantages of admitting students whose parents did not participate in the organizing process?

How can parents be involved in admissions decisions?

Parent Voice

What does it mean to have parent leaders in the school?

What would it mean for parents to have "voice and vote" within a school?

How can we value the voice and vote of parents?

How does it affect parents when their decisions are not respected?

How do you feel when you are heard? How do you feel when you are not heard?

What does it mean to have equality between parents and teachers?

What are the consequences of insincerity toward parents (on the part of the school)?

How do you recognize and value the interest of parents in participating the school, and how do you maintain it?

How do you define communication among staff at the school?

How do you define communication with parents?

What are the advantages of getting to know and understand the different cultures of our community?

What does it mean to have trust *(confianza)* between school staff and parents, and what are the consequences of mistrust?

What factors affect the ability (or inability) to have good communication among parents?

What should be the role of parents in the selection of personnel for the school?

General

In what ways is social justice reflected in this school?

How are the most important aspects of the school reflected?

What does it mean to be an autonomous school? In what ways are we applying autonomy in this school?

We know there is a system of conflict resolution for students. How is conflict resolution handled between staff and parents? Among the staff?

Notes

Introduction

1. The concept of *testimonio*, elaborated by the Latina Feminist Group (2001), will be explained more fully in chapter 5. See Nuñez-Janes and Robledo (2009) for a similar use of *testimonio*.
2. For a review of these stories, sometimes called "deficit theories," about Latino families in the educational research literature, see Flores (2005) and Valencia and Solorzano (2004). For further critique of deficit stories about Latino parents, see Villenas and Deyhle (1999), Lopez (2001), and Hurtig and Dyrness (forthcoming).
3. See Kozol (2005), Chapa (2002), and Orfield and Lee (2005b). Latino students are the most segregated minority group in U.S. schools, and they face the highest dropout rates (Chapa 2002; Orfield and Lee 2006). Their segregation is clearly related to their low participation in higher education (Chapa 2002).
4. According to Richard Wood (2002), faith-based organizing is the second-largest social-justice movement in the United States today, after the labor movement. In a national study of faith-based community organizing, Warren (2001) found 133 local and metropolitan-area federations operating in thirty-three states and the District of Columbia. The Pacific Institute for Community Organizations (PICO) is one of four major national networks linking these federations.
5. Data from 2000. The Academic Performance Index is a statewide ranking assigned to schools based on their performance on statewide standardized tests.
6. These figures represent an early snapshot of teachers who expressed interest in starting new schools, and are not necessarily representative of all teachers who ultimately opened new small schools.
7. Amanda Lashaw (2006) explores the phenomenon of dreaming and the role that it played in the small schools movement.
8. The mothers later named the group Madres Unidas (Mothers United), placing themselves in a long history of mothers organizing in Latin America and the United States.
9. Participatory research as a method and form of activist research will be explained in greater detail in the concluding chapter.
10. In this book I use the term "Latina" rather than "Chicana," as used by

Delgado-Bernal (2006), because the women I worked with, who included immigrants from Central America, did not identify as Chicana.

1. Separate Journeys

1. My translation from the Spanish.
2. We later discussed the book in Madres Unidas, and, at Ofelia's request, I photocopied passages from my book for all of them to read.
3. The first small school organizing effort in Oakland, which failed.
4. Both teachers and parents participated on a later OCCA trip to visit the small schools in Chicago, but the teacher from UCS who had been on this trip did not mention it in the focus group.

2. Baudelia's Leadership

1. The Request for Proposals for new small schools was described in the Introduction.
2. All quotes in English are my translation from the Spanish, unless otherwise indicated.
3. She later gave me a copy of this. Out of respect for her words I have included both the original Spanish and my English translation of her statement.
4. Baudelia's response to the RFP, question 5.2; my translation from the Spanish.

3. Contested Community

1. For more information, see Wood (2002).
2. Ibid., 31.
3. "Why Immigrants Select Oakland," *Oakland Tribune*, March 25, 2002.
4. Gregory uses these terms to describe the managing of citizen participation in an urban development project by the Port Authority of New York. See Apple (1996) for a discussion of similar processes in education.
5. In addition to Valenzuela (1999), see Delgado-Gaitán 2001; Valdés 1996. Bruce Fuller (2007) provides a review of the literature on Latino parent socialization practices, highlighting several studies that found this meaning of *educación* in Latino communities.
6. There is some research supporting this; see Lareau (1989) and Lewis and Forman (2002).

4. The Good Parent, the Angry Parent, and Other Controlling Images

1. Findings from this interview are discussed in chapter 1.
2. Although the Madres invited parents they knew who had been involved since the beginning, they also invited parents who were suggested to them by teachers. Getting parents to participate in focus groups proved to be an unexpected challenge, and the groups were ultimately composed of those parents who were willing and able to attend.

3. Pseudonym for a new small middle school that did not have a site for the following year.
4. The district's required reading program, phonics-based and highly scripted.
5. See Wood (2002) for an explanation of this organizing model.

5. Ofelia's Kitchen

1. La Virgen de Guadalupe is the patron saint of the Americas. Latinos from around the world make pilgrimages to Our Lady of Guadalupe in Mexico City, where, according to Catholic teaching, the Virgin first appeared to an indigenous man. La Virgen de Guadalupe has become highly significant in Latino Catholic identity.
2. See Solorzano and Yosso 2001 and Yosso 2006 for a discussion of counterspaces in the context of Chicana students in the university setting.
3. Michelle Fine, "Contesting Injustice/Insisting on Human Rights: Participatory Action Research by and for Youth," keynote address given at Crossroads II: Community-based Collaborative Research for Social Justice, Hartford, Connecticut, June 8, 2007.

6. En Confianza

1. See also Chela Sandoval's (2000) analysis of Frantz Fanon's work, describing the methodology of the oppressed as "the bursting of the self and its re-formation" (129).
2. See Wood (2002) and Warren and Wood (2001) for a lengthy description of the organizing model.
3. BACEE job description for school change facilitators, from the BACEE Web site.
4. The UCS student population at this time was 76 percent Latino, 10 percent African American, 10 percent Asian, and less than 2 percent white.
5. I have reproduced the poem, with Carmen's permission, at the end of this chapter.
6. My translation from her Spanish, as are all excerpts from here on.
7. Samuel, whose daughter was then in fifth grade and would soon graduate, was no longer a candidate.
8. "Latino Majority Arrives—among State's Babies," *Los Angeles Times*, February 6, 2003.
9. See Anyon 1997 and 2005 for a description of how political and economic forces shaping the city impact urban schooling.

Conclusion

1. Checker, Vine, and Wali (2010). See Hale (2006, 2008) and Speed (2006) for a succinct review of the roots of activist research in anthropology.
2. For some examples, see Lipman 2005; Foley and Valenzuela 2005; Emihovich 2005; González 2005; Weis and Fine 2000; Nygreen 2006.
3. Revised mission statement, bylaws, Council on Anthropology and

Education (CAE), May 2007. Available at http://www.aaanet.org/sections/cae/aboutcae.html. CAE is a subsection of the American Anthropological Association.

4. See the introduction to Hale's edited volume for further elaboration of the ways in which activist scholarship is "a privileged source of theoretical innovation" (Hale 2008, 19).

5. In addition to Hale (2006), see Nygreen 2006; Lipman 2005; González 2005.

6. Bell hooks (1989, 1990) wrote especially eloquently about this, critiquing blacks who sought to reverse the poles of domination but not its logic.

References

Anyon, Jean. 1997. *Ghetto Schooling: A Political Economy of Urban Educational Reform.* New York: Teachers College Press.

———. 2005. *Radical Possibilities: Public Policy, Urban Education, and a New Social Movement.* New York: Routledge.

Anzaldúa, Gloria. 1987. *Borderlands/La Frontera: The New Mestiza.* San Francisco: Spinsters/Aunt Lute.

Apple, Michael W. 1996. *Cultural Politics and Education.* New York: Teachers College Press.

Avila, Inés Hernández. 2001. "Telling to Live: *Devoro la Mentira, Resucitando Mi Ser.*" In the Latina Feminist Group, *Telling to Live: Latina Feminist Testimonios.* Durham, N.C.: Duke University Press, 298–301.

Barrera, Mario. 1979. *Race and Class in the Southwest: A Theory of Racial Inequality.* Notre Dame, Ind.: University of Notre Dame Press.

Bell, Lee Anne. 2003. "Telling Tales: What Stories Can Teach Us about Racism." *Race, Ethnicity and Education* 6:1: 3–28.

Benmayor, Rina. 1991. "Testimony, Action Research, and Empowerment: Puerto Rican Women and Popular Education." In *Women's Words: The Feminist Practice of Oral History*, ed. Sherna Gluck and Daphne Patai. New York: Routledge, 159–74.

Benmayor, Rina, Rosa M. Torruellas, and Ana L. Juarbe. 1997. "Claiming Cultural Citizenship in East Harlem." In *Latino Cultural Citizenship: Claiming Identity, Space, and Rights*, ed. W. Flores and R. Benmayor. Boston: Beacon Press, 152–209.

Bickham Mendez, Jennifer. 2008. "Globalizing Scholar Activism: Opportunities and Dilemmas through a Feminist Lens." In *Engaging Contradictions: Theory, Politics, and Methods of Activist Scholarship*, ed. Charles R. Hale. Berkeley: University of California Press, 136–63.

Brown, Wendy. 1995. *States of Injury: Power and Freedom in Late Modernity.* Princeton, N.J.: Princeton University Press.

Brown, Wendy, and Janet Halley. 2002. *Left Legalism/Left Critique.* Durham, N.C.: Duke University Press.

Carrillo, Rosario. 2006. "Humor Casero Mujerista—Womanist Humor of the Home: Laughing All the Way to Greater Cultural Understandings and Social Relations." In *Chicana/Latina Education in Everyday Life: Feminista Perspectives on Pedagogy and Epistemology*, ed. Dolores Delgado-Bernal,

C. Alejandra Elenes, Francisca Godinez, and Sofia Villenas. Albany: State University of New York Press, 181–95.

Chapa, Jorge. 2002. "Affirmative Action, X Percent Plans, and Latino Access to Higher Education in the Twenty-first Century." In *Latinos Remaking America*, ed. M. Suarez-Orozco and M. M. Paez. Berkeley: University of California Press, 375–88.

Checker, Melissa, David Vine, and Alaka Wali. 2010. "A Sea Change in Anthropology?" Public Anthropology Reviews. *American Anthropologist* 112:1: 5–6.

Clifford, James, and George E. Marcus. 1986. *Writing Culture: The Poetics and Politics of Ethnography*. Berkeley: University of California Press.

Collins, Patricia Hill. 2000. *Black Feminist Thought: Knowledge, Consciousness, and the Politics of Empowerment*. 2d ed. New York: Routledge.

Crawford, Jim. 2000. *At War with Diversity: US Language Policy in an Age of Anxiety*. Tonawanda, N.Y.: Multilingual Matters, 1–30, 84–103.

Crozier, Gill. 2001. "Excluded Parents: The Deracialization of Parental Involvement." *Race and Ethnicity in Education* 4:4: 329–41.

Delgado-Bernal, Dolores. 2006. "Learning and Living Pedagogies of the Home." In *Chicana/Latina Education in Everyday Life: Feminista Perspectives on Pedagogy and Epistemology*, ed. Dolores Delgado-Bernal, C. Alejandra Elenes, Francisca Godinez, and Sofia Villenas. Albany: State University of New York Press, 113–32.

Delgado-Bernal, Dolores, C. Alejandra Elenes, Francisca Godinez, and Sofia Villenas, eds. 2006. *Chicana/Latina Education in Everyday Life: Feminista Perspectives on Pedagogy and Epistemology*. Albany: State University of New York Press.

Delgado-Gaitán, Concha. 1996. *Protean Literacy: Expanding the Discourse on Empowerment*. London: Falmer Press.

———. 2001. *The Power of Community: Mobilizing for Family and Schooling*. Lanham, Md.: Rowman and Littlefield.

Dyrness, Andrea. 2004. "Speaking Truth to Power: Immigrant Parents, Progressive Educators, and the Politics of Change in an Urban School." Dissertation, University of California, Berkeley.

———. 2007. "'*Confianza* Is Where I Can Be Myself': Latina Mothers' Constructions of Community in Education Reform." *Ethnography and Education* 2:2 (June): 257–71.

Emihovich, Catherine. 2005. "Fire and Ice: Activist Ethnography in the Culture of Power." *Anthropology and Education Quarterly* 36:4: 305–14.

Fals-Borda, Orlando, and Mohammed A. Rahman. 1991. *Action and Knowledge: Breaking the Monopoly with Participatory Action-Research*. New York: Apex Press.

Faltis, Christian, and Sarah Hudelson. 1998. *Bilingual Education in Elementary and Secondary School Communities*. Boston: Allyn and Bacon.

Fine, Michelle. 1991. *Framing Dropouts: Notes on the Politics of an Urban Public High School*. Albany: State University of New York Press.

————. 1993. "[Ap]parent Involvement: Reflections on Parents, Power, and Urban Public Schools." *Teachers College Record* 94:4 (summer): 682–729.

Fine, Michelle, and Janis Somerville, eds. 1998. *Small Schools, Big Imaginations: A Creative Look at Urban Public Schools.* Chicago, Ill.: Cross City Campaign for Urban School Reform.

Flores, Barbara. 2005. "The Intellectual Presence of the Deficit View of Spanish-Speaking Children in the Educational Literature during the 20th Century." In *Latino Education: An Agenda for Community Action Research,* ed. P. Pedraza and M. Rivera. Mahwah, N.J.: Lawrence Erlbaum Publishers, 75–98.

Foley, Douglas, Bradley A. Levinson, and Janise Hurtig. 2001. "Anthropology Goes Inside: The New Educational Ethnography of Ethnicity and Gender." *Review of Research in Education* 25 (2000–2001): 37–98.

Foley, Douglas, and Angela Valenzuela. 2005. "Critical Ethnography: The Politics of Collaboration." In *The Sage Handbook of Qualitative Research,* ed. Norman K. Denzin and Yvonna S. Lincoln. Thousand Oaks, Calif.: Sage Publications, 217–34.

Freire, Paulo. [1970] 2005. *Pedagogy of the Oppressed.* New York: Continuum.

————1973. *Education for Critical Consciousness.* New York: Continuum.

Fuller, Bruce. 2007. "Early Learning in Latino Communities." In *Standardized Childhood: The Political and Cultural Struggle over Early Education.* Stanford, Calif.: Stanford University Press, 227–70.

Gaventa, John. 1993. "The Powerful, the Powerless, and the Experts: Knowledge Struggles in an Information Age." In *Voices of Change: Participatory Research in the United States and Canada,* ed. Peter Park, Mary Brydon-Miller, Budd Hall, and Ted Jackson. Westport, Conn.: Bergin and Garvey, 21–40.

Gilroy, Paul. 1987. *"There Ain't No Black in the Union Jack": The Cultural Politics of Race and Nation.* Chicago: University of Chicago Press.

González, Norma. 2001. *I Am My Language: Discourses of Women and Children in the Borderlands.* Tucson: University of Arizona Press.

————. 2005. "Reflections on the Field: Anthropology and Education—Past Present, and Future." Paper presented at the American Anthropological Association Annual Meetings, Washington, D.C.

Gregory, Steven. 1998. *Black Corona: Race and the Politics of Place in an Urban Community.* Princeton, N.J.: Princeton University Press.

Hale, Charles R. 2006. "Activist Research v. Cultural Critique: Indigenous Land Rights and the Contradictions of Politically-Engaged Anthropology." *Cultural Anthropology* 21:1: 96–120.

————, ed. 2008. *Engaging Contradictions: Theory, Politics, and Methods of Activist Scholarship.* Berkeley: University of California Press.

Hall, Budd. 1993. "From Margins to Center? The Development and Purpose of Participatory Research." *American Sociologist* 23:4: 15–28.

Hernández-Castillo, R. Aída. 2006. "Knowledge for What? Socially Committed Anthropology: Between Local Resistance and Global Powers." Paper presented at the Abriendo Brecha III: Activist Scholarship Conference, Austin, Texas, February 16–18, 2006.

Hondagneu-Sotelo, Pierrette. 2001. *Doméstica: Immigrant Workers Cleaning and Caring in the Shadows of Affluence*. Berkeley: University of California Press.

Hondagneu-Sotelo, Pierrette, and Ernestine Avila. 2003. "'I'm Here, but I'm There': The Meanings of Latina Transnational Motherhood." In *Gender and U.S. Immigration: Contemporary Trends*, ed. Pierrette Hondagneu-Sotelo. Berkeley: University of California Press, 317–40.

hooks, bell. 1989. *Talking Back: Thinking Feminist, Thinking Black*. Boston: South End Press.

———. 1990. *Yearning: Race, Gender and Cultural Politics*. Boston: South End Press.

Hurtado, Aida. 1989. "Relating to Privilege: Seduction and Rejection in the Subordination of White Women and Women of Color." *Signs* 14:4 (summer): 833–55.

———. 2003. *Voicing Chicana Feminisms: Young Women Speak Out on Sexuality and Identity*. New York: New York University Press.

Hurtig, Janise. 2005. "Resisting Assimilation: Mexican Immigrant Mothers Writing Together." In *Latino Language and Literacy in Ethnolinguistic Chicago*, ed. Marcia Farr. Mahwah, N.J.: Lawrence Erlbaum, 247–303.

———. 2008. "Community Writing, Participatory Research, and an Anthropological Sensibility." *Anthropology and Education Quarterly* 39:1 (March): 92–106.

Hurtig, Janise, and Andrea Dyrness. Forthcoming. "Parents as Critical Educators and Ethnographers of Schooling." In *A Companion to the Anthropology of Education*, ed. Bradley Levinson and Mica Pollock. Malden, Mass.: Wiley Blackwell.

Kozol, Jonathan. 2005. *The Shame of The Nation*. New York: Crown Publishers.

Lareau, Annette. 1989. *Home Advantage*. London: Falmer Press.

Lareau, Annette, and Erin McNamara Horvat. 1999. "Moments of Social Inclusion and Exclusion: Race, Class, and Cultural Capital in Family–School Relationships." *Sociology of Education* 72 (January): 37–53.

Lashaw, Amanda. 2006. "Experiencing Immanence: The Presence of Hope in a Movement for Equitable Schooling." Berkeley: Institute for the Study of Social Change, ISSC Fellows Working Papers.

Latina Feminist Group. 2001. *Telling to Live: Latina Feminist Testimonios*. Durham, N.C.: Duke University Press.

Lewis, Amanda E., and Tyrone A. Forman. 2002. "Contestation or Collaboration? A Comparative Study of Home–School Relations." *Anthropology and Education Quarterly* 33:1: 60–89.

Lipman, Pauline. 2005. "Educational Ethnography and the Politics of Globalization, War, and Resistance." *Anthropology and Education Quarterly* 36:4: 315–28.

Lopez, Gerardo. 2001. "The Value of Hard Work: Lessons on Parent Involvement from an (Im)migrant Household." *Harvard Educational Review*
71:3: 416–29.

López, Nancy, and Chalane Lechuga. 2007. "'They Are like a Friend':
Othermothers Creating Empowering School-Based Community Living
Rooms in Latina and Latino Middle Schools." In *Urban Girls Revisited:
Building Strengths*, 2d ed., ed. Bonnie J. Leadbeater and Niobe Way. New
York: New York University Press, 97–120.

Lorde, Audre. 1978. "A Litany of Survival." In *The Black Unicorn*. New York:
W. W. Norton, 31–32.

Luykx, Aurolyn. 1996. "From *Indios* to *Profesionales:* Stereotypes and Student
Resistance in Bolivian Teacher Training." In *The Cultural Production of the
Educated Person: Critical Ethnographies of Schooling and Local Practice*, ed.
Bradley A. Levinson, Douglas E. Foley, and Dorothy C. Holland. Albany:
State University of New York Press, 239–72.

———. 1999. *The Citizen Factory: Schooling and Cultural Production in Bolivia.*
Albany: State University of New York Press.

Maguire, Patricia. 1987. *Doing Participatory Research: A Feminist Approach.*
Amherst, Mass.: Center for International Education.

———. 1993. "Challenges, Contradictions, and Celebrations: Attempt-
ing Participatory Research as a Doctoral Student." In *Voices of Change:
Participatory Research in the United States and Canada*, ed. Peter Park, Mary
Brydon-Miller, Budd Hall, and Ted Jackson. Westport, Conn.: Bergin and
Garvey, 157–91.

———. 2001. "Uneven Ground: Feminisms and Action Research." In *Handbook of Action Research*, ed. Peter Reason and Hilary Bradbury. Thousand
Oaks, Calif.: Sage Publications, 59–69.

Marcus, George E., and Michael M. J. Fischer. 1986. *Anthropology as Cultural
Critique.* Chicago: University of Chicago Press.

Meier, Deborah. 1995. *The Power of Their Ideas: Lessons for America from a
Small School in Harlem.* Boston: Beacon Press.

Menjívar, Cecilia. 2000. *Fragmented Ties: Salvadoran Immigrant Networks in
America.* Berkeley: University of California Press.

Moll, Luis, and Richard Ruiz. 2002. "The Schooling of Latino Children." In
Latinos Remaking America, ed. Marcelo Suárez-Orozco and Mariela M.
Páez. Berkeley: University of California Press, 362–74.

Moraga, Cherríe. [1981] 2002. "Preface." In *This Bridge Called My Back*, ed.
Cherríe Moraga and Gloria Anzaldúa. Berkeley: Third Woman Press,
xliv–li.

Moraga, Cherríe, and Gloria Anzaldúa, eds. 1981. *This Bridge Called My Back:
Writings by Radical Women of Color.* New York: Kitchen Table: Women of
Color Press.

Murillo, Enrique G. 2002. "How Does It Feel to Be a *Problem?*: 'Disciplining'
the Transnational Subject in the American South." In *Education in the New
Latino Diaspora: Policy and the Politics of Identity*, ed. Stanton Wortham,

Enrique G. Murillo, and Edmund T. Hamman. Westport, Conn.: Ablex Publishing, 215–35.

Nabudere, Dani Wadada. 2008. "Research, Activism, and Knowledge Production." In *Engaging Contradictions: Theory, Politics, and Methods of Activist Scholarship*, ed. Charles R. Hale. Berkeley: University of California Press, 62–87.

Naples, Nancy. 2003. *Feminism and Method: Ethnography, Discourse Analysis, and Activist Research*. New York: Routledge.

Nuñez-Janes, Mariela, and Andrea Robledo. 2009. "*Testimoniando:* A Latina/Chicana Critical Feminist Approach to Racism in College." *Chicana/Latina Studies* 9:1: 72–102.

Nygreen, Kysa. 2006. "Reproducing or Challenging Power in the Questions We Ask and the Methods We Use: A Framework for Activist Research in Urban Education." *Urban Review* 38:1 (March): 1–26.

Orfield, Gary, and Chungmei Lee. 2005a. *New Faces, Old Patterns? Segregation in the Multiracial South*. Cambridge, Mass.: The Civil Rights Project.

———. 2005b. *Why Segregation Matters: Poverty and Educational Inequality*. Cambridge, Mass.: The Civil Rights Project.

———. 2006. *Racial Transformation and the Changing Nature of Segregation*. Cambridge, Mass.: The Civil Rights Project at Harvard University.

Pardo, Mary S. 1998. *Mexican-American Women Activists: Identity and Resistance in Two Los Angeles Communities*. Philadelphia: Temple University Press.

Park, Peter. 1993. "What Is Participatory Research?: A Theoretical and Methodological Perspective." In *Voices of Change: Participatory Research in the United States and Canada*, Peter Park, Mary Brydon-Miller, Budd Hall, and Ted Jackson. Westport, Conn.: Bergin and Garvey, 1–19.

Pastor, J., J. McCormick, and M. Fine. 2007. "Makin' Homes: An Urban Girl Thing." In *Urban Girls Revisited: Building Strengths*, 2d ed., ed. Bonnie J. Leadbeater and Niobe Way. New York: New York University Press, 75–96.

Pollock, Mica. 2008. *Because of Race: How Americans Debate Harm and Opportunity in Our Schools*. Princeton, N.J.: Princeton University Press.

Reason, Peter, and Hilary Bradbury. 2001. "Inquiry and Participation in Search of a World Worthy of Aspiration." In *Handbook of Action Research: Participative Inquiry and Practice*, ed. Peter Reason and Hilary Bradbury. London: Sage Publications, 1–14.

Sandoval, Chela. 2000. *Methodology of the Oppressed*. Minneapolis: University of Minnesota Press.

Scheper-Hughes, Nancy. 1995. "The Primacy of the Ethical: Propositions for a Militant Anthropology." *Current Anthropology* 36:5 (June): 409–40.

Scott, James. 1990. *Domination and the Arts of Resistance: Hidden Transcripts*. New Haven: Yale University Press.

Shirley, Dennis. 1997. *Community Organizing for Urban School Reform*. Austin: University of Texas Press.

Solorzano, Daniel, Miguel Ceja, and Tara Yosso. 2000. "Critical Race Theory, Racial Microaggressions, and Campus Racial Climate: The Experiences of African American College Students." *Journal of Negro Education* 69:1/2 (winter/spring): 60–73.

Solorzano, Daniel, and Dolores Delgado Bernal. 2001. "Examining Transformational Resistance through a Critical Race and LatCrit Theory Framework: Chicana and Chicano Students in an Urban Context." *Urban Education* 36:3 (May): 308–42.

Solorzano, Daniel, and Tara Yosso. 2001. "Critical Race and LatCrit Theory and Method: Counter-Storytelling." *Qualitative Studies in Education* 14:4: 471–95.

Speed, Shannon. 2006. "At the Crossroads of Human Rights and Anthropology: Toward a Critically Engaged Activist Research." *American Anthropologist* 108:1: 66–76.

Tejeda, Carlos, Manuel Espinoza, and Kris Gutierrez. 2003. "Toward a Decolonizing Pedagogy: Social Justice Reconsidered." In *Pedagogies of Difference: Rethinking Education for Social Change*, ed. P. P. Trifonas. New York: Routledge, 9–37.

Torre, María Elena, Emily Genao, Michelle Fine, and Natasha Alexander. 2007. "'Don't Die with Your Work Balled Up in Your Fists': Contesting Social Injustice through Participatory Research." In *Urban Girls Revisited: Building Strengths*, ed. Bonnie J. Leadbetter and Niobe Way. New York: New York University Press, 221–42.

Trinidad Galván, Ruth. 2006. "Campesina Epistemologies and Pedagogies of the Spirit: Examining Women's Sobrevivencia." In *Chicana/Latina Education in Everyday Life: Feminista Perspectives on Pedagogy and Epistemology*, ed. Dolores Delgado-Bernal, C. Alejandra Elenes, Francisca Godinez, and Sofia Villenas. Albany: State University of New York Press, 161–79.

Valdés, Guadalupe. 1996. *Con Respeto: Bridging the Distances between Culturally Diverse Families and Schools*. New York: Teachers College Press.

Valencia, Richard, and Daniel Solorzano. 2004. "Today's Deficit Thinking about the Education of Minority Students." in *Tongue-Tied: The Lives of Multicultural Children in Public Education*, ed. Otto Santa Ana. Lanham, Md.: Rowman and Littlefield, 124–33.

Valenzuela, Angela. 1999. *Subtractive Schooling: U.S.-Mexican Youth and the Politics of Caring*. Albany: State University of New York Press.

Villenas, Sofia. 2001. "Latina Mothers and Small-Town Racisms: Creating Narratives of Dignity and Moral Education in North Carolina." *Anthropology and Education Quarterly* 32:1: 3–28.

———. 2005. "Latina Literacies in *Convivencia*: Communal Spaces of Teaching and Learning." *Anthropology and Education Quarterly* 36:3: 273–77.

———. 2006a. "Latina/Chicana Feminist Postcolonialities: Un/tracking Educational Actors' Interventions." *International Journal of Qualitative Studies in Education* 19:5 (September–October): 659–72.

———. 2006b. "Mature Latina Adults and Mothers: Pedagogies of Whole-ness and Resilience." In *Chicana/Latina Education in Everyday Life: Feminista Perspectives on Pedagogy and Epistemology*, ed. Dolores Delgado-Bernal, C. Alejandra Elenes, Francisca Godinez, and Sofia Villenas. Albany: State University of New York Press, 143–45.

Villenas, Sofia, and Donna Deyhle. 1999. "Critical Race Theory and Ethnographies Challenging the Stereotypes: Latino Families, Schooling, Resilience and Resistance." *Curriculum Inquiry* 29:4: 413–45.

Warren, Mark. 2001. *Dry Bones Rattling: Community Building to Revitalize American Democracy*. Princeton, N.J.: Princeton University Press.

Warren, Mark, and Richard Wood. 2001. *Faith-Based Community Organizing: The State of the Field*. Jericho, N.Y.: Interfaith Funders.

Weis, Lois, and Michelle Fine. 2000. *Speed Bumps: A Student-Friendly Guide to Qualitative Research*. New York: Teachers College Press.

Willis, Paul. 1977. *Learning to Labor*. Lexington, Mass.: D. C. Heath.

Wood, Richard L. 2002. *Faith in Action: Religion, Race, and Democratic Organizing in America*. Chicago: University of Chicago Press.

Yosso, Tara J. 2006. *Critical Race Counterstories along the Chicana/Chicano Educational Pipeline*. New York: Routledge.

Index

academic achievement: in flatlands schools vs. hills schools, 9
Academic Performance Index (API) ranking, 15, 225n.5
Action for New Small Schools, 7
activist research, 199–208, 227n.1; challenges of, 200; competing loyalties in, 200, 201–2; continuum from least to most direct involvement in political action, 203; cultural critique compared to, 201–2, 205–6; defined, 201; as exercise in solidarity, 221; feminist critique of, 203–4; need to recognize structures of social inequality within social movements, 215; participatory research as distinct from other models of, 201–8; policy-oriented model of, 201, 205, 217; researcher role in, 202, 203; social change defined as policy change in, 201
Adam Bede (Eliot), 155
admissions in new small school: anxieties over, 86–87; the chosen and the excluded, 99–107, 209; debate over fair admissions policy, 81–82; diversity issue, 86; lottery for, 90, 98–99; mistakes in, 100–106, 111; negotiating, 79–107; parents' perspective on, 99–106; questions prepared by Madres Unidas for teachers to discuss about, 223; teachers and, 100–101, 102, 106–7
African Americans. *See* black people
agency: denial of intellectual, to

Latino parents, 70; planning of focus groups and interviews and experience of own, 152–54; professionals' denial of Madres' legitimacy in their own right, 168. *See also* change agents, immigrant parents as
Alexander, Natasha, 157
Alinsky, Saul, 11
American Anthropological Association journal: "Public Anthropology Reviews" section of, 199
anger: affirmed by Madres Unidas as healthy alternative to self-blame, 156–57; censorship of, 110, 114–15, 167–68; controlling image of angry parent, 131, 132, 133, 138; as first step toward transformative action, 157; at inequities, as basis for public actions, 128–30, 132, 138
anti-immigrant discourse: connecting mothers' personal experiences with statewide, 189–91
Anyon, Jean, 227n.9
Anzaldúa, Gloria, 5, 145, 206
Apple, Michael W., 115, 226n.4
Arnold, Allen, 7
authentic form of caring: Latino concept of *educación* and, 92
autonomy: deconstructing, in new small autonomous schools, 208, 211–14; teachers' resentment at lack of, 126–28; use of "autonomous school" against parents' rights, 113, 117

Andrea Dyrness is assistant professor of educational studies at Trinity College in Hartford, Connecticut.